CONTENTS

Introduction: Understanding the specification and the assessment package   iv

Theme 1: Life in Modern Britain   1

Chapter 1:   Principles and values in British society   1

Chapter 2:   Identity   6

Chapter 3:   The media and the free press   16

Chapter 4:   The UK's role in key international organisations   24

Chapter 5:   Making a difference in society   36

Theme 2: Rights and Responsibilities   46

Chapter 6:   Laws in contemporary society   46

Chapter 7:   Rights and responsibilities within the legal system   52

Chapter 8:   How laws protect the citizen and deal with criminals   62

Chapter 9:   Universal human rights   77

Chapter 10:   Bringing about change in the legal system   84

Theme 3: Politics and Participation   93

Chapter 11:   Political power in the UK   93

Chapter 12:   Local and devolved government   102

Chapter 13:   Where does political power reside?   121

Chapter 14:   How do others govern themselves?   143

Chapter 15:   Bringing about political change   149

Theme 4: Taking Citizenship Action   161

Chapter 16:   Taking citizenship action   161

Glossary   172

Index   180

Introduction: Understanding the specification and the assessment package

This textbook is a starting point for your journey along a citizenship pathway. Its aim is to inform you so that you will become a responsible and involved citizen who understands how you can play a part and try to make a difference in modern British society. The textbook develops the content of the specification and assists in your understanding and application of citizenship skills and processes, and provides background to the assessment structure and how to complete your own active citizenship Investigation.

Course structure

The layout of this book mirrors the structure and the content of the AQA specification. In this course, you are required to be taught the entire content of the specification. This, like the book, is divided into three Themes:

- Life in modern Britain
- Rights and responsibilities
- Politics and participation

Each of the three Themes is made up of five chapters and they have a common structure:

- The first chapter sets out the 'big picture' concepts, issues and ideas relating to the Theme.
- Then we look at the local context in regard to the Theme.
- The third chapter reviews the national context in regard to the Theme.
- Next we examine the international or global aspects of the Theme.
- The final chapter discusses the active citizenship aspects of the Theme; that is, how individual citizens and groups of citizens can try to make a difference.

This course emphasises the use of contemporary case studies to help develop your knowledge and understanding of citizenship skills and processes. Where important issues arise relating to the content of the book prior to any further edition, updates will appear on the following website. Answers to the Exam practice questions and additional resources can be found at: www.hoddereducation.co.uk/AQAGCSECitizenshipStudies

Citizenship skills, processes and methods

For AQA GCSE (9–1) Citizenship Studies, the specification requires that you need to develop your knowledge and application of **citizenship skills, processes** and **methods**. Some are demonstrated through your active citizenship Investigation, while others can be examined through questions about the subject content.

- **Citizenship skills:** Many skills associated with citizenship are not specific to citizenship but are a necessary component of becoming a participating citizen. A skill is an ability to undertake something proficiently. Some of the skills associated with citizenship are critical-thinking, problem-solving, collaboration, advocacy, representation, initiative, social interaction and teamwork.
- **Citizenship processes:** These are activities and events that are linked in order to achieve an outcome. For example, changing a law or being involved in a court case each have an agreed process that must be followed to achieve an outcome.
- **Citizenship methods:** These are the individual elements or actions that citizens can take; some like voting are a part of a formal state/political process, while others such as protesting can be an individual or group activity, be planned or improvised.

Within this book you can develop your understanding of these aspects of citizenship studies through the case studies, differing points of view and the activities.

AQA
GCSE (9–1)

Citizenship Studies

SECOND EDITION

Association for Citizenship Teaching
QUALITY MARK
CITIZENSHIP RESOURCES

Mike Mitchell

HODDER
EDUCATION
AN HACHETTE UK COMPANY

Although every effort has been made to ensure that website addresses are correct at time of going to press, Hodder Education cannot be held responsible for the content of any website mentioned in this book. It is sometimes possible to find a relocated web page by typing in the address of the home page for a website in the URL window of your browser.

Hachette UK's policy is to use papers that are natural, renewable and recyclable products and made from wood grown in well-managed forests and other controlled sources. The logging and manufacturing processes are expected to conform to the environmental regulations of the country of origin.

Orders: please contact Hachette UK Distribution, Hely Hutchinson Centre, Milton Road, Didcot, Oxfordshire, OX11 7HH. Telephone: +44 (0)1235 827827. Email education@hachette.co.uk Lines are open from 9 a.m. to 5 p.m., Monday to Friday. You can also order through our website: www.hoddereducation.co.uk

ISBN: 9781398322936

© Mike Mitchell 2021

First published in 2016

This edition published in 2021 by

Hodder Education,

An Hachette UK Company

Carmelite House

50 Victoria Embankment

London EC4Y 0DZ

www.hoddereducation.co.uk

Impression number   10 9 8 7 6 5 4 3 2

Year   2025 2024 2023 2022 2021

Cover photo © Jacob Lund/stock.adobe.com

Illustrations by Aptara Inc.

Typeset in Myriad Pro-Light, 11/13 pts. by Aptara, Inc.

Printed in Italy

A catalogue record for this title is available from the British Library.

Active citizenship

The term 'active citizenship' underpins the nature of this specification. The course is not just intended to provide you with knowledge and information, but also to give you the skills and the understanding of processes that can enable you to become an 'active citizen'.

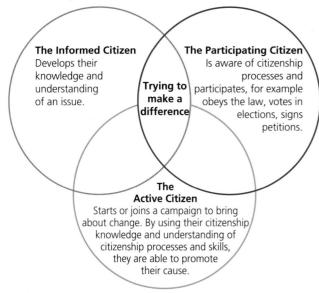

Figure 1 Becoming an active citizen

Figure 1 illustrates the relationship between the interlocking levels of citizenship involvement. An example of these three stages could be a person who is concerned about a local issue that they have read about or seen online.

- They research the issue and believe something should be done: The **Informed Citizen**.
- They see that there is an online petition about the issue and they sign it: The **Participating Citizen**.
- They attend a meeting of the protest group and join. They agree to become a candidate in the local elections on behalf of the group to campaign about the issue and bring about change: The **Active Citizen**.

Assessment structure

While it is important that you have a clear understanding of the content of the AQA GCSE (9–1) Citizenship Studies specification, it is also important to understand the nature of the assessment as it is your performance in the examinations that will determine your GCSE grade.

Table 1 indicates how the content of the course relates to the assessment structure.

Table 1 Course content: You are expected to answer **all** the questions in both exam papers

EXAMINATION PAPER	PERCENTAGE OF TOTAL MARKS OF THE GCSE	PART OF THE SPECIFICATION	SECTION OF THE SPECIFICATION
Paper 1 **Section A**	25%	Active Citizenship Section A is divided into two parts: Part 1: Questions about the nature of active citizenship, drawing upon the last section in each of the three themes about how citizens can try to make a difference in society (10%) Part 2: Questions about your own Investigation (15%)	Part 1: 3.2.5 How can citizens make their voice heard and make a difference in society? 3.3.5 How do citizens play a part to bring about change in the legal system? 3.4.5 How can citizens try to bring about political change? Part 2: 3.5.2 The Investigation: taking citizenship action
Paper 1 **Section B**	25%	Politics and participation	3.4.1 Where does political power reside in the UK and how is it controlled? 3.4.2 What are the powers of local and devolved government and how can citizens participate? 3.4.3 Where does political power reside: with the citizen, parliament or government? 3.4.4 How do others govern themselves?

EXAMINATION PAPER	PERCENTAGE OF TOTAL MARKS OF THE GCSE	PART OF THE SPECIFICATION	SECTION OF THE SPECIFICATION
Paper 2 **Section A**	25%	Life in modern Britain	3.2.1 What are the principles and values that underpin British society? 3.2.2 What do we mean by identity? 3.2.3 What is the role of the media and the free press? 3.2.4 What is the UK's role in key international organisations?
Paper 2 **Section B**	25%	Rights and responsibilities	3.3.1 What laws does a society require and why? 3.3.2 What are a citizen's rights and responsibilities within the legal system? 3.3.3 How has the law developed over time, and how does the law protect the citizen and deal with criminals? 3.3.4 What are universal human rights and how do we protect them?

You can find the detailed AQA GCSE (9–1) Citizenship Studies specification, along with specimen examination papers and mark schemes, at the AQA website: www.aqa.org.uk.

Assessment objectives

Clearly the marks you achieve in the exam are based upon how well you answer the unseen questions on the examination paper. But how are the judgements made about your answers? Every GCSE subject has several Assessment Objectives. These link to the requirements of the subject and specification. Each question that appears on an exam paper links to an Assessment Objective. Assessment Objectives can give you information about what you are expected to deliver in your answers, therefore it is important for you to spend some time studying the specific Assessment Objectives for each GCSE course you are studying.

Table 2 shows the Assessment Objectives for GCSE Citizenship Studies and indicates the weighting of these AOs across the examination papers.

The questions across the exam papers are worth a variety of different marks. The more marks a question is given, the longer and more detailed the required response. For your AQA GCSE (9–1) Citizenship Studies exams you will be given a printed booklet with allocated response spaces for each question. These spaces offer guidance as to how long the response should be.

Each question on Paper 1 Section B and on all of Paper 2 assesses only a single Assessment Objective. The Assessment Objective that is being assessed is indicated by the number of marks allocated for that question.

Paper 1 Section A includes questions that follow a different pattern. The questions shown in Table 3 relate to two Assessment Objectives as you are required to write about your own citizenship activity or reflect upon the actions of others.

Table 2 Assessment Objectives (AOs)

AO AND MARKS ALLOCATED	WEIGHTING OF THE AO IN THE EXAMINATION	WORDING OF THE AO	NOTES ABOUT THE AO
AO1 (1 or 2 marks)	30%	Demonstrate knowledge and understanding of citizenship concepts, terms and issues.	Consider how this AO can be broken down into differing questions that could be asked: *Knowledge of*: citizenship concepts or terms or issues. *Understanding of*: citizenship concepts or terms or issues.

AO AND MARKS ALLOCATED	WEIGHTING OF THE AO IN THE EXAMINATION	WORDING OF THE AO	NOTES ABOUT THE AO
AO2 (4 marks)	30%	Apply knowledge and understanding of citizenship concepts, terms and issues to contexts and actions.	Again, this AO can be broken down into several types of question that can be asked. Like AO1 above it is about your knowledge and/or understanding of concepts, issues and terms, but also how you can apply these to a context, for example a case study, or actions, such as a citizenship process or skill you demonstrated in your Investigation.
AO3 (8 marks)	40%	Analyse and evaluate a range of evidence relating to citizenship issues, debates and actions, including different viewpoints, to develop reasoned, coherent arguments and make substantiated judgements.	This AO is related to longer responses where you have to make a case, defend a position, draw together a range of evidence, arrive at a conclusion or sustain an argument.

Table 3 Mark allocation for Paper 1 Section A

QUESTION NUMBER	QUESTION FORMAT	MARKS ALLOCATED TO QUESTION	ASSESSMENT OBJECTIVE
1.6	Relates to a case study of other people taking citizenship action	8	4 marks for AO2 4 marks for AO3
2.3	Relates to your own citizenship Investigation	6	2 marks for AO1 4 marks for AO3
2.4	Relates to your own citizenship Investigation	12	4 marks for AO2 8 marks for AO3

The different styles of questions

A range of different question styles is used across the exam papers. It is helpful if you become familiar with each style.

AO1 questions

These questions will often require short responses – a single word or a sentence. 2-mark questions may require two distinct answers. Some questions may be in a multiple-choice style, where you choose one correct or two correct responses. Here are two examples of AO1 questions:

1 Name one member country of the Commonwealth other than the UK. [1]

2 Identify which two of the following preside over debates in the United Kingdom Parliament. [2]

   A Black Rod

   B Lord Chamberlain

   C The Speaker

   D Sergeant at Arms

   E The Lord Speaker

   F Chairman of Ways and Means

Question 1 requires a one-word answer, for example Canada – where 1 mark is awarded.

Question 2 requires you to select the two correct answers – C and E. 2 marks would be awarded for this; if only one is correct, only 1 mark is awarded.

AO2 questions

These questions will normally be based upon source material, which can be a short statement or quotation, a diagram, data or a chart. Here is an example of an AO2 question:

3 Using the source below, consider how central government formation differs in France from that in the United Kingdom. [4]

Source

In 2017, the French held elections for their President. The elections for the President normally take place over two rounds of voting. Every elector has one vote. If the candidate who comes first after the first round of voting has over 50 per cent of the total votes cast, they are elected. If no candidate achieves 50 per cent of the vote, there is a second round of voting a week later at which only the names of the top two candidates from the first round appear on the ballot paper. At the conclusion of the second ballot the candidate who comes top is elected for five years. Once elected the President appoints the Prime Minister and government ministers. Members of the French Parliament are elected separately from the President.

These sources may be unfamiliar to you, as in the example given above, which is about France. However, the question asks you to apply your knowledge and understanding of the UK situation to the situation described in France. Your answers will not be found within the sources but they can support the structure of your answer. You are applying your knowledge of the UK system to the information given about the French system provided in the source.

To answer question 3, you would have to identify the following points from the source and compare them against your knowledge of the UK:

- France has two types of election – one to elect the President and a separate one to elect members of the French Parliament. The UK has one – a General Election where we elect MPs for the whole of the UK, after which a government is formed. The Prime Minister is the leader of the largest party in the House of Commons, having been elected as an MP at the General Election. After the election the Queen asks the leader of the party with a majority of MPs in the House of Commons to become the Prime Minister.
- The UK does not have an elected President like France, but a constitutional monarch who is non-political.
- In the UK, the Prime Minister appoints people to government posts from members of their political party in the House of Commons and Lords.

AO3 questions

These questions demand an extended response where you can develop a case, review evidence and draw conclusions. There may be a short supporting statement placed prior to the question to give a context. Here is an example:

4 'Young people who commit crime should always be given non-custodial sentences. Locking up young people is not helpful to them or society.'

Considering a range of views, examine the arguments for and against the statement. [8]

This question requires you to consider arguments for and against a statement. The phrase 'a range of views' relates to your ability to draw upon a number of differing opinions and views when answering the question. You may want to make some notes on these before writing your response. For example:

- **Points FOR:** Young people should not be taken away from their families and friends. Locking people up can make them become more hardened criminals. Younger people often do not know the consequences of committing crime. Better to change behaviour and reform a character than lock them up.
- **Points AGAINST:** Even young criminals can be a danger to society and need to be in prison (the Bulger case), to teach them a lesson and lead them to change their behaviour. They often come from troubled families so prison can help them. The safety of society should come first.

Examining an argument will lead you to comment on each point that you make. You must try to ensure that there is a balanced number of points made for each case.

AO3 synoptic questions

In this course you are synoptically assessed in three questions: the last 8-mark question from each of the three content themes. Synoptic questions are where you are expected to draw upon your understanding of citizenship issues from across different parts of the specification and integrate them into your answer. The synoptic questions are: Paper 1 Section B final question; Paper 2 Section A final question; and Paper 2 Section B question 10.2.

Here is an example of a synoptic question:

5 'Judges in the UK like many in the USA should be made to stand for election so they are fully accountable to the people.'

Considering a range of views, analyse the case for and against making judges in the UK accountable through elections.

In your answer you should consider:
- the principles relating to judicial appointments in the UK
- the nature of elections and the political process in the UK. [8]

The structure of these questions is slightly different in that two bullet-pointed statements are added to provide some limited scaffolded structure for a response. When you look at these three questions you first have to recognise which other sections of the content they are expecting you to draw upon. This question would come from Paper 2 Section B Rights and responsibilities, and is about how judges are appointed. The other section of the course the question relates to is Politics and participation, as the question relates to elections. These could be the notes you would make before writing your response:

- Judges in the UK are appointed after an independent interview – no political involvement.
- Judges are not allowed to be political.
- They are appointed for life (until they retire).
- In the UK, judicial independence is a very important concept within our democracy.
- The judiciary is seen as a distinct element, separate from Parliament.
- **Points about the case FOR:** Makes judges accountable to the people; allows for changing public opinion about the implementation of laws to be reflected in those chosen to enforce the law; could broaden the type of people elected as judges, making the judiciary more representative.
- **Points about the case AGAINST:** It makes judicial appointments political; do you want judges who have party political labels; should judges express their own views on issues?

The style of question is not specifically asking you to draw conclusions but rather to analyse, deconstructing the arguments made by both points of view.

Assessing active citizenship – Paper 1 Section A

This section of Paper 1 is different from the three sections that make up the rest of Paper 1 and Paper 2. Section A Active Citizenship of Paper 1 comprises two sets of questions:

- The first set of questions (10 per cent of the GCSE marks) relates to your understanding of active citizenship based upon the last bullet point of each of the three Themes.
- The second set of questions (15 per cent of the GCSE marks) is based upon your own citizenship Investigation.

Most of the questions about active citizenship are like the questions on the other papers in that they assess only a single Assessment Objective. The exception is question 1.6, which is about the case study. Question 1.6 is based on a source: a text, a photo, an artwork or data, or a combination of these regarding a case study.

Throughout the course, and built into the assessment, is the use of contemporary case studies. These help develop your understanding of often complex issues and concepts and also enable you to undertake further research. See Chapter 16 for example case studies and research questions on them.

Citizenship Investigation

It is a requirement of the specification that you undertake an in-depth investigation of a citizenship issue of your own choice, which should involve using and developing a range of citizenship processes and skills that lead to some form of citizenship action. On AQA's website there is an Investigation Portfolio, which will help you to record your progress.

The questions set in the exam on your Investigation can ask you to:

- describe and analyse your own experiences of planning and taking practical citizenship actions with others
- critically reflect on your own experiences of planning and taking practical citizenship actions
- advocate a viewpoint and represent the viewpoints of others in relation to the issues, causes and situations studied and citizenship actions you have undertaken in relation to citizenship concepts.

You have to answer four questions about your Investigation. Two assess a single Assessment Objective and two assess two Assessment Objectives. These account for two out of only three questions across both papers that assess more than one Assessment Objective, all of which are in Section A of Paper 1 (see Table 3 on page vii for how the marks for these questions are split for the different Assessment Objectives).

Other supporting resources are available by the same author to help you develop your knowledge and understanding of GCSE Citizenship and its assessment requirements:

AQA GCSE (9–1) Citizenship Workbook (IBSN 978-1-3983-1720-8) contains over 270 sample questions and online responses to help you understand the nature of the GCSE assessment requirements.

My Revision Notes: AQA GCSE (9–1) Citizenship Studies (ISBN 978-1-5104-1830-1) provides a structured approach to preparing and revising for the GCSE question papers.

Table 4 AQA GCSE Citizenship assessment at a glance

PAPER 1	PAPER 2
What is assessed? Section A: ● Active Citizenship: 25% ● Chapters 5, 10 and 15 and your Investigation Chapter 16 Section B: ● Politics and Participation: 25% ● Chapters 11, 12, 13 and 14	**What is assessed?** Section A: ● Life in Modern Britain: 25% ● Chapters 1, 2, 3 and 4 Section B: ● Rights and Responsibilities: 25% ● Chapters 6, 7, 8 and 9
How is it assessed? ● Written paper: 1 hr 45 mins ● 80 marks (40 per section) ● 50% of the GCSE	**How is it assessed?** ● Written paper: 1 hr 45 mins ● 80 marks (40 per section) ● 50% of the GCSE
Format Q&A booklet. All questions to be answered.	**Format** Q&A booklet. All questions to be answered.

How to get the best out of this book

This textbook is designed to follow every element that makes up the AQA specification for GCSE Citizenship.

Each of the three Themes comprises five chapters, each one matching an element of the specification. Chapter 16 outlines the nature of the Citizenship Investigation you have to undertake.

Each chapter is made up of text to support your learning and the following components:

The **Spec coverage** outlines the main element of the learning as stated in the specification:

Spec coverage
- The role of international law in conflict situations:
  - to protect victims of conflict
  - how international humanitarian law helps establish the rules of war.

All the elements described below are intended to promote your application of citizenship skills and understanding of citizenship processes.

A **Discussion point** is where key questions are posed about the text. These questions can form part of your review of your learning, stimulate a class or group debate or form a question that you can research.

The example below is taken from page 10 and relates to issues surrounding a multicultural society and immigration.

Discussion point

The issue of **immigration** and its impact upon society is often the focus of debate.

The UK has, over its history, seen people from all over the world come and settle in this country. At the same time many people have returned home and UK citizens have emigrated to live abroad, for example in recent years to retire and live in Spain. The numbers of people coming to live in the UK and those leaving the UK to live elsewhere are shown in Table 2.4.

Consider what issues arise from living in a modern multicultural society.

Some people are concerned about issues relating to immigration. How would you answer the concerns they raise?

The book also includes numerous **case studies** to help support your learning.

A case study helps you focus on a real-life example relating to your learning.

Every case study is followed by a **Different viewpoints** section that poses questions relating to the case study. It might challenge the basis for the case study, or make you consider the evidence supporting the case study.

This approach is intended to make you consider the evidence presented. Is it biased? Is it partial? Are there other viewpoints?

The example below is taken from page 26 regarding the Commonwealth.

Case study

Commonwealth helps St Lucia build climate resilience

St Lucia is a small country with limited resources to deal with the impact of severe weather.

With help via finance and technical assistance from the Commonwealth, the aim is to prepare post-disaster business plans, use new technology and enable schools to be used as emergency shelters.

Different viewpoint

Does the Commonwealth have a useful function in the twenty-first century?

The Different viewpoints represent opinions; they are not factual statements.

To respond to these you should have a point of view that is supported by evidence that makes a rational argument, or you should consider the issue from a different viewpoint.

The book also contains a number of **Activity** boxes. See page 142 for an example.

This Activity allows you as a class or group to select an issue that concerns you and, after researching the issue, to contact your MP and, hopefully, follow up any response you receive.

The Activities are designed to help support development of your active citizenship skills, enabling you to consider and apply the skills and processes you will need when carrying out your own Investigation.

Activity

Consider as a class or a group writing to your local MP about an issue of concern. The issue can be local, national or international. Research your issue, ask the MP to respond to your questions and ask whether they will raise the matter with the appropriate minister. After any response, arrange for your MP to visit your school and discuss the issue with you. Keep a log of the process and ask the MP (when they visit or in a follow-up letter) about the process of citizens making their voice heard and how it might be improved.

Another feature is the **Learning review points** at the end of each chapter. This enables you to check your understanding of the core ideas in the chapter you have completed.

Learning review points
- What are the key values and principles that underpin the UK?
- What are the main factors that help determine a person's identity?

Review questions are quick-fire questions to assess your learning and understanding.

Exam practice boxes are exam paper questions:

- AO1 questions are worth 1 or 2 marks. These are short responses.
- AO2 questions are worth 4 marks. These responses are 2 to 4 lines.
- AO3 questions are worth 8 marks. These short essay-style responses are between 12 and 15 lines.

Some of the active citizenship questions assess two AOs.

In the examination, the booklet will indicate the space available for each response.

EXAM PRACTICE

1 Identify one benefit to a community of Neighbourhood Watch schemes. (AO1) [2 marks]
2 Referring to the INQUEST case study on page 88, consider two arguments you could put forward to support its aims. (AO2) [4 marks]
3 Analyse the arguments put forward by those who wish to abolish trial by jury. (AO3) [8 marks]

Answers to the Exam practice questions and additional resources can be found at: www.hoddereducation. co.uk/AQAGCSECitizenshipStudies

Websites: Each section contains a list of websites to enable you to check the nature of the evidence contained in the book and to carry out your own research.

Websites
Freedom House: www.freedomhouse.org
Global Witness: www.globalwitness.org/en
Amnesty International UK: www.amnesty.org.uk
European Parliament: www.europarl.europa.eu/portal/en

The **glossary** on page 172 provides helpful reminders of key citizenship terms. The same term often appears in several chapters and this glossary provides the definitions together in one place.

Supplementary vote – a voting system used in the UK where voters have a second vote that is used in the election process if no candidate gets 50 per cent of the first-choice votes (see page 124).

Chapter 1: Principles and values in British society

Key question

● What are the principles and values that underpin British society?

Principles and values in British society today

Spec coverage

● The key principles and values underpinning British society today.

Figure 1.1 A new British citizen receiving their citizenship certificate after taking their oath

People who currently hold citizenship in another country but wish to become citizens of the United Kingdom have to undertake a **citizenship** test as a part of the process. The book on which the test is based has a section entitled 'The values and principles of the UK'. It identifies five fundamental **principles** of British life. It is stated that these **values** and principles are based upon history and traditions. They are protected by law, custom and expectations.

The expression '**British values**' is often quoted in the media and by politicians. This phrase means those values associated with contemporary British society. It does not mean that these values are solely British nor that they were invented by the British.

The values and principles of the UK

Democracy

The rule of law

Individual liberty

Tolerance of those with different faiths and beliefs

Participation in community life

Figure 1.2 The fundamental principles of British life as stated in the official study guide for the citizenship test (Source: Life in the United Kingdom – Official Study Guide)

Most values in any society are based upon the culture, religious nature and history of that society. Many values and principles are now seen as universal and are identified in international law or treaties such as the Universal Declaration of Human Rights, or the Human Rights Act 1998 in the United Kingdom.

While many people would agree with the broad principles of British society outlined above, there can be many different interpretations of what these principles and values actually mean.

● **Democracy** is a fundamental aspect of British life:
  – All citizens should be able to participate in the democratic process.
  – Every vote should be of equal importance.
  – There should be fair, open and regular elections to public offices.
● The **rule of law** implies that no individual or group is above the law.
● **Individual liberty** means that individuals are free to act according to their wishes, but if the actions they take are deemed illegal by the state they then face the consequences through the legal system.

- **Tolerance** of others of a differing faith or belief is seen as vital in a modern **multicultural society**.
- For those who live in the UK, is **participation in community life** a value or a principle or is it an aspiration or wish? Should one be compelled to join in with others? Should living a separate lifestyle be penalised?

- **Equality** – as well as tolerance, it is important that there is equality of treatment and consideration for all members of society irrespective, for example, of their race, gender, ethnicity, age, sexuality or religion. **The Equality Act 2010** safeguards these rights.

Discussion point

Each of the values and principles mentioned raises questions about its true meaning in modern society.

- Many people challenge the nature of our current democracy and wish to introduce changes that they feel would enhance democracy in the UK; for example:
  - lowering the voting age
  - making voting compulsory
  - having regular referendums
  - changing the voting system
  - abolishing the House of Lords
  - having equal electorates for each MP
  - ensuring a government has a mandate from at least 50 per cent of the electorate.

- Campaigners on the rule of law question whether there is equal access to the law, especially for those on limited means. While citizens facing criminal charges have access to some free legal support, there is no free legal support in most civil cases.
- When is someone's individual liberty and freedom to take an action an infringement on someone else's freedom and liberty?
- Is there a limit to which a society should tolerate the views and beliefs of some of its citizens or those living in this country?

These questions and others asked about British values go to the heart of the nature of contemporary British society and are key issues that form the backdrop to citizenship studies.

Rights, duties and freedoms of citizens

Spec coverage

- The human, moral, legal and political rights and the duties, equalities and freedoms of citizens.

While we use the words and phrases 'rights', 'responsibilities', 'freedoms' and 'the rule of law' in everyday conversation, with regard to citizenship they have exact meanings. There is also a debate within society about the balance between rights and responsibilities/duties. What rights should citizens have and what duties or responsibilities can the state expect from its citizens? For example, in a time of war the state increases the duties it places upon its citizens – from calling citizens up to fight to rationing food – and limits citizens' rights, for example the freedoms of movement and speech.

- **Rights** are the legally binding social and ethical entitlements that are considered the building blocks of a society. All citizens within our society should enjoy them equally. The idea of freedom of speech is an essential part of our way of life, but society does limit that right where it conflicts with other rights. Rights within a society structure the way government operates, the content of laws and the morality of society. Table 1.1 on page 3 shows legislative changes relating to individual rights in the UK. Rights are often grouped together and debates take place about human rights or children's rights or prisoners' rights, for example.

- **Morals** are the rules that govern which actions are believed to be right and which to be wrong. They are often related to personal behaviour. A society can claim to live by certain moral values and individuals can state that they live their life by certain moral values.

- **Duties/responsibilities** (these two terms often are interchangeable, but the term 'duty' often implies a legal/moral underpinning) relate to those responsibilities a society places upon its citizens. For example, you are expected to pay your taxes, obey the law and take part in the judicial system as a jury member if required. Duties are not optional and are often enshrined in law.

- **Freedoms** are the power or right to speak and act or think as one wants. We often explain freedom in

Table 1.1 Examples of legislative changes to individual rights and equality issues in the UK

RIGHTS OF WOMEN	SEXUAL RIGHTS
• Representation of the People Act 1928 • Equal Pay Act 1970 • Sex Discrimination Acts 1975 and 1986 • Employment and Equality Regulations 2003 and 2006 • Equality Acts 2006 and 2010	• Sexual Offences Act 1967 • Disability Discrimination Act 1995 and 2005 • Sexual Offences Act 2003 • Gender Recognition Act 2004 • Civil Partnerships Act 2005 • Marriage (Same Sex Couples) Act 2013
RACIAL EQUALITY	**RIGHTS OF THE CHILD**
• Race Relations Acts 1965, 1968, 1976 and 2000	• The United Nations Convention on the Rights of the Child came into force in 1992 – every child in the UK is entitled to more than 40 specific rights

relation to a context. Expressions such as freedom of choice, the freedom of the press and freedom of movement relate to some basic beliefs in our society.

• **Equality** means treating all individuals equally. Where inequality or discrimination occur, the state often attempts to remedy the situation, either through policy or legislative action. Table 1.1 shows legislative changes relating to equality issues in the UK.

Race audit could lead to new laws

In 2017 the UK government published consolidated data for the first time that indicated the experience of public services by differing racial groups in the UK. The government stated that the information contained in the data might lead to changes in legislation to attempt to overcome some of the issues raised. To find out more about what this data tells us about the UK today, use the following website: www.ethnicity-facts-figures.service.gov.uk

Identities

Spec coverage
• Key factors that create individual, group, national and global identities.

The factors that create identity are multi-dimensional and they influence different individuals in different ways. Table 1.2 identifies some factors that influence the creation of identity.

For each individual, group or nation, identity and the weight given to any, all or more than those factors listed can vary from person to person, group to group and from one nation to another.

National identity can also relate to the nature of the society within which one lives and works. In the UK we have a British identity, and some have a Scottish, Welsh, English, Irish or Cornish identity that they would put before or in place of their British identity. National identity can also link back to shared values, as long as citizens believe and support those values that the nation state holds together.

In order to make judgements and consider issues relating to life in modern Britain, it is necessary to base any argument or point of view upon evidence, data and information. Figure 2.2 on page 7 indicates how wealth is distributed in the UK.

Table 1.2 Factors that influence the creation of identity

IDENTITY	FACTOR		COMMENT
Individual	• Gender • Education • Race • Employment • Family • Peer group	• Ethnic group • Location • Social class • Culture • Religion • Media	Each of these factors can have varying levels of importance for each individual.
Group	• Employment • Peer group	• Social interests • Political views	While these repeat individual identity factors, they also represent groups to which one is attached and can therefore allow one to be influenced by the identity of the group.
National	• Shared values • Homogeneity		National identity and its association with national values gets confused with national characteristics and stereotyping. Factors influencing national identity could be the role of monarchy providing a feeling of continuity.
Global	• Political and social awareness		Increasingly in this interconnected world of 24-hour news, individuals can readily identify with global issues and concerns.

As a citizenship student you need to ensure you have up-to-date information relating to modern Britain, but you will need to ensure your data and information is robust and cannot be challenged as being partial, out of date, unreliable or biased.

Websites

Office for National Statistics: www.ons.gov.uk

The process of becoming a UK citizen: www.gov.uk/becoming-a-british-citizen

British Council: http://esol.britishcouncil.org/content/learners/uk-life/life-uk-test/values-and-principles-uk

Activity

1   Study the information provided in this chapter. What conclusions can you draw about the values and principles that the government believes underpin British society?
2   If you could select **three** collections of data to present a fuller picture of modern Britain, which would you select and why?
3   Carry out a survey in your local community to find out what people consider to be important British values. Draw up a list of what the government suggests and others that you consider important. Ask those who you contact to rank your list in order of importance. Either as a class, as groups or individually, collate your results and consider what conclusions can be drawn.

Discussion point

What does Table 1.2 on page 3 tell us about the difficulty in holding a discussion about an individual's identity?

Review questions

1   Identify two freedoms enjoyed by UK citizens.
2   Using examples, what is the difference between a right and a duty?
3   Which law passed in 1998 was about the rights of UK citizens?

Learning review points

● What are the key values and principles that underpin the UK?
● What are the main factors that help determine a person's identity?

EXAM PRACTICE

1   In what year was the first Race Relations Act passed?
     A 1958   **C** 1979
     B 1965   **D** 2003 (AO1) [1 mark]
2   Identify and explain the importance of two symbols of UK national identity that are shown in Figure 1.1 on page 1. (AO2) [4 marks]
3   Justify a case for stating that some factors influence the creation of a person's identity more than others. (AO3) [8 marks]

SUGGESTED ANSWERS

The following are answers and possible routes through the higher-mark questions.

Answers and possible routes through all the Exam practice questions in this book can be found at: www.hoddereducation.co.uk/ AQAGCSECitizenshipStudies

1 Answer: B.

2 This 4-mark question breaks down into four distinct parts:

1 and 2 identify two symbols – the Union flag and the photo of the Queen = 2 marks.

3 and 4 explain the importance of each – the flag is the national flag of the UK, combining the flags of the nations of the UK; the Queen is the monarch of the whole of the UK and is seen as a symbol of the nation and the concept of a constitutional monarchy = 2 marks.

Total 4 marks (AO2)

3 This is an open-ended question in that there is no single correct response. You are expected to present a justification for certain factors being more important than others. For each, you would explain why you think it is important. For example, you may wish to make a case for:

- Education – often linked to economic advancement.
- Moving from local area to go to university – broader peer group can have a lifetime impact upon the individual.
- Social class – many believe that social class is an important predictor of your future life and is linked to many of the other factors related to identity.
- Family – the nature of and support from your family, especially in your early years, is seen as important in shaping a person's identity.

If you select too many you will not have time to develop a brief case for each. In the concluding sentence you may wish to add that, while the three or four you have selected are important, others could have been included (give examples) or are interrelated with the ones you have selected – this demonstrates further background knowledge.

8 marks (AO3)

Formal mark schemes for 8-mark questions are awarded according to levels:

Levels 7–8: Developed and sustained justification for the choices made. The views expressed relate to the citizenship issue. Developed and reasoned justifications are provided that relate to the evidence provided. The justifications put forward form a coherent argument.
Levels 5–6: Justification is offered for the selection made. A range of evidence and views related to the citizenship issue. The evidence is used to support the justification of the choice but these points are not always completely developed. Conclusions drawn from the arguments may not be completely coherent.
Levels 3–4: Basic justification in regard to a limited range of evidence related to the citizenship issue. Weak arguments for selection are made that are not necessarily related to the evidence presented. Some attempt is made to integrate the justification into concluding remarks.
Levels 1–2: Limited evidence is presented and/or evidence presented is not directly related to the citizenship issue. Little or no attempt is made to justify the evidence presented. Little or no attempt is made to integrate the points made.

Theme 1: Life in Modern Britain

Chapter 2: Identity

Key question
- What do we mean by identity?

The UK and identity

Spec coverage
- The United Kingdom of Great Britain and Northern Ireland and how it is comprised of England, Northern Ireland, Scotland and Wales.
- The impact of this on identity debates.

During the last 50 years the population of the UK has grown by over 10 million people. About half of this growth has taken place since 2001.

The nature of the population of any given country can be studied in many different ways. Table 2.1 indicates the total population by individual country of the UK and shows each country as a percentage of the total population of the UK. The table also indicates the projections for the UK population until 2043.

The age structure of the population from 1974 and projected to 2039 (Table 2.2 on page 7) enables one to understand the number of young people and hence the educational needs of the population. The number of people past retirement age indicates costs relating to state pensions and health services.

The size of the workforce indicates levels of taxation that can be expected to support services and the number of homes that may need to be built. Thus differing ways of looking at a country's population can help governments plan ahead.

Figure 2.1 The nations of the UK

Table 2.1 Estimated and projected population of the UK and constituent countries, mid-2019 to mid-2043 (in millions)

	2019 (%)	2023*	2028*	2033*	2038*	2043*
United Kingdom	66.9 (100)	68.1	69.4	70.5	71.4	72.4
England	56.3 (84.3)	57.6	58.8	59.8	60.8	61.7
Wales	3.2 (4.7)	3.2	3.2	3.2	3.2	3.3
Scotland	5.5 (8.2)	5.5	5.5	5.6	5.6	5.6
Northern Ireland	1.9 (2.8)	1.9	2.0	2.0	2.0	2.0

* Projected

Table 2.2 Age distribution of the UK population, 1974 to 2039

	% POPULATION AGED 0 TO 15	% POPULATION AGED 16 TO 64	% POPULATION AGED 65 AND OVER
1974	25.2	61.0	13.8
1984	21.0	64.1	14.9
1994	20.7	63.4	15.8
2004	19.5	64.5	15.9
2014	18.8	63.5	17.7
2024*	19.0	61.1	19.9
2034*	18.1	58.5	23.3
2039*	17.8	57.9	24.3

* Projected

Numbers may not sum to 100 due to rounding

Another way of looking at the nature and composition of the UK population is to study the distribution of wealth. The UK is one of the richest countries in the world, but how is its wealth distributed? According to the **Office for National Statistics (ONS)**, the richest 1 per cent of Britain's population has as much wealth as the poorest 55 per cent of the population. There is also a geographical pattern to this wealth distribution. The average wealth of households in the South East of England in 2018 was £381,000. In the North East the average household wealth was £163,000.

The UK is a very diverse society, having attracted people from all over the world to live, work and settle here. The numbers of people living in the UK in 2018 by country of origin are shown in Table 2.3.

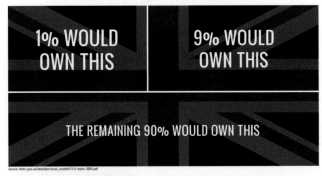

IF THE UK FLAG WAS DIVIDED LIKE UK WEALTH

1% WOULD OWN THIS

9% WOULD OWN THIS

THE REMAINING 90% WOULD OWN THIS

WE'RE **NOT** ALL IN THIS TOGETHER

Figure 2.2 UK flag divided up to indicate wealth ownership

Table 2.3 Immigration to the UK by country

COUNTRY OF ORIGIN	NUMBER
Poland	832,000
India	832,000
Pakistan	535,000
Romania	392,000
Ireland	369,000
Germany	309,000
Italy	253,000
South Africa	246,000
Bangladesh	241,000
China	207,000

In 2011, after English, the next most common language spoken was Polish.

The nature and culture of a society are often linked to the nature and importance in that society of religious faith. In the 2011 Census:

- 59.3 per cent of the population identified as Christian.
- The second largest group was 4.8 per cent who identified as Muslims.
- 25 per cent of the population reported no religious affiliation.

The ethnic groups that made up the UK population in 2011 were:

- White – 86.0 per cent
- Asian/Asian British – 7.5 per cent
- Black/African/Caribbean/Black British – 3.3 per cent
- Mixed/multiple ethnic groups – 2.2 per cent
- Other ethnic groups – 1 per cent.

So many of the things we take for granted that make up 'the British way of life' are not in fact British but owe their origins to other cultures and to the many peoples over the centuries who have come to live in the UK.

The impact of nations and regions upon identity debates

Until the start of **devolution**, the UK operated as a centralised state with almost all political power centred on London and Parliament. Identity within the nations and regions of the United Kingdom has related to historical situations, for example Scotland has different education and legal systems from the rest of the UK. National identity within the nations has been shown through cultural identity, based upon literature, customs, music, language and sport.

- Northern Ireland, which only came into existence in 1921 as a result of the establishment of the then Irish Free State (now the Irish Republic), has a divided cultural identity between those who are nationalist and support the re-unification of Ireland, and the unionists who support Northern Ireland and its union with the UK. Within Northern Ireland the identity factors based upon culture follow the two strands within society: each identifies with differing sports; one supports a recognition of the Irish language, the other does not.

- In Wales, the national identity is shown through the cultural factors indicated above, from the importance of Welsh rugby to the Eisteddfod (a cultural festival celebrating the Welsh people and language).

- Within England, regions and counties have their own histories and traditions that have led to regional identities forming. In many areas, such as the West Country or counties such as Yorkshire and Lancashire, these identities are very strong.

- With the increasing movement of people within the United Kingdom and increasing **migration** to the UK, these identity factors may differ in importance across the population.

The impact of this national debate about identity can be seen as one of the factors that has led to the growth of the devolution of power to the nations and regions of the UK. Scotland once again has its own Parliament, and Wales and Northern Ireland their own Assemblies, so more decisions that impact upon the lives of the people of those nations are decided by their own politicians in their own capital cities. Will the recognition of separate identities within the United Kingdom lead to the breakup of the United Kingdom? Already Scotland has had a referendum on independence.

Is there a clear acceptance by the population of what it means to be British? Do the British have a clear identity, or is it a matter of being Scottish, Welsh, Irish or English first and British second? All the values and principles that underpin society are shared values and are also shared by numerous other countries. The importance of being British is often summed up by the political slogan 'Stronger together', which was used to persuade people in Scotland to continue to support the Union.

The UK's changing population

Spec coverage

- Changes and movement of population over time:
   – the impact on different communities in the UK
   – the nature of immigration and migration to and from the UK.

The United Kingdom has a long tradition of people from other countries coming to live here. Some were invaders. More recently, others have come to escape persecution.

- In the seventh century BC, the Celts arrived in Britain. In the first century AD, the Romans invaded. After they left in the fifth century AD, the Angles, the Saxons and the Jutes from present-day Germany and Denmark arrived.

- In 1066, the Normans from France conquered England. Under the Normans, Jewish people came to live in England. They were expelled in 1290. In the Middle Ages, skilled tradespeople from Germany and Belgium settled in Britain.

- By the sixteenth century, there were black people living in this country. Protestants escaping persecution in France, Holland and Belgium came to live here.

- In the nineteenth century, the population of Ireland suffered as a result of the potato famine. Many came to live in mainland Britain. Many others settled in the United States of America. Many Irish navigators, as they were called, built the canals and later the railway system in England. The word 'navigator' got shortened over time to navvy, meaning a person carrying out heavy manual work. During the nineteenth century, Indian and Chinese people arrived in Britain, as did many Jewish people escaping persecution in Russia.

- During the Second World War, many people from Czechoslovakia and Poland fled to Britain and set up their own communities. Many were not able to return to their homelands after the war and settled here.

- In the post-war period, the government encouraged people from the Commonwealth to come and work here, especially in the public services and transport. In the 1950s, large numbers came from the West Indies. In the 1960s, many immigrants came from Pakistan and India. In the 1970s, Ugandan Asians came to the UK to flee persecution.

Case study

The Windrush generation scandal

In April 2018 the UK government was forced to apologise over deportation threats made to children of Commonwealth citizens who had been living and working in the UK for decades.

They had been told they were here illegally as they lacked official paperwork. They were told they needed evidence to continue working, get NHS treatment, or even to remain in the UK.

These Commonwealth citizens who arrived in the UK from 1948 until 1971 have been labelled the Windrush generation. The term refers to the ship HMT *Empire Windrush*, which arrived in the UK in April 1948 bringing workers from the Caribbean countries. These people had been invited to come here by the UK government due to major labour shortages after the Second World War.

A review of the Home Office files found that at least 83 individuals who had arrived before 1973 had been removed from the country.

The Prime Minister Theresa May apologised for their treatment. An inquiry was announced and a compensation scheme established.

The inquiry reported in March 2020 that the scandal was 'foreseeable and avoidable'. It criticised 'a culture of disbelief and carelessness' at the Home Office.

The Windrush Compensation Scheme was established in April 2019. About 15,000 claims are expected, costing an estimated £200 million.

Source: **www.bbc.co.uk/news/topics/c5qj4d564jkt/ windrush-generation**

Different viewpoint

Immigrants over the history of the UK have made a major contribution to the life and culture of its society.

Consider drafting a report on the changes in population that have occurred in your local area over the last 150 years and the impact of these changes. Information can be obtained from past Census returns, local newspapers and records held by local historical societies and local record offices. Much of this information is available online.

- When the UK was a member of the European Union, the concept of free movement of labour meant that many EU citizens came to the UK to work and settle.

During our history there has also been a pattern of **emigration** from the UK. Some people returned to their home countries following a change in political or economic circumstances. Many UK citizens have gone to live in other countries, especially in the eighteenth, nineteenth and twentieth centuries. Many Scots were forced to leave the Highlands during what is called the Clearances. Many went to live in the USA. Others left to find a new life in the expanding British Empire, especially in Canada, Australia, New Zealand, South Africa and the countries of East Africa. Others settled in India. In recent years, many have moved to live and work or retire in EU countries.

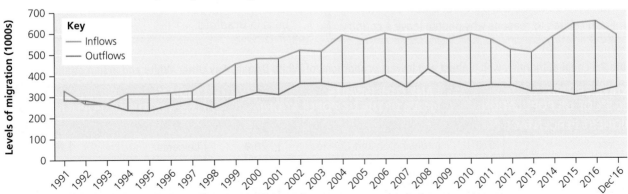

Figure 2.3 The number of people leaving and coming to live in the UK since 1991 (UK **net migration**) (Source: **http://economicshelp.org**)

There have also been major movements of the population within this country. This country has changed from a society that was largely agricultural, where most of the population lived in rural areas, to an industrialised urban society where most people live in cities and large towns.

Table 2.4 The nature of migration in the UK in 2019

	TOTAL NUMBER
Immigration	677,000
Emigration	407,000
Net migration	270,000

Discussion point

The issue of **immigration** and its impact upon society is often the focus of debate.

The UK has, over its history, seen people from all over the world come and settle in this country. At the same time many people have returned home and UK citizens have emigrated to live abroad, for example in recent years to retire and live in Spain. The numbers of people coming to live in the UK and those leaving the UK to live elsewhere are shown in Table 2.4.

Consider what issues arise from living in a modern multicultural society.

Some people are concerned about issues relating to immigration. How would you answer the concerns they raise?

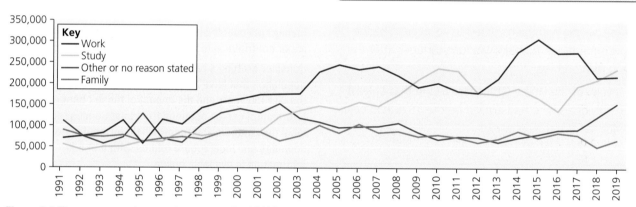

Figure 2.4 The reasons why people come to the UK (Source: **https://public.tableau.com/profile/migobs#!/vizhome/Netmigration2020/Figure3**)

Push and pull migration

When discussing issues surrounding migration numbers, a number of reasons arise why people leave a country or come to a new country. These are identified using the terms 'push' and 'pull':

- Pull relates to the attraction of a new country.
- Push relates to reasons why people leave a country.

Manchester and Bradford

- Manchester saw its population grow by 600 per cent between 1771 and 1831.
- Bradford's population grew by 50 per cent every ten years between 1811 and 1851.
- In 1851, only 50 per cent of its population had been born in Bradford.

Table 2.5 Local authorities with highest and lowest proportions of White British, Any Other White and Indian ethnic groups

WHITE BRITISH (80.5% OF UK POPULATION)		ANY OTHER WHITE (4.4% OF THE UK POPULATION)		INDIAN (2.5% OF THE UK POPULATION)	
HIGHEST PERCENTAGE (%)					
Redcar	97.6	Kensington and Chelsea	28.9	Leicester	28.3
Allerdale	97.6	Westminster	24.1	Harrow	26.4
Staffordshire	97.5	Haringey	23.0	Hounslow	19.0
Blaenau Gwent	97.3	Hammersmith and Fulham	19.6	Brent	18.6
Copeland	97.3	Camden	19.0	Oadby and Wigston	17.7

WHITE BRITISH (80.5% OF UK POPULATION)		ANY OTHER WHITE (4.4% OF THE UK POPULATION)		INDIAN (2.5% OF THE UK POPULATION)	
LOWEST PERCENTAGE (%)					
Newham	16.7	Redcar	0.6	Isles of Scilly	0.0
Brent	18.0	Torfaen	0.6	Torridge	0.1
Ealing	30.4	Knowsley	0.7	Rydaye	0.1
Harrow	30.9	South Tyneside	0.7	Redcar	0.1
Tower Hamlets	31.2	South Staffordshire	0.7	Purbeck	0.1

Many immigrants were drawn to the UK to work in certain industries and therefore settled together in the same locality. As others from their homeland came to the UK, they also settled into the same local area. Therefore, the pattern of immigration into the UK has varied from region to region. London, as the capital and a major employer, has always attracted a large number of immigrant workers. About 35 per cent of all the people who were born abroad and now live in the UK, live in London.

According to the 2011 Census, the local authorities shown in Table 2.5 had the highest and lowest proportions of White British, Any Other White and Indian ethnic groups. These figures indicate that the make-up of the UK population varies from area to area. So the impact on communities also varies.

Values in a democratic and diverse society

Spec coverage
- The need for mutual respect and understanding in a diverse society.
- The values that underpin democratic society.

For many years, the accepted views across all major political parties and other groups in society was that the UK aimed to be a multicultural society where people from all countries and backgrounds were accepted and able to practise their faith and live their lives in peaceful co-existence with their neighbours. As time passed, the older generation and their children would integrate into the norms and values of British society. In other countries a more integrationist approach was taken, whereby newcomers were expected to accept and adopt that country's way of life. Research has shown that **multiculturalism** has succeeded in fostering a sense of belonging among minorities, but it has paid too little attention to how to sustain support for multiculturalism among parts of the white population.

In the UK in recent years, politicians have begun to challenge the nature and impact of the multiculturalism approach. In 2011, the then Prime Minister David Cameron made a speech claiming that multiculturalism had failed. He defined state multiculturalism as a policy that 'encouraged different cultures to live separate lives, apart from each other and apart from the mainstream'. He claimed that the UK needed a clear sense of shared national identity that was open to everyone.

He then outlined the values he associated with this sense of national identity as:

- freedom of speech
- freedom of worship
- democracy
- the rule of law
- equal rights regardless of race, sex or sexuality.

He also said 'We must say to our citizens: this is what defines us as a society. To belong here is to believe in these things.'

These values identified by David Cameron are those associated with all modern Western liberal democracies and are included in human rights agreements.

In order to bring about the changes he wanted, David Cameron believed there were a number of practical things that needed to be done:

- Immigrants should speak English.
- Britishness classes and British history should be taught in schools.
- A National Citizenship Service should be introduced for 16-year-olds.
- He wanted to develop the concept of 'the Big Society' – relating to voluntary activity by citizens.

The term 'community cohesion' has come to demonstrate how in a local community the principles underpinning multiculturalism can be delivered. On the next page is a case study from Stoke-on-Trent.

Discussion point

Consider each of the following values and the associated questions:

- **Freedom of speech:** Can you have total freedom of speech? Should you be able to say anything about anybody or anything?

- **Freedom of worship:** If society allows freedom of worship, to what extent, if any, should religious views and opinions impact on the way society operates?

- **Democracy:** The UK claims to be a democracy. Citizens are entitled to vote and can elect representatives or stand for election themselves. Can we claim to have a democratic society when so many do not participate and governments are elected on the support of a minority of those who do vote?

- **The rule of law:** All citizens are equal before the law and have equal access, and will be treated the same according to the offence committed, not according to their background. Many challenge this statement. Does the justice system treat everybody equally?

- **Equal rights:** All citizens have their rights protected and should not be subject to discrimination. Are we an equal society where we all have equal rights and where there is no discrimination?

Case study

Stoke-on-Trent Pathfinder

The Stoke-on-Trent Pathfinder developed a community cohesion charter to present community cohesion in a user-friendly way that addresses local issues. A conference was held at which key stakeholders were invited to discuss and sign up to the charter. Politicians, public sector organisations and local agencies engaged in wide discussion of how community cohesion principles could be applied to local needs. The charter states that Stoke-on-Trent should be a place where:

- the diversity of people's backgrounds is appreciated and valued
- there are positive relationships between individuals from different backgrounds in the workplace, schools and the community
- all have a right to be part of a just society, where racial, religious or cultural differences exist in an atmosphere of mutual understanding and respect
- every individual is treated equally and has the same life opportunities
- together, listening and responding with openness and respect, we will move forward in ways that acknowledge genuine differences, building on shared hopes and values.

This commitment will establish a strong and cohesive community based upon a common understanding of respect, security and justice.

We will strive to ensure that we:
- respect other people's freedom within the law to express their beliefs and convictions
- learn to understand what others believe and value and allow them to express this in their own terms
- recognise that all of us at times fall short of the ideals of our own traditions, and never compare our ideals with those of others
- work to prevent disagreement from leading to conflict
- respect the right of others to disagree with us.

(Source: adapted from **www.london.gov.uk/sites/default/files/communitycohesionactionguide.pdf**)

Different viewpoint

How does your local community attempt to deal with issues relating to community cohesion and diversity? Are any initiatives led by the community via volunteer groups, or is the lead taken by the local authority?

Threats to multiculturalism

The debate over values was originally occasioned by the changing population structure of the UK and the settlement pattern of newcomers into the country. The growth in the number of individuals from a number of countries (including from the UK itself) who have joined and support terrorist groups has also caused many to reflect on how successful the UK has been with its multiculturalism policy.

Increasingly, Western countries are becoming concerned about how citizens come to be influenced and then take part in military actions abroad and return home and pose a threat to national security, and also how others are influenced within the UK and elsewhere to undertake terrorist acts within their own countries.

An example of a terrorist attack in England that was carried out by someone born in this country was carried out on 29 November 2019. Convicted terrorist Usman Khan, armed with two knives and wearing a fake suicide vest, attacked and killed two people on London Bridge, after attending a prisoner-rehabilitation programme. He was shot and killed by the police at the scene after being subdued by a member of the public.

Identity and multiple identities

Spec coverage
- Identity and multiple identities.
- The diverse nature of the UK population.

Individuals gain their **identity** in numerous ways. Some people study the impact of a person's biological background, while others study the nature of how people are brought up. This scientific discussion is called the **nature v. nurture** debate. It revolves around which of these two aspects is most important in an individual's personal development and the creation of their identity. Within citizenship studies we are concerned with the influences of society upon individuals and their relationships to each other and to the society in which they reside.

If you had to identify yourself, what categories would you use? Looking at the image in Figure 2.5, can you construct a statement about your identity?

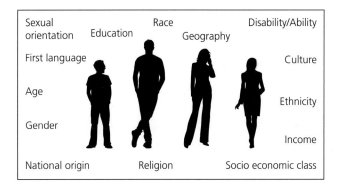

Figure 2.5 Factors that create identity

Like our fingerprints and our DNA, each of us is different, so there is no correct answer to the order and importance of which factors create our identity. Some people will use more categories; some fewer. Each of the headings helps towards creating your personal identity. As Figure 2.5 indicates, none of us has a single identity. Instead, we use multiple classifications in order to arrive at our identity. This is what is called having a **multiple identity**. A **group identity** is when one associates with an identifiable group within society.

Often a person's identity is used to associate with a country: I am British, I am Welsh, I am Scottish. This is called a **national identity** and relates to a sense of belonging to a country. Clearly, if you were born in Scotland and both your parents were born and brought up in Scotland, the label you would most likely use to describe your identity may be Scottish. You may consider yourself primarily British with a Scottish background, thereby assuming two national identities.

In the modern world, most people have multiple identities and, depending upon a given situation, the primary identity they use may change.

Consider the person in Figure 2.6 and their portrait of their identity. How would you describe them?

As well as personal identity, we often submerge our identity within a group or assume a national identity or a global identity.

According to a UK government report in 2013, 'Identity in the UK is changing; the power of high speed communication, the spread of social media and the increase of online personal information are all key factors which will influence identity in the next decade.' 'Global is now the new local' means that whatever happens anywhere in the world is known everywhere within a short period of time, and can alter opinions and set new social and political agendas.

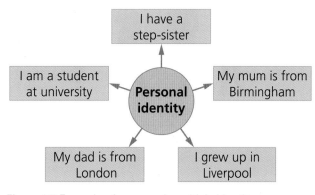

Figure 2.6 Example of a person's multiple identity

Group, national and global identity

Consider a young person who is an avid supporter of Manchester United football club:

- When they attend matches, they adopt the group identity of a supporter of that club and do not support the players from the team playing against Manchester United.
- Watching the English football team playing in the World Cup, this supporter adopts a national identity – being an English supporter – and supports the English players, whichever club they come from.
- At the World Cup, this fan may meet people from other countries across the world wearing Manchester United tee shirts and they then adopt a **global identity**, because Manchester United, like many other football teams, is a global brand.

National identity

Over many years the British Social Attitudes survey has asked questions about what people feel are important aspects of being British. The results are shown below.

Important aspects of being British

How important do you think each of the following is?
- *To have British citizenship*
- *To share customs/traditions*
- *To have been born in Britain*
- *To have lived here for most of your life*
- *To be able to speak English*
- *To be a Christian*
- *To respect British political institutions and laws*
- *To feel British*
- *To have British ancestry.*

In 2013 the answers were:
- *Speak English – 95 per cent*
- *Have British citizenship – 85 per cent*
- *Respect political institutions and laws – 85 per cent*
- *Feel British – 78 per cent*
- *Live life in Britain – 77 per cent*
- *Have been born in Britain – 74 per cent*
- *Have British ancestry – 51 per cent*
- *Share customs/traditions – 50 per cent*
- *Be Christian – 24 per cent.*

Discussion point

Look at the list in the box showing the points people think are important about being British. Do you agree with the answers given in 2013? If not, what suggestions would appear on your list?

Websites

British Social Attitudes survey: www.bsa-data.natcen.ac.uk

Migration Watch: www.migrationwatchuk.org/statistics-net-migration-statistics

Office of National Statistics: www.ons.gov.uk/peoplepopulationandcommunity/populationandmigration

UK Parliament: http://researchbriefings.files.parliament.uk/documents/SN06077/SN06077.pdf

Review questions

1 Which country makes up the largest percentage of the UK population?
2 Which language was the most often spoken after English in 2011?
3 What is the difference between immigration and emigration?
4 Identify three factors that are claimed to influence identity.

Activity

You have to design a survey asking questions about what people feel are important aspects of being British.
a) Construct your survey and ask 100 people to answer your questions.
b) Think of interesting ways you can present your answers, to gain the attention of an audience.

Learning review points

- What factors and elements make up one's identity?
- What is the make-up of modern UK society?
- What freedoms and values do we associate with living in a democratic society?
- What are the differing elements that can contribute to a person's identity?

EXAM PRACTICE

1 Explain using an example what is meant by the term 'multiple identity'. (AO1) [2 marks]
2 Referring to Table 2.2 on page 7, consider two issues that arise for government policy in regard to the projected population profile of the UK population in 2039. (AO2) [4 marks]
3 Examine the factors that have led to concentrations of immigrants from certain countries living together in parts of the UK. (AO3) [8 marks]

Key question

- What is the role of the media and the free press?

The rights, responsibilities and role of the media

Spec coverage

- The rights, responsibilities and role of the media and a free press in:
  - informing and influencing public opinion
  - providing a forum for the communication and exchange of ideas and opinions
  - holding those in power to account.

Figure 3.2 Examples of social media platforms

Figure 3.1 Examples of traditional media platforms

Today the story of the media in society often relates to news or stories arising from the internet or **e-media**. In the past, discussions about the media centred upon the role and importance of newspapers as against television. These means of mass media are often called **traditional media**, while those relating to the internet age are called **new media**. Today much of our interaction with the media is via another form of new media – **social media** – where we as individuals communicate with each other.

In today's world, the power and influence of social media are increasing. During the ongoing civil war in Syria, many news outlets rely upon the concept of citizen journalists to gather news and distribute it via social media and news organisations to a worldwide audience.

'Media' as a term relates to communication, whereas the phrase '**mass media**' indicates the ability to communicate with a large number of people at the same time. The basic function of media, whatever its format, is the communication of information or opinion to others, whether through news, views, comment or entertainment. A film, whether watched at the cinema, at home on a subscription channel or on catch-up TV, is a form of mass media and is normally aiming to entertain, whereas a newspaper covers the range of functions identified. It normally has an editorial line – a sort of policy viewpoint, linked to political or social values, on major issues – and it may support a specific political party at an election. Table 3.1 on the next page shows national newspaper circulation figures for January 2020.

Television stations in the UK also carry out the same range of functions as a newspaper, but by law they are not allowed to have an editorial position and have to be politically impartial, ensuring all political parties have access to the station, especially when an election is being held.

When it was established, the BBC also had as one of its functions 'to educate', to provide programmes on the radio and on television that inform people about issues as well as entertaining them. How does the traditional media hold up in the new media age?

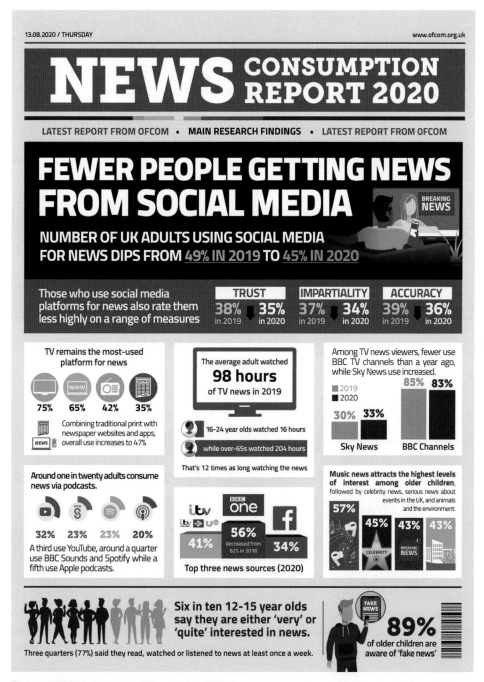

Figure 3.3 News consumption report, 2020
(Source: **www.ofcom.org.uk/research-and-data/tv-radio-and-on-demand/news-media/news-consumption**)

Table 3.1 UK national newspaper circulation figures for January 2020 – all these newspapers have seen a decline in circulation in the past year (Source: ABC)

PUBLICATION	ABC TOTAL JANUARY 2020
Metro (free)	1,426,535
The Sun	1,250,634
Daily Mail	1,169,241
The Sun on Sunday	1,042,193
The Mail on Sunday	967,043
Evening Standard (free)	798,198
The Sunday Times	645,108
Daily Mirror	451,466
The Times	368,929
Sunday Mirror	367,244
Daily Express	296,079
Daily Star	277,237
Sunday Express	252,733
i	217,182
Daily Star – Sunday	162,345
Financial Times	157,982
The Observer	156,217
Sunday People	139,698
Guardian	132,341
Sunday Mail	105,451
Daily Record	104,343
Sunday Post	86,953
City AM (free)	85,521

How does the media hold those in power to account?

In this country, we use the phrase 'a free press' to describe how the media is able to operate. This term should not be confused with 'free newspapers', which are give-away news/advertising sheets. A 'free press', or freedom of the press, is a concept that states that for a free, open and democratic society to exist, the press should be free from political and judicial interference and be able to print the stories they wish. Clearly, within any society there needs to be laws to protect individuals from newspapers printing false stories, but restrictions upon the press should be limited.

The term 'free press' is now more widely interpreted to mean freedom of any form of mass media. Television in the UK is governed by legislation and has to be politically impartial; a formal charter governs the way the BBC operates. The current charter expires in 2027. Newspapers claim that the stories they publish are in the public interest. This is a basic principle of journalism and provides its moral authority. Public interest can be defined as what matters to everyone in society. That is different from what might be of interest to people.

In 2009, *The Daily Telegraph* published information about the expenses claims made by **Members of Parliament** (MPs). This information had been leaked to the newspaper.

The police refused to investigate how this data was removed from the House of Commons. In the following weeks the circulation of the *Telegraph* increased by more than 600,000 copies. Many MPs were forced to resign. Others were charged and went to prison. The release of this information led to changes in the rules for MPs claiming expenses, and had a major impact on the public's perception of politicians.

The power of the media is now almost instant, especially when it involves the internet.

Freedom of Information Act

The Freedom of Information Act 2000 provides public access to information held by public authorities. These include government departments, local authorities, the NHS, state schools and police forces. The Act also requires public bodies to automatically publish certain information. There is an Information Commissioner to monitor the working of the Act.

(Source: **Information Commissioner's Office**)

Case study
Exam grades

In 2020, due to the Covid-19 pandemic, students throughout the UK were not able to take their public exams. The government decided to issue results based upon a mixture of teachers' estimated grades and an algorithm that attempted to adjust the grades and produce fair results. This resulted in large numbers of students not achieving the grades they expected and differing types of schools achieving different degrees of success. Within hours of the results being published, MPs and ministers were being attacked about the unfairness of the results and the impact upon students and their futures. Within days the government was forced to climb down and issue fresh results.

This was an example where all forms of the media were involved in the campaign, which was based upon individuals using the media to present their case.

Different viewpoint

How does this case study indicate the campaigning power of traditional and social media in bringing about change?

Case study
EU membership

A referendum on the UK's membership of the European Union (EU) was held in June 2016. A large section of the print media was opposed to our membership, while a majority of MPs supported the UK's continued membership of the EU. Several newspapers and social media campaigns, some of which lasted many years, played a significant role in convincing people that they should vote against EU membership. These included campaigns by *The Sun* and *Daily Express* newspapers. The role of the press in this matter showed the power of the media to influence the political direction of the country.

Different viewpoint

Why do you think that newspapers were more influential than television in influencing public opinion about EU membership?

The right of the media to investigate and report

Spec coverage
- The right of the media to investigate and report on issues of public interest subject to the need for accuracy and respect for people's privacy and dignity.

The following two case studies help our understanding of the role of the media and the possible limits on its ability to investigate:

- The first case study relates to the way in which newspapers hacked into people's phones and used the information they found.
- The second case study relates to the way *The Daily Telegraph* exposed what came to be called the MPs' expenses scandal by printing details of financial claims made by MPs that were reimbursed from public funds.

The first case study led to the police investigating and arresting several newspaper reporters, editors and private investigators and the second led to many MPs retiring at the next election and others being arrested and facing court proceedings.

Case study
Phone hacking

In 2011, the 168-year-old *News of the World* newspaper ceased publication following the allegation that many of its reporters and editors had been involved in hacking people's phones for information that would then provide stories in the newspaper. It led to a former editor being jailed. He served 5 months of an 18-month sentence. At the time he was charged he was the Prime Minister's official spokesperson. Those who had their phones hacked included celebrities, politicians and victims of crime. Five of those who were charged pleaded guilty before the trial.

A private investigator had been paid to target the phones of certain people of interest to the newspaper. In one year the investigator was paid £100,000 for his work.

These events led to the government establishing a public Inquiry presided over by a judge, Lord Hutton, to investigate the issues surrounding the phone hacking scandal and to look at the role of the media and its regulation.

Following the closure of the *News of the World*, its owners published a new Sunday newspaper called *The Sun on Sunday*, which in 2020 was selling over 1 million copies a week.

Different viewpoint

Often the media state that what they do is in the public interest. Do you think this was the case in regard to phone hacking?

Case study
MPs' expenses

For a long time the press had been trying to use the Freedom of Information Act to find out about MPs' expenses. The Information Commissioner was involved and ordered the release of a detailed breakdown of the expenses. The campaign by journalists continued to try to get further information. Eventually in 2009

it was announced that there would be an inquiry into MPs' expenses, but it would report after the General Election. Seven weeks later, *The Daily Telegraph* published the first of a series of details about MPs' and ministers' expenses claims. It had purchased these files for £110,000. *The Daily Telegraph* continued publishing details about expenses over several weeks. The Speaker of the House of Commons resigned.

At the General Election in 2010, 232 new MPs were elected, mostly replacing MPs who decided not to stand again, many as a result of the expenses scandal.

A new body has since been established to regulate both MPs' expenses and salaries – the Independent Parliamentary Standards Authority (IPSA).

Different viewpoint

Does this case study meet the requirement of being in the public interest?

Should the fact that *The Daily Telegraph* paid for information that was illegally downloaded have an impact on whether it is still in the public interest?

Press regulation and censorship

Spec coverage
- The operation of press regulation and examples of where censorship is used.

In 2011, the government set up the Leveson Inquiry into the press, following allegations that the press acquired material for their stories by illegally hacking into people's phones and recording their conversations. This far-reaching inquiry looked into the role of the media in a modern society and also came up with a number of proposals about the balance between the rights and responsibilities of the press and how the press should be regulated.

It emerged that thousands of people had been subject to press intrusion. Many celebrities gave evidence at the inquiry as well as ordinary people, including Gerry McCann, father of the missing girl Madeleine McCann, and the parents of Milly Dowler. Lord Justice Leveson found that the press had 'wreaked havoc with the lives of innocent people'. His report was published in 2012 and made the following recommendations:

- The newspaper industry should continue to be self-regulated and the government should not try to control what papers publish.
- The old Press Complaints Commission (PCC) was not fit for purpose and should be replaced.
- A new body should be established to promote high standards, including the power to investigate complaints and impose penalties.
- This new body should be established by the industry with a new code of conduct.
- This new body should be backed up by legislation designed to ensure that it carried out its work properly.

Lord Justice Leveson believed this new system would give the public confidence that their complaints would be dealt with and it would ensure that the press was protected from government interference.

Following the Report's publication, a Royal Charter was eventually agreed that would establish a new regulator. This was opposed by the newspaper industry, which felt it gave too much power to politicians. The newspaper industry went ahead and established its own regulator outside the charter arrangements.

Discussion point
Is it better for the government to pass laws controlling the media or for the media to regulate itself?

The **Independent Press Standards Organisation (IPSO)** was set up in September 2014 by the newspaper industry. It handles complaints and conducts investigations into standards and compliance. It has the power to require published corrections, and can fine publications. Over 1400 print titles have signed up to IPSO. The *Guardian*, *The Independent* and the *Financial Times* have not joined IPSO. It has already adjudicated in over a thousand complaints. IPSO looks at complaints in relation to the Editors' Code of Practice, which is the ethical code under which journalists are expected to work.

The code relates to the following aspects of reporting:
- Accuracy
- Opportunity to reply
- Privacy
- Harassment
- Intrusion into grief or shock
- Children
- Children in sex cases
- Hospitals
- Reporting of crime
- Clandestine devices and subterfuge
- Victims of sexual assault
- Discrimination
- Financial journalism
- Confidential sources
- Witness payment in criminal trials
- Payments to criminals.

This code of conduct can be considered a form of self-censorship by the newspaper and magazine industry. Regarding all of these points, journalists should be able to state that the story was in the public interest and so was not in violation of the code.

The government approved a new body called **IMPRESS** to be the new press regulator, but very few newspapers have signed up to be a part of its regulatory structure. It has a complaints system that the public can use and does offer some financial protection for publishers facing court action.

Most newspapers belong to IPSO, but it is not government approved and doesn't provide the same legal safeguards as IMPRESS.

Censorship

Censorship is the ability to suppress or prevent the publication of information. As well as censorship by outside bodies, the press themselves at times exercise self-censorship where they refuse to use materials they are offered either individually or collectively as an industry. An example of this was in regard to the use of photographs surrounding the death of Diana, Princess of Wales in a car crash in Paris.

The media, like everyone else in society, is limited in certain areas by laws relating to libel, obscenity and blasphemy. In regard to national security, the government can issue DA-Notices that request that editors do not report a matter as it is against the national interest. The Terrorism Act 2006 made it an offence to 'glorify terrorism'. Some see this as a limit upon free speech. In 2013, the offices of the *Guardian* newspaper were raided by the police following the publication of stories about surveillance. The stories were based upon leaked material provided by Edward Snowden, a former National Security Agency (NSA) employee in the USA.

Censorship and social media

Increasingly, people are using social media platforms to access news and opinion. Social media allows ordinary people to comment upon news and even to report on unfolding events. We have all seen images and footage of events as they are happening, taken by people using their phones and posted to social media. These people are known as 'citizen journalists', and they report first-hand on events.

However, the fact that anyone can use social media means that there is no regulation on what is published. False claims and stories can be easily spread and in recent years conspiracy theories have become more common. Not only that, but there has been some evidence that states have used social media to influence the outcome of elections and referendums (most notably in the US elections).

While these drawbacks to social media raise the question of censorship, owners of these media

platforms deny they are responsible for the content published on them. Increasingly, they are trying to enforce some controls, rather than working within a legal framework.

Discussion point

Should social media platforms be treated any differently than newspapers with regard to censorship?

Censorship and other media forms

Censorship does exist in relation to other media formats. Films are classified as to their suitability for certain age groups by the British Board of Film Classification. If they are not approved, they cannot be shown in British cinemas. The Broadcast Advertising Clearance Centre approves all television advertising before it is shown. The Advertising Standards Authority (ASA) governs other advertising formats and **Ofcom**, a government body, has regulatory powers with regard to the media.

Websites

UK government: www.gov.uk

BARB (Broadcasters' Audience Research Board): www.barb.co.uk

Ofcom: www.ofcom.org.uk

IMPRESS: www.impress.press/about-us

Independent Parliamentary Standards Authority (IPSA): www.parliament.uk/about/mps-and-lords/members/pay-mps

Independent Press Standards Organisation: www.ipso.co.uk

Activity

Select a day when an interesting news story is going to appear. Select a range of newspapers and watch TV news stations on that day and use the internet. Produce a report showing how the different formats presented the news story.
a) Did any give it a specific slant?
b) How prominent was the story within their news agenda?
c) What commentary did they offer?
d) Which format did you think presented the news story most fairly?

Review questions

1 What is meant by the phrase a 'free press'?
2 What is the role of Ofcom?
3 Give two examples of social media.
4 Why was the *News of the World* closed down?

Learning review points

- What do we mean by the phrase 'the media'?
- Why is it important to have a 'free press'?
- What controls should operate with regard to the media?

EXAM PRACTICE

1 Name the government-appointed newspaper regulator. (AO1) [1 mark]
2 Referring to Figure 3.3 on page 17, consider two reasons why television is still the most used format for accessing news. (AO2) [4 marks]
3 Examine the case for and against *The Daily Telegraph*'s publication of materials it purchased about MPs' expenses (see page 20). (AO3) [8 marks]

Chapter 4: The UK's role in key international organisations

The role of the UK within key international organisations

The UK has played a major role in the establishment of many of the key international organisations and bodies that exist today. Many of these bodies came into existence in the period immediately after the end of the Second World War. In a recent poll of the power and influence of countries, the United Kingdom came top as the country that has more soft power influence than any other country. With regard to hard power, in the year ending March 2020, the UK spent £51.3bn, 2.85 per cent of its **Gross Domestic Product (GDP)**, on defence. Its defence budget is the fifth largest in the world. The USA had the largest defence budget, over the same period spending 3.5 per cent of its GDP.

United Nations (UN)

The UN was established in 1945 when representatives of 51 countries met in San Francisco in the USA to draw up the **United Nations Charter**. The United Nations officially came into existence on 24 October 1945. This day is now celebrated as United Nations Day.

Figure 4.1 UN Headquarters, New York

The UN has its headquarters in New York, where all member countries meet to decide the policy and actions to be taken by the UN. The General Assembly is the forum to which all member countries belong. The **Security Council** is made up of 15 members, five of whom are permanent and have the ability to **veto** any proposals. The UK was a founder member of the UN and has a permanent seat on the Security Council.

Today the UN is one of the most important international bodies in the world, with 193 members. In 1948, after much discussion and debate, the UN adopted the **Universal Declaration of Human Rights (UNDHR)**, which identified rights to which all people are entitled.

The four purposes set out in the Charter of the UN are:
1. to maintain international peace and security
2. to develop friendly relations among nations
3. to cooperate in solving international problems and in promoting respect for human rights
4. to be a centre for harmonising the actions of nations.

While it was established to help maintain peace, the work of the UN and its **agencies** now has an impact on many aspects of people's lives, from agriculture to health and education.

Some examples of UN Agencies and international bodies linked to the UN:
- FAO – the Food and Agricultural Organization aims to improve agricultural productivity.
- IAEA – the International Atomic Energy Authority works for the safe use of atomic power.
- ILO – the International Labour Organization aims to improve working conditions and set standards.
- UNESCO – the UN Educational, Scientific and Cultural Organization promotes education for all.
- WHO – the World Health Organization works to improve standards of health throughout the world.

The 30 member states of NATO (listed alphabetically) and the year they joined:

Albania (2009)	Iceland (1949)	Norway (1949)
Belgium (1949)	Italy (1949)	Poland (1999)
Bulgaria (2004)	Latvia (2004)	Portugal (1949)
Canada (1949)	Lithuania (2004)	Romania (2004)
Croatia (2009)		Slovakia (2004)
Czech Republic (1999)	Luxembourg (1949)	Slovenia (2004)
		Spain (1982)
Denmark (1949)	Montenegro (2017)	Turkey (1952)
Estonia (2004)	Netherlands (1949)	United Kingdom (1949)
France (1949)		
Germany (1955)	North Macedonia (2020)	United States of America (1949)
Greece (1952)		
Hungary (1999)		

The UN has often undertaken a peace-keeping role. It has no standing armed forces of its own and relies on member states **volunteering** forces and resources to support the UN's peace-keeping function. The United Kingdom has long been an active contributor to UN peace-keeping missions and is a major contributor to the peace-keeping budget. Since 1948, there have been 68 peace-keeping missions. At the beginning of 2020, the UN had 14 active peace-keeping operations.

British personnel are currently supporting three UN peace-keeping missions in:

- Cyprus (UNFICYP)
- The Democratic Republic of Congo (MONUSCO)
- South Sudan (UNMISS).

North Atlantic Treaty Organization (NATO)

NATO is an intergovernmental military defence alliance. It was established in 1949 and the UK was a founder member. It has its HQ in Brussels in Belgium. The organisation provides for a system of collective defence – if a member country is attacked, the other members come to its defence.

There are currently 30 member states of NATO (see box). Recent countries to become members are Albania and Croatia in 2009, Montenegro in 2017 and North Macedonia in 2020. Besides European countries, its membership includes the USA, Canada and Turkey.

NATO also has a number of partnership arrangements with other countries and organisations from the Atlantic to Central Asia and cooperates with a network of international organisations. While NATO has not been called upon to use its members' armed forces to defend its members' borders, it did take command of the UN-mandated International Security Assistance Force (ISAF) in Afghanistan in August 2003. Its mission was to enable the Afghan government to provide effective security across the country and to ensure that it would never again be a safe haven for terrorists. Its mission was completed at the end of 2014.

NATO member countries' combined military spending accounts for over 70 per cent of the world's defence spending. NATO has set a target for member countries to spend 2 per cent of their GDP on defence. Following the 2015 General Election, the Conservative government pledged to maintain UK defence spending at the 2 per cent target figure set by NATO for the next ten years.

European Union (EU)

The European Union (EU) was formerly known as the European Economic Community (EEC) and more usually as the Common Market. The six founding member countries that signed the Treaty of Rome in 1957 were France, West Germany, Belgium, the Netherlands, Luxembourg and Italy. The Community aimed to encourage trade between member countries, allow for the free movement of people between countries and work towards 'an ever-closer union'.

Sir Winston Churchill first suggested the idea of a United States of Europe in 1946. The EEC was seen as a way of preventing future wars. Twice in the twentieth century there had been war in Europe, with the six member countries taking opposing sides.

In 2020 there were 27 members of the EU, of which 19 used the **euro** as their currency. The United Kingdom joined in 1973, after being refused membership by the French President in 1961 and 1968. The headquarters of the Union is divided between Brussels in Belgium and Strasbourg in France. In June 2016 in a national referendum, the UK voted to leave the EU. The UK ceased to be a member of the EU in January 2020, and set a target of achieving a new treaty arrangement with the EU by January 2021. See page 27 for more details about the relationship between the UK and the EU.

The Union has its own directly elected Parliament, which is elected every four years.

The decision-making process within the European Union is different from that which operates in its member states. Proposals for new laws, directives or initiatives are drafted by the **European Commission**. These are then considered by the member state governments at **Council of the European Union** meetings. The **European Parliament** is then consulted. Four times a year, heads of government from all the member states meet at the **European Council** to discuss the political direction and priorities of the Union.

Council of Europe

The **Council of Europe** is the continent's leading human rights organisation. Forty-seven countries are members, of which 27 are also members of the European Union. The Council of Europe is not itself a part of the European Union. All member countries agreed to abide by the **European Convention on Human Rights**. The convention was adopted in 1950 and came into force in 1953. The **European Court of Human Rights** oversees the implementation of the Convention. The Court is made up of judges from all its member countries. The UK was a founder member of the Council of Europe and helped draft the Convention. Individual citizens can bring complaints of human rights violations to the Strasbourg Court, once all possibilities of appeal have been exhausted in the member state concerned.

The European Convention on Human Rights

The Convention enshrines the basic human rights and fundamental freedoms of everyone within the jurisdiction of any member state. These include rights:

- to life
- to protection against torture and inhuman treatment
- to freedom and safety
- to a fair trial
- to respect for private and family life
- to freedom of expression (including freedom of the press), thought, conscience and religion
- to freedom of peaceful assembly and association.

Commonwealth

Formerly known as the British Commonwealth, the Commonwealth has 54 member countries, which span Africa, Asia, the Americas, Europe and the Pacific. Thirty-one of the members are small states with fewer than 1.5 million people. It represents about 30 per cent of the world's population. Its members include some of the richest and some of the poorest countries in the world. All members must agree with the values set out in the **Commonwealth Charter**. The Commonwealth is a voluntary organisation and its Charter brings together the values that unite the Commonwealth – democracy, human rights and the rule of law. The Head of the Commonwealth is Queen Elizabeth II, and its headquarters are in London. Heads of government of the member states meet every two years at the Commonwealth Heads of Government Meeting (CHOGM).

Case study

Commonwealth helps St Lucia build climate resilience

St Lucia is a small country with limited resources to deal with the impact of severe weather.

With help via finance and technical assistance from the Commonwealth, the aim is to prepare post-disaster business plans, use new technology and enable schools to be used as emergency shelters.

Different viewpoint

Does the Commonwealth have a useful function in the twenty-first century?

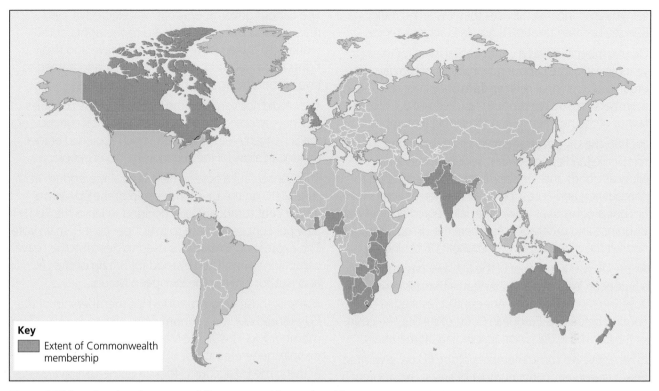

Figure 4.2 Map showing the extent of Commonwealth membership

World Trade Organization (WTO)

The World Trade Organization came into being in 1955 as the successor body to the General Agreement on Tariffs and Trade (GATT), which was set up at the end of the Second World War. The United Kingdom was a member of GATT from 1948 and joined the WTO in 1955. The WTO has 164 member countries and its headquarters are in Geneva, Switzerland. The WTO is the only global organisation dealing with trading rules between nations.

The WTO claims to:

- cut living costs and raise living standards
- settle trade disputes and reduce trade tensions between nations
- encourage economic growth and employment
- cut the cost of doing business
- encourage good governance
- help countries develop
- give the weak a stronger voice
- help support health and the environment
- contribute to peace and stability.

Discussion point

It is often said that 'the UK punches above its weight' when it comes to international affairs. To what extent do you think the statement is correct?

The UK and the EU

Spec coverage

- The UK's membership of the EU and its impact upon the UK.

The UK joined the then European Economic Community (EEC), usually known at the time as the Common Market, in 1973, 16 years after it was set up. By joining the EEC, the UK agreed to pool and share elements of our **sovereignty** over some policy areas. In those areas where the EU has been given **competence**, member governments cannot change or undermine the rules it has laid down. Where the EU has no competence, a national government can decide its own policy. For example, if the UK tried to amend its competition policy on takeovers and state aid to business, the EU would intervene as these rules are set at a European Union level. However, the Chancellor of the Exchequer could set whatever income tax rates they wished in their Budget, because taxation is not an EU competence.

Our membership was a controversial issue for many years. In 1975, the Labour government of the day organised a national **referendum** about our continued membership. The referendum resulted in a 2:1 vote in favour of the new terms and remaining a member.

In 1986, the UK government was fully supportive of the Single Market Agreement, which promised to allow all goods and services to be traded and open to competition and accessible to all businesses across the EU, but progress was slow, especially regarding financial, insurance and other services where the UK government had felt the agreement would benefit UK businesses.

As the UK was a member of the EU, laws passed at a European level had a higher status than UK laws covering the same issues. Any conflict resulted in cases coming before the European Court of Justice, the court of the EU whose decisions are binding on members.

In recent years, some members of the EU have wanted closer cooperation in a number of areas. This approach is often called **federalist** and UK governments ensured that the UK had opt-outs from many of the initiatives.

The Labour government that was elected in 1997 reversed this policy with regard to the rights of UK workers to maternity and paternity leave and the rights of casual and part-time workers, and agreed to implement the Social Chapter of EU policies.

The UK did not sign up to the Eurozone (those countries that have adopted the euro as their common currency) nor the Schengen Area Agreement, which abolished border controls to allow for the free movements of people.

The Conservative government held a referendum in June 2016 on the UK membership of the EU. With a 72 per cent turnout, voters decided to leave the EU by a 51.9 per cent Leave vote to a 48.1 per cent Remain vote. The expression '**Brexit**' was used to describe the Leave campaign's aims. The 'Br' stood for Britain or the UK, and 'exit' for leaving the European Union.

Many of those who supported UK membership of the EU pointed out the economic benefits to the UK of our membership. The Single Market, with its 500 million people, generates about £10 trillion of economic activity. The EU accounts for half of the UK's overall trade and investments. Around 3.5 million jobs in the UK are linked to our EU trade.

Case study
The EU In–Out Referendum, 2016

Since the 1990s, the gap between those who wanted to 'stay in' the EU and those who wanted to 'get out' narrowed significantly. The 1975 Referendum had been 2:1 in favour of remaining in the then EEC.

In the 2015 General Election, the United Kingdom Independence Party (UKIP) – whose main aim was for the UK to leave the European Union – achieved 3.9 million votes (12.6 per cent of the votes cast), but won in only one constituency. In the 2014 elections to the European Parliament, UKIP topped the poll with 27.5 per cent of the vote and had 24 MEPs elected.

Following the 2015 General Election, the re-elected Prime Minister, David Cameron, reiterated a Conservative Party manifesto commitment to hold an 'in–out' referendum on Britain's membership of the European Union by the end of 2017, following renegotiations with EU leaders. The referendum took place on 23 June 2016.

For the third time in its history, all the electors within the UK were able to take part in a referendum. In 1975 the referendum was about the UK membership of the European Economic Community, and in 2011 it

was about changing the voting system regarding how we elect MPs.

Both sides of the debate received taxpayer funding to promote their cause in the run-up to the 2016 referendum. Politicians from different political parties found themselves debating and disagreeing with members of their own parties.

While the television channels have to be politically neutral, the press was divided over our membership. The *Daily Mail*, *The Sun*, *Daily Express* and *Daily Telegraph* supported a Leave vote, while the *Daily Mirror*, *The Times*, *Guardian* and *Financial Times* supported a Remain vote. The Remain campaign was led by the Prime Minister and the Chancellor of the Exchequer, while two of the leading Leave campaigners were also important members of the Conservative Party: Boris Johnson and the Justice Minister, Michael Gove.

The case for Brexit

The slogan used by the Leave campaign in 2016 encapsulated its stance: 'Take Back Control'. It believed that for over 40 years the EU had undermined the sovereignty of the UK Parliament by taking control of many policy areas. It argued that the EU was basically undemocratic, with all its officials being appointed rather than directly elected. It thought the EU was leading to the end of the nation state and moving towards a federal United States of Europe. Also, issues such as the number of EU citizens migrating into the UK had caused resentment. It argued that, by moving away from the trade regulations of the EU, the UK could enter into more favourable trade agreements with the nations of the world.

The result

- Votes to Leave: 17,410,742 (51.9 per cent)
- Votes to Remain: 16,141,241 (48.1 per cent)

The turnout was 72 per cent. The results in Table 4.1 showed some interesting voting patterns:

Table 4.1 The results of the 2016 EU referendum

Nation	Vote to Leave (%)	Vote to Remain (%)	Turnout (%)
England	53.4	46.6	73.0
Scotland	38.0	62.0	67.2
Wales	52.5	47.5	71.7
Northern Ireland	44.2	55.8	62.9

In England, every counting region with the exception of London voted by a majority to leave the EU.

The morning after the count, David Cameron announced his resignation as Prime Minister and leader of the Conservative Party.

The UK and the EU after the separation – the divorce agreement

Following the referendum in 2016, there was political turmoil in the UK. The new Conservative Prime Minister, Theresa May, tried to make progress regarding leaving the EU, but Parliament was often deadlocked, so in May 2017 she called a General Election on the issue of Brexit.

The official opposition party, the Labour Party, also had a new leader, Jeremy Corbyn, from the far left of his party, who energised the party and was an effective campaigner. Following the election, the Conservatives lost their overall majority so had to make an

arrangement with the DUP (Democratic Unionist Party) from Northern Ireland, to have a majority in the House of Commons. The result of the election only added to the political turmoil at Westminster. The EU had insisted that the negotiations regarding the UK leaving the EU should fall into two parts, firstly a withdrawal agreement, detailing the process of leaving, and secondly a treaty about the future relationship of the UK and the EU.

Eventually Mrs May was forced to ask for an extension to the leaving date as she was not able to get a majority to support her in the House of Commons. The EU agreed that the UK membership could be extended until October 2019.

Mrs May was forced to stand down due to an inability to make progress on Brexit. In July 2019, Boris Johnson was elected as the new Conservative leader and Prime Minister. He called the third General Election in four years, in December 2019, and campaigned under the slogan 'Get Brexit Done'. The Conservatives won the election with a majority of 80 seats.

With this majority won by the Conservative government, it was able to agree the Withdrawal Agreement and formally leave the EU in January 2020, three months later than the original extension date under Mrs May. The impact of leaving was delayed for 12 months as the UK maintained the rights of membership until January 2021. At the time of writing, a treaty between the UK and the EU had been agreed in December 2020, but many matters are still to be resolved with further talks. The relationship between the UK financial sector and the EU is a major issue that is still outstanding.

Different viewpoints

'Referendums should not be used in the UK; we have an elected Parliament to make decisions on our behalf.' Carry out a survey to see who agrees and disagrees with this statement. What are the key points made by each side?

After more than 40 years' membership, the decision by the British people means that the UK has to negotiate a new arrangement with the EU.

What would be your priorities within these negotiations regarding, for example, trade, freedom of movement of peoples, accepting EU laws or paying to have access to the EU Single Market?

Table 4.2 The UK's possible future trade relations with the EU

		LEAVE SINGLE MARKET AND CUSTOMS UNION BUT NEGOTIATE BILATERAL TRADE AGREEMENT	LEAVE SINGLE MARKET AND CUSTOMS UNION WITH NO DEAL
KEY POINTS THE UK WANTS TO ACHIEVE BY LEAVING THE EU	Central migration from the EU	✔	✔
	End ECJ jurisdiction	✔	✔
	End applicability of EU regulations	✔	✔
	Pursue an independent trade policy	✔	✔
	Stop obligatory budgetary contributions to the EU	✔	✔
	Exit CAF and CFP	✔	✔
WHAT THE UK WANTS FROM THE EU	Tariff-free trade with the EU	✔	✔
	Access to the EU Single Market for services	Very limited	✗
	Seamless and frictionless border, including in Northern Ireland	✗	✗
	Voluntary participation in EU programmes	Partial	✗

The Lisbon Treaty, which includes a section about a country leaving the EU (Article 50), requires a country to formally announce it wants to leave. Then for a period of two years that country remains a member of the EU, but undertakes negotiations with the EU about their future relationship.

Table 4.2 outlines the options available for the UK's future relationship with the EU.

The second column indicates what the UK wishes to achieve from the talks.

> ### Discussion point
> Looking at the table of votes for each nation within the UK (Table 4.1 on page 29) what impact could leaving the EU have on the future cohesion of the UK?

International disputes and conflicts

> ### Spec coverage
> - How the UK has assisted in resolving international disputes and conflicts, and the range of methods used.

The UK has played an active part in attempting to resolve international disputes and conflicts. The methods used have varied from **mediation** to **humanitarian aid** (**soft power**), from the use of **sanctions** to the use of force (**hard power**). In recent years, the UK government has been involved in trying to resolve a number of international disputes and has worked with international bodies and agencies and directly with other nations to help resolve issues. Some of these interventions have been controversial and still divide public opinion in the UK. The UK's intervention in Iraq, 2001–09, was subject to a public Inquiry that eventually led to the publication of the Chilcot Report.

There was a huge anti-war demonstration in London to protest about British participation in the conflict. It happened just prior to a vote in the House of Commons in February 2003 about the UK taking part in the war. Police claimed it was the UK's biggest ever demonstration, with at least 750,000 taking part. The organisers put the figure closer to two million.

Mediation

The UK has been involved in numerous mediation attempts to resolve disputes and conflicts by seeking a peaceful resolution or sponsoring international conferences that lead to a peaceful resolution.

From 1968 until 1998, the history of Northern Ireland was linked to the phrase 'the Troubles'. Several attempts to seek a peaceful solution to the civil unrest and conflict between the opposing Unionist and Nationalist communities had failed. The UK

government imposed direct rule from Westminster. The bombing and killing spread from Northern Ireland to the UK mainland. By 1993, a framework had been agreed for a peaceful agreement to the Troubles, based upon the idea of 'consent': that any agreement could only proceed if the people of Northern Ireland consented. In 1996, the former US Senator George Mitchell agreed to chair the Northern Ireland peace talks. After all-party talks, an agreement was announced on Good Friday 1998.

This Good Friday Agreement was put to the people of both Northern Ireland and the Republic of Ireland (Eire) in a referendum, and both voted in favour of the agreement, which is still in force today. In this case, it took the influence of an outside but interested party – the USA – to enable an agreement, which involved the UK government, the government of the Irish Republic and all the political parties in Northern Ireland, to be reached.

Case study
'The Troubles' in Northern Ireland

	DATE	EVENT
1971	February	First soldier shot dead in Northern Ireland
	December	15 people killed in attack on Belfast pub (Ulster Volunteer Force)
1972	January	13 Catholic protesters killed by British troops
	July	9 killed in 22 IRA bombs in Belfast
1974	May	22 killed in car bombs in Dublin
	October	5 killed in a Guildford pub
	November	21 killed in two Birmingham pubs
1978	February	12 killed in hotel in County Down
1979	March	Conservative MP Airey Neave killed in car bomb attack
	August	Lord Mountbatten killed when his boat was blown up
		19 people died when a bomb exploded under a bus
1981	May	10 Republican (Nationalist) prisoners starve to death
1984	October	5 killed when IRA bombed Conservative Party Conference hotel
1987	November	11 killed during Remembrance service in Enniskillen
1988	March	Three IRA suspects shot by British Special Forces in Gibraltar
1990	July	Ian Gow, Conservative MP, murdered by IRA car bomb
1993	March	Warrington – 2 children killed by IRA bomb
1996	February	IRA bombed Canary Wharf, London, killing 2 people
	July	Manchester – IRA bombed shopping centre

Different viewpoint
To what extent is the peace settlement in Northern Ireland a good example of a mediation process?

Sanctions

The UK government operates a range of sanctions, from arms embargoes and trade control restrictions, to defence export policies against a number of countries and terrorist organisations. These sanctions are normally imposed as a part of a collective action by international bodies such as the EU, NATO or the UN.

In 2020, arms embargoes or controls were being imposed on 20 countries, ranging from Mali, Syria and Zimbabwe to Belarus and Russia.

Sometimes sanctions can take the form of **boycotts**, where citizens and organisations refuse to buy goods or use services relating to a specific country or company to express their opposition to a policy or action. Sometimes the government undertakes a boycott. In 2012, the UK government refused to send a minister to attend the UEFA football European Championship due to the actions of the then Ukraine government. Increasingly, the UK government is targeting individual citizens in foreign countries who have committed human rights abuse, and placing them under financial sanctions.

In the past, groups and citizens boycotted South African goods when the country was run by the **apartheid** regime. Nestlé, the Swiss-based company, has faced a boycott from consumers because of its policy of selling baby-feeding products in Africa.

Use of force

The United Kingdom armed forces have been involved in numerous military actions since 1990 (see Table 4.3). Most of the actions of British armed forces have involved working with others in alliances or the allocation of troops to an international force

Table 4.3 The UK's use of force since 1990

DATE	EVENT
1991	The Gulf War
1992–96	UN peace-keeping mission in the former Yugoslavia
1998	Operation Desert Fox – a four-day bombing campaign against targets in Iraq
1999	NATO-led campaigns in the former Republic of Yugoslavia and Kosovo
1999	East Timor, as part of a multinational peace-keeping force
2000	Sierra Leone, evacuating non-combatants and rescuing captured British troops
2001–14	Afghanistan – British troops were involved in combat operations as part of a US-led campaign
2003	EU-led crisis management in the Democratic Republic of the Congo
2003	Invasion of Iraq. British troops remained in Iraq until 2011
2011	Military intervention in Libya
2014	Iraq and Syria - Operation Shader
2019	Persian Gulf Crisis

under the control of an international body like the EU, NATO or the UN. Many of these actions have proved to be controversial. One parliamentary convention that developed following the Iraq war is that governments should obtain the approval of the House of Commons before committing British troops to action abroad.

The two case studies on this page are examples of the UK using military force to try to resolve an issue abroad.

Case study
Military intervention in Afghanistan

Quote from the National Army Museum website:

The war in Afghanistan spanned the tenures of three prime ministers, and cost the lives of 453 British service personnel and thousands of Afghans. What was accomplished after 13 years of conflict, which included eight years of heavy fighting in Helmand, still remains open to debate.

(Source: **www.nam.ac.uk/explore/war-afghanistan**)

Case study
Military intervention in Sierra Leone

The UK sent troops into Sierra Leone, a former British colony in Africa, in May 2000, to bring the civil war there to an end. The rebel Revolutionary United Front (RUF) was using extreme violence against its opponents in the conflict. Through Operation Palliser, the UK was able to support and re-establish a stable and democratic Sierra Leone under President Ahmad Tejan Kabbah, who achieved his office through an election declared as 'free and fair' by international observers.

Different viewpoint

Looking at these two case studies, do you think the use of force is an acceptable way to bring about change?

How non-governmental organisations respond to humanitarian crises

Spec coverage

● How non-governmental organisations (NGOs) respond to humanitarian crises.

Whenever there is a natural disaster or civil war, appeals are made to provide funds to help those in need. Many of these appeals are by single organisations, but they are often made by umbrella groups such as the Disasters Emergency Committee (DEC), which works with a range of **NGOs** to provide urgent help and relief. DEC works with 13 leading UK aid charities in times of crisis. Since its launch in 1963, it has run 67 appeals and raised more than £1.4 billion.

The UK government is the first country in the **G7** to honour the UN target set in 1970 of ring-fencing 0.7 per cent of its **GNI** for international aid spending. In 2020 the government announced that it would reduce our international aid funding to 0.5 per cent of GNI. The government allocates some of its funding to the work of NGOs.

The Department for International Development, which is currently responsible for allocating funding, has been subsumed into the Foreign Office and renamed the Foreign, Commonwealth and Development Office (FCDO). Announcing the merger in July 2020, the Prime Minister Boris Johnson stated, 'The merger is an opportunity for the UK to have even greater impact and influence on the world stage as we recover from the Covid-19 pandemic and prepare to hold the G7 presidency and host COP26 next year.'

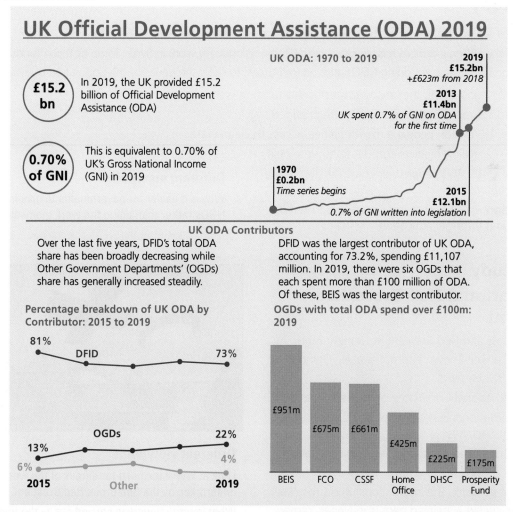

Figure 4.3 UK Official Development Assistance, 2019 (DFID is Department for International Development; BEIS is Department for Business, Energy & Industrial Strategy; FCO is Foreign & Commonwealth Office; CSSF is Conflict, Stability and Security Fund; DHSC is Department of Health and Social Care) (Source: **https://assets.publishing.service.gov.uk/government/uploads/system/ uploads/attachment_data/file/878395/Statistics-on-International-Development-Provisional-UK-Aid-Spend-2019.pdf**)

Case study

Oxfam

Oxfam is a UK-based international humanitarian relief NGO. This organisation dates back to 1942, when the Oxford Committee for Famine Relief was set up to pressure the wartime government to help starving children in Belgium and Greece. Today, Oxfam is a worldwide organisation providing a range of services and help.

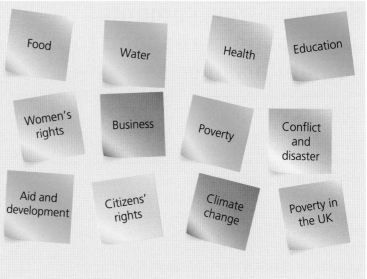

Different viewpoint

Look at www.oxfam.org.uk for details of the work of Oxfam.

Why in the twenty-first century is there still a need for charities like Oxfam?

Case study

The government working with NGOs and others in Syria

Since 2012 the UK government has allocated over £2.8bn to ongoing work in Syria. Some of those funds have assisted over 30 partners, including NGOs and the Red Cross, to meet the needs of the population of Syria.

Between 2012 and 2015, the key outcomes of this funding were:

- **Food** – 13.3 million ration portions were provided.
- **Water** – 1.6 million people a month gained access to clean water.
- **Health** – 2 million medical consultations were held.
- **Shelter** – 409,000 people were given shelter in the whole region.
- **Education** – 224,000 children were supported in formal and informal education.

Different viewpoint

Why is it easier for governments to give money to NGOs rather than doing the work themselves?

Case study

International Red Cross/Red Crescent

The Red Cross and Red Crescent movement is an example of a well-known international NGO and is made up of three parts:

1 The International Committee of the Red Cross (ICRC)
2 The International Federation of Red Cross and Red Crescent Societies
3 189 national Red Cross and Red Crescent societies around the world, including the British Red Cross.

As a part of its work, the International Red Cross/Red Crescent is currently helping people in Nepal, Yemen, Africa, Iraq, South Sudan and Syria.

Different viewpoint

Look at www.icrc.org for details of the work undertaken by the Red Cross/Red Crescent.

What important work is carried out by the International Red Cross/Red Crescent organisation?

Case study
MSF Factfile – Ukraine

Médecins Sans Frontières (Doctors without Borders, a medical charity that helps in humanitarian emergencies), set up in 1971, now operates in over 60 countries. In Ukraine, MSF has 62 staff working with 130 Ukrainian staff, providing basic health care and medicines in 25 locations on both sides of the disputed border. As the conflict has progressed, it has had to expand its psychological support and mental health provision and is helping people at 30 locations on both sides of the frontline.

Different viewpoint

Look at www.msf.org.uk for details of the work undertaken by Médecins Sans Frontières.

How does MSF help those in need?

Websites

United Nations: www.un.org/en

NATO: www.nato.int

EU: www.europa.eu/index_en.htm

Council of Europe: www.coe.int/en

Commonwealth: www.thecommonwealth.org

WTO: www.wto.org

International Committee of the Red Cross: www.icrc.org

MSF: www.msf.org.uk

Oxfam: www.oxfam.org.uk

FCDO: www.gov.uk/government/organisations/foreign-commonwealth-development-office

Review questions

1 Identify two international bodies to which the UK belongs.
2 Which body oversees human rights issues in Europe?
3 What is soft power?
4 Where can the UK use a veto?

Learning review points

● What is the role of the UK within:
   – the UN
   – NATO
   – the Council of Europe
   – the WTO
   – the Commonwealth?
● What is the relationship between the United Kingdom and the European Union?
● How are international disputes and conflicts resolved?
● What is the role and work of NGOs?

Activity

What actions do you think your school or local community could take in response to a humanitarian crisis? Consider inviting an NGO representative to come in to school to discuss the work of their organisation.

EXAM PRACTICE

1 Define the role of the UK at the United Nations. (AO1) [2 marks]
2 Referring to Table 4.2 on page 30, consider two consequences of leaving the EU without a treaty for the UK's relationship with the EU. (AO2) [4 marks]
3 Examine the arguments put forward that the UK spends too much on international aid. (AO3) [8 marks]

Chapter 5: Making a difference in society

- How can citizens make their voice heard and make a difference in society?

The opportunities and barriers

Spec coverage

- The opportunities and barriers to citizen participation in democracy.

Within a democracy like the United Kingdom, citizens have the right to participate in a variety of ways in issues that concern them. Some are formalised as a part of the democratic process:

- voting or access to elected members like **councillors** or Members of Parliament
- standing for election
- using e-democracy formats to set up online petitions on issues that may be discussed by the UK Parliament.

Citizens can also access the legal system and try to get the judiciary to make a decision about an issue that concerns them. They can work with others in pressure or interest groups to bring about change.

Money   Regulatory agencies
Business interest   Decisions
Associations   Morality
Influence   Lobbying groups   Public
Ethics
Laws   Critics   Advocacy
Corporations   Conflicts
Government   Legislators   Professional

Although in recent years there have been concerns about the decline in the number of people who vote in elections, especially young people, there has been an increase in the number of people who participate in pressure and interest groups and in the informal use of social network platforms, often in single-issue campaigns.

One such organisation is 38 Degrees. The organisers chose this name as 38 degrees is the tipping point for an avalanche to take place. 38 Degrees allows individuals to set up campaigns on issues they care about. If 38 Degrees accepts a campaign idea, it will help individuals set up petitions and organise action to get as much exposure and support as possible for the campaign. On its website, individuals can propose new campaigns and can support existing ones.

One of its earliest successful campaigns was about the proposed sell-off of the state-owned forests in the UK.

Save our Forests campaign

- Over 500,000 people signed the petition.
- Over 100,000 people wrote to or emailed their local MP.
- Raised money to carry out opinion polls and newspaper advertising.
- Over 220,000 people shared the campaign details on Facebook.

This campaign was ultimately successful as the Bill to sell off the state-owned forests was withdrawn.

38 Degrees' campaigns can be on local, national or international issues as they are generated by individuals or groups. The case studies on the next page are examples of recent campaigns.

Save our Human Rights Act

This was a national campaign in 2019 trying to prevent the government making changes to human rights laws in the UK. Over 300,000 people signed in support.

Save Staffordshire Countryside and AONB

Some petitions are local and achieve smaller numbers of supporters, but are still successful. The campaign to save Staffordshire countryside and AONB is an example. In 2015 the sponsors of the petition, which was signed by 11,978 people, wrote to supporters:

Today has been a very good day! The councillors voted unanimously to accept our petition, and voted to never sell the Staffordshire Countryside and Green Spaces to private investors.

Save the BBC

In 2019, over 300,000 people signed a petition against changes that were proposed to the ways the BBC operates.

United for Grenfell

The tragedy of the Grenfell Tower fire in 2017 led to a petition about combustible building materials.

Within a week the petition had 59,000 signatures.

The campaign led to the government setting new standards for cladding on new buildings. It also helped to fund the removal of dangerous cladding on social housing tower blocks and to ensure that companies remove dangerous cladding from buildings in the private sector.

Voter turnout since 1945 in UK General Elections

The issue of **voter turnout** shown in Table 5.1 does not just concern people in the UK. Table 5.2 shows voter turnout in national elections across a range of countries. One of the major concerns regarding voter turnout has been in regard to young people. Figure 5.1 (on page 39) indicates that young people in the UK are the least likely to have voted in a General Election, compared with other young people in Europe.

Table 5.1 Voter turnout in General Elections in the United Kingdom from 1945 to 2019

GENERAL ELECTION DATE	TURNOUT (%)
1945	72.8
1950	83.9
1951	82.6
1955	76.8
1959	78.7
1964	77.1
1966	75.8
1970	72
Feb 1974	78.8
Oct 1974	72.8
1979	76
1983	72.7
1987	75.3
1992	77.7
1997	71.4
2001	59.4
2005	61.4
2010	65.1
2015	66.1
2017	68.8
2019	67.3

Table 5.2 How Britain's voter turnout measures up: voter turnout in selected developed nations (most recent national election)

COUNTRY AND YEAR OF ELECTION	PERCENTAGE TURNOUT
Belgium* (2014)	87.2%
Turkey* (2011)	86.4%
Sweden (2014)	82.6%
Australia* (2013)	80.5%
South Korea (2012)	80.4%
Israel (2015)	76.1%
Greece* (2015)	71.9%
France (2012)	71.2%
United Kingdom (2019)	67.3%
United States (2020)	67.0%
Germany (2013)	66.0%
Spain (2011)	63.3%
Canada (2011)	54.2%
Japan (2014)	52.0%
Switzerland (2011)	40.0%

* National law makes voting compulsory, though this is not necessarily enforced.
In addition, one Swiss canton has compulsory voting.

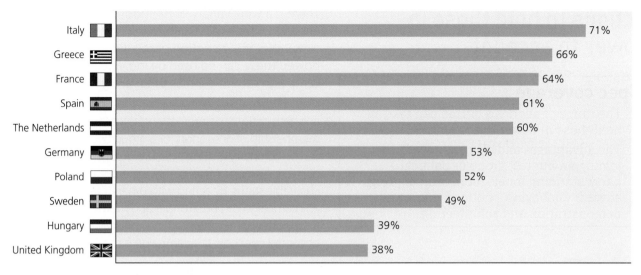

Figure 5.1 Percentage of people aged 18–24 who have voted in at least one political election, by European country, 2014 (Source: Eurobarometer, ONS)

> ### Discussion point
> Why should we be concerned about low levels of voter turnout? Is the answer to make voting compulsory or should people have the right not to take part?

Table 5.3 Turnout by age group in the 2019 General Election

AGE	TURNOUT
18–24	47%
25–34	55%
35–44	54%
45–54	63%
55–64	66%
65+	74%

What are the barriers to participation in the democratic process?

People who do not participate give a wide range of reasons why:

- Lack of interest or apathy
- A belief that their participation will not make a difference
- A lack of faith in politicians and the political process
- A lack of information or understanding about how to participate
- The issues are not important to them
- They lead busy lives.

Some attempts have been made to make voting and registering to vote easier, but many of the points above relate to the motivation or interest of the individual and this was one of the reasons why Citizenship was introduced as a compulsory national curriculum subject, to introduce students to the nature of participation in a democratic society. Suggestions to increase voter participation include:

- Compulsory voting
- Lowering the voting age to 16
- Allowing online voting.

It does appear that, if people and especially young people are motivated about an issue, they will take part. The referendum on Scottish Independence in 2014 shows that, when people think their vote will make a difference and the issue they are voting about is clearly defined, they are prepared to take part. In this referendum, 16- and 17-year-olds were able to vote and over 109,000 in that age group registered to vote. Overall, the referendum turnout was 84.6 per cent.

Actions to hold those in power to account

Spec coverage

- The range of actions a citizen can take to hold those in power to account.
- The advantages and disadvantages of joining an interest group or political party, standing for election, campaigning, advocacy, lobbying, petitions, joining a demonstration and volunteering.

There is a wide variety of methods citizens can use to engage with the political process, to bring their views to others' attention or to influence those in power. These can be used by individual citizens or by campaign groups such as **pressure groups**.

Many people now get involved in their local communities and with national or international issues through membership of or support for a group or cause. These can be voluntary groups, pressure groups, **trade unions** or interest groups. Many of these groups also have charitable status. By acting with others, the message of any campaign can be stronger and more effective. But as a supporter or member, you may not have so much say or control over how the campaign is run.

Petitions – collections of signatures indicating support for an agreed statement. These are used to show the strength of support for the statement. Increasingly, petitions are now completed online and are called e-petitions.

Leafleting – distributing materials that support a particular point of view, often asking for support and/or financial help.

Lobbying – a general term about making your views known to those whose opinions you wish to influence. The specific term relates to citizens approaching their MP to raise an issue. This is done in the Lobby of the House of Commons. Advocacy is a form of lobbying, where a person or a group puts forward their ideas to advocate a certain position. Often this is done verbally, but it can be in writing.

Direct action – this can take either a non-violent or a violent form. Non-violent examples include strikes, occupation of buildings and sit-ins. This can lead to protesters being arrested, for example for refusing to leave property or blocking roads. Violent direct action is criminal activity. Examples include when protesters seek to destroy property, assault others or instigate a riot. The term 'civil disobedience' also relates to direct action. This normally involves citizens disobeying rules or laws with which they disagree.

Boycotts – deciding not to purchase certain goods or services because of a particular cause.

Demonstrations – these can take many forms, from small groups to mass marches and rallies.

Media promotion – staging events and protests to attract media attention and publicity.

Use of celebrity – by attracting celebrities, causes are often able to gain media coverage and boost the number of their supporters.

Use of e-media – this format of campaigning has become increasingly important. E-media enables groups to contact their supporters quickly, give them the latest information and correct any media stories. It also enables groups to quickly contact the traditional media (newspapers and television).

Joining a political party can be another way of campaigning on issues that concern you. Whereas a pressure group, such as the RSPB or the RSPCA, may have specific campaigning issues around bird and animal welfare, political parties have to have a position on every aspect of public life, from defence, to the economy, to welfare issues including animal welfare, to levels of taxation.

Joining a political party allows a citizen to be supported if they wish to stand for election to a public office, provided their party wishes to support them. They could stand for election as a councillor, a **Police and Crime Commissioner**, or as an MP or MEP. In the 2015 General Election, Mhairi Black of the Scottish National Party (SNP), who was 20 years old and still a university student, was elected to the UK Parliament. She represents the Paisley and Renfrewshire South constituency. She was the youngest MP since the seventeenth century.

The youngest MP elected at the 2019 General Election was Nadia Whittome, who was elected as the Labour MP for Nottingham East at the age of 23. She has vowed to give half of her annual salary away to charities in her constituency.

Figure 5.2 Nadia Whittome, Labour MP

The role of organisations

Spec coverage
- The role of organisations such as: public services, interest groups, pressure groups, trade unions, charities and voluntary groups, and how they play a role in providing a voice and support for different groups in society.

Often by working with others, citizens can help achieve the changes they wish.

Table 5.4 gives an indication of the range of groups where citizens working together are trying to promote change.

Table 5.4 Range of organisations

RSPCA	Animal Liberation Front	Shelter	European Movement
Confederation of British Industry	Countryside Alliance	Welsh Language Society	Greenpeace
Friends of the Earth	Surfers Against Sewage	Rowers Against Thames Sewage (RATS)	Fathers4Justice
Mothers Apart from their Children	NSPCC	Campaign for Real Ale	Amnesty International
Liberty	Christian Aid	Oxfam	Charter88
Electoral Reform Society	Migration Watch UK	Muslim Council of Britain	TaxPayers' Alliance
British Humanist Association	Fawcett Society	FOREST	Animal Aid

Many pressure groups and interest groups are local; others are national and some international. Not all pressure groups operate in the same way. They are classified in different ways by: their status, the nature of the issue they are concerned about or the methods they use.

- **Single-cause groups:** These pressure groups focus on a single issue: for example, those opposed to the (HS2) high-speed rail development.
- **Multi-cause groups:** These are groups that seek to influence policy and decisions over a range of issues, such as trade unions that seek to influence policy on pay, hours of work, health and safety, pensions, discrimination, etc., for example the RMT.
- **Protective:** Groups that seek to protect the interests of their members: for example, the British Medical Association, which is the professional body that speaks on behalf of doctors.
- **Promotional:** These are groups that wish to promote views to their members and other interested parties on a particular topic. For example, Greenpeace is interested in environmental issues.

Groups are also classified by their status as insider or outsider groups:

- Insider status implies that the group is able to discuss with, meet and be consulted by those it wishes to influence. For example, if there were to be changes to rural planning regulations, the government would consult the Campaign to Protect Rural England (CPRE), but it would be unlikely to involve the Countryside Alliance, which is seen as an outsider group, in direct talks or negotiations.

- Outsider status implies that the group does not have direct access to those making decisions and is not consulted or directly involved in discussions.

Some groups often seek outsider status, not wishing to be a part of the 'system' of talks and negotiations. They are often deemed to be outsiders because the methods they use involve direct action. Fathers4Justice was labelled an outsider group.

Figure 5.3 Campaigning to stop the sale of forests in the UK

In recent years, membership of political parties has been in decline while that of single-issue groups has been increasing (Table 5.5).

Table 5.5 The comparative membership of political parties, trade unions and pressure groups

POLITICAL PARTY MEMBERSHIP	TRADE UNIONS	PRESSURE, INTEREST AND VOLUNTARY GROUPS
Labour 580,000	Unite 1,400,000	National Trust 5,600,000
Conservatives 180,000	Unison 1,300,000	Greenpeace 2,800,000 internationally
SNP 125,482	GMB 631,000	RSPB over 1 million
Lib Dems 120,845	USDAW 450,000	Women's Institute 220,000
Greens 48,500	NEU 450,00	Countryside Alliance 100,000
UKIP 26,447	NASUWT 313,000	TaxPayers' Alliance 18,000

While there are benefits to pressure or interest groups working with decision-makers, there are those who say that they have too much influence (Table 5.6).

Discussion point

Which point of view do you agree with about the role of pressure groups?

Table 5.6 Arguments for and against pressure groups

POINTS THAT SUPPORT THE VIEW THAT PRESSURE GROUPS STRENGTHEN THE INFLUENCE OF THE CITIZEN	POINTS THAT DO NOT SUPPORT THE VIEW THAT PRESSURE GROUPS STRENGTHEN THE INFLUENCE OF THE CITIZEN
More people belong to pressure groups than to political parties.	Pressure groups have too much influence, as they are concerned about a narrow issue.
Pressure groups speak up for the public on issues that politicians do not discuss.	Politicians pay too much attention to pressure groups, all of which are unrepresentative.
Pressure groups exert pressure on issues between elections.	Pressure groups are themselves undemocratic and often use non-democratic methods.
If pressure groups did not exist, politicians could ignore a large number of issues.	Some insider groups exert too much power and influence, to the detriment of the whole population.
Pressure groups can raise immediate issues with politicians.	Politicians are too concerned with immediate headlines and over-react to every protest.

Voluntary groups are playing an increasingly important part in the life of many local communities. Many 16-year-olds have taken part in the National Citizenship Service programme, which involves an element of volunteering. Volunteering in this context is about helping others by giving your time free of charge. This might involve helping at the local library or assisting at a local hospital.

Increasingly, the public sector looks to volunteers to help provide services and support. The Covid-19 pandemic demonstrated the importance of volunteering to community life. Individuals signed up to help each other, through delivering medicines, providing food, and looking out for the lonely. Many became NHS volunteers and Facebook groups sprang up in every community to offer help to those in need.

How citizens work together to change communities

Spec coverage

- Two different examples of how citizens working together, or through groups, attempt to change or improve their communities through actions to either address public policy, challenge injustice or resolve a local community issue.

Throughout this book, case studies of individuals and groups taking action are used to explain why and how people try to bring about change and the outcomes they achieve.

These case studies can be locally based, about national government or be global issues, but they are all about trying to bring about a change, be that in people's attitudes or in policy. Examples of how people can bring about change in their local communities are shown below.

Case study

Westmill wind farm

Westmill wind farm is a community-owned onshore wind farm in Oxfordshire in the South East of England. It was a partnership arrangement with the landowner. Windpower Over Westmill (WOW), the community group, established a cooperative society among people who live in the 2500 homes that use its electricity. This is an example of an environmental issue linked to cooperative community thinking.

Different viewpoint

Carry out a survey in your class or local community to find out people's views about wind farms on land or at sea. Why do people take such opposing views about the development of new wind farms?

Case study

Surfers Against Sewage

Surfers Against Sewage (SAS) launched a new campaign to clean up UK beaches following the Covid-19 pandemic, which they say caused a new wave of plastic pollution. They say they saw an explosion of discarded masks and plastics on beaches and in rivers. They intend to use social media to name and shame individual companies whose waste they most frequently find.

(Source: **www.bbc.co.uk/news/uk-england-bristol-53947161**)

Different viewpoint

Surfers Against Sewage is not a large or powerful pressure group so why do you think it is so successful?

How those who wish to bring about change use the media

Spec coverage

- How those who wish to bring about change use the media.

We all now live in a new 24-hour society, where within minutes millions know about something happening on the other side of the world. The media – both traditional and the new e-media – is still important to those who wish to influence public opinion. It often helps set the political agenda because politicians have to respond to stories published in the media or appearing on social media platforms. Individuals and groups use a range of methods to attract media attention and support. The following case studies illustrate different ways in which media attention can be gained.

Case study

Marcus Rashford fights for school meals

During the Covid-19 pandemic, schools were closed for much of the academic year. For many children, the midday school lunch is a very important meal. The government started a scheme, giving food vouchers to the poorest families. When the government announced the scheme would end over the summer, the Manchester United and England footballer Marcus Rashford wrote to the Prime Minister stating how important it was that the poorest had access to food. Speaking from personal experience, he explained that he had grown up in poverty so was aware of the issue many were facing. The government changed its decision and Rashford got together with the largest food suppliers to establish a Food Foundation to help those in need.

Different viewpoint

Why do you think the government took notice of Marcus and his campaign?

Case study

The European migrant crisis

In recent years, the issue of migration into the European Union and the UK has received prominent news coverage. Many of these migrants have travelled from areas of the world where there are civil wars or they face persecution for their beliefs or faith and they are forced to flee their homelands. Others are economic migrants who wish to find work and better economic prospects for themselves and their families. Charities such as Save the Children have run campaigns seeking financial help and support from the public.

The famous street artist Banksy bought the MV Louise Michel, an ex-French Navy vessel to help rescue migrants in the Mediterranean. At one stage it became so overloaded with rescued migrants that other boats

had to come to its assistance. Sea-Watch International, a charity working with Banksy, said there were 353 people on board who had been at sea for several days. The MSF Sea Team were treating many for dehydration, traumatic injuries, hypothermia and fuel burns. Surrounding countries were refusing to allow the ship to dock.

(Source: **https://news.sky.com/story/migrants-from-banksy-funded-boat-stranded-as-italy-and-malta-refuse-safe-port-charity-says-12059823**)

Different viewpoint

To what extent have the media and charities been able to influence public opinion and the UK government regarding the issue of migration? Use a range of internet sources to support your point of view.

Websites

38 Degrees: https://you.38degrees.org.uk

National Council for Voluntary Organisations: www.ncvo.org.uk

Nadia Whittome MP: https://members.parliament.uk/member/4869/contact

Mhairi Black MP: https://mhairiblack.scot

Surfers Against Sewage: www.sas.org.uk

Chefs in Schools: www.chefsinschools.org.uk

Sea-Watch: https://sea-watch.org/en

Extinction Rebellion: https://extinctionrebellion.uk/the-truth/about-us

Review questions

1 Using an example, explain the term 'volunteering'.
2 What is meant by the term 'turnout'?
3 Name one single-cause pressure group.
4 What is a Police and Crime Commissioner?

Activity

You are asked to make a presentation to your class about the work of three different types of pressure group (i.e. single cause, protective group, insider group, and outsider group).

One example must be a local group, another a national group and the last an international group. Use your presentation to test the knowledge of your class about pressure groups.

Learning review points

- How can citizens play an active part in our democratic process?
- Why is taking part in elections important?
- What barriers are there to citizens taking part in the democratic process?
- What are pressure groups?
- What methods do individuals and groups use to bring about change?

EXAM PRACTICE

1 Identify two national campaigns for change that have used celebrities to promote their cause. (AO1) [2 marks]
2 Referring to Table 5.3 (page 39), discuss two reasons why voter turnout is as shown in the table. (AO2) [4 marks]
3 Examine why some pressure groups are more successful than others. (AO3) [8 marks]

- What laws does a society require and why?

The fundamental principles of law

Spec coverage

- The fundamental principles of law to ensure rights and freedoms; the presumption of innocence and equality before the law.

Desert island scenarios

Look at the illustration below, which shows two situations occurring after a shipwreck. On the desert island on the left, the person is living on their own. They have to build their own home, find and cook their own food, and they can use everything from the wreck. There is nobody to tell them what to do or what not to do. They must survive by themselves and cope on their own and they are totally responsible for themselves and their survival.

On the desert island on the right, a group of people must learn to live together. For every situation, from finding and cooking food to building a shelter, they have to consider questions such as:

- Should they work together or alone?
- If they are working together, should someone become the leader?
- How should they decide on a leader?
- What rules would they have on the island and how would they agree on them?
- What would happen to people who didn't follow the rules, and who would enforce this?

Each of these is an important question that has a number of other questions within it – see the Discussion point box on the next page.

Discussion point

- **How do they decide issues?**

  Should this involve everybody? Should there be an age limit to those who can help decide? Should they decide by meeting, discussion and voting? Should the voting be open or secret? Should everybody's vote be of equal worth? Or should the group select a person or people to make these decisions on their behalf, because they are busy doing the tasks that enable the group to survive on the island? These are basic questions about how you organise decision-making in a society.

- **Who makes the rules?**

  Should everybody be involved or should a few be selected? If there are people in the group who have experience of legal issues, should they be left to sort out the rules? What sort of rules does the island need? Should they be about protecting the resources, like the food and water available to the group? Who owns the goods from the shipwreck? Are rules needed to stop theft or violence? Would rules stop any person or group taking advantage of any other person or group on the island? Should there be rules about doing work on the island for the benefit of all in order to receive food and shelter?

- **Who enforces the rules?**

  Is it the responsibility of everybody on the island to enforce the rules, report those breaking the rules and call those who break the rules to account? Or should the group select someone to do this on their behalf? Who decides what happens to those who break the rules? Should everybody take part in the decision-making process about guilt or innocence? Should any punishment be decided case by case or should there be agreed punishments for each rule that is broken? Is the person who is said to have broken the rules assumed to be innocent or guilty? Do they have to prove their innocence or it is up to others to prove them guilty?

While these might seem abstract questions about an imaginary group on a desert island, the questions posed go to the heart of the principles relating to law in our society. By answering these questions, we are drafting our own views about the concepts of justice, fairness, presumption of innocence and equality before the law, which are the basic building blocks of our legal system.

- **Justice** is defined as a behaviour or treatment that is morally right and fair. At times, there are differences of opinion between countries about what justice is. Each country's justice system is based upon its system of morality, which can be different from another country's system.

- **Fairness** relates to treating people equally and appropriately according to the circumstances. Two people from differing circumstances who each commit the same offence for the first time should not be dealt with differently.

- Within our legal system there is a 'presumption of innocence'. This assumes that a person brought before a court is innocent and it is up to the state to prove their guilt beyond reasonable doubt rather than the accused having to prove their innocence.

- Equality before the law is about the law treating every person equally, allowing every person equal access to the justice system.

These concepts are incorporated into the more general concept of 'the rule of law', which is a doctrine whereby every person, no matter whom they are, is subject to the law, and every person should be treated equally. This concept incorporates the following principles:

- The idea of legal certainty
- That laws are properly enacted and clear in their purpose
- That there is equality and fairness
- That laws cannot be retrospective: that is, you cannot be charged with doing something that is now an offence but which you carried out before the law came into force
- That there is due legal process.

Another fundamental aspect of our legal system is the role of the citizen. Many trials are determined by the decision of a jury made up of randomly selected citizens. Citizens can also become **magistrates** (justices of the peace – JPs) in their local communities. The Magistrates' Courts deal with a large percentage of all criminal cases.

When considering the elements that comprise a legal system, look at Figure 6.1 on page 48 and think about the consequences of each of the missing elements indicated by a cross.

(a) Laws   Police   Courts and punishment

Each of these elements is required for a successful legal system: laws are made that apply to everyone; the police are expected to enforce the law and apprehend those suspected of breaking the law; those accused appear before a court and if guilty are punished.

(b)

No courts – there would be no examination of the evidence to prove guilt or innocence and there would be no form of punishment.

(c)

No police – it is unlikely that offenders would be brought to court.

(d)

No laws – the police could arrest anybody for any offence and the courts could hand out any punishment they liked.

Figure 6.1 The importance of every element of the legal system

Rules and laws

Spec coverage

- The nature of rules and laws in helping society deal with complex problems of fairness, justice and discrimination.

Rules and laws

The term 'rules' is used in relation to the way a group or organisation operates, while laws relate to the way in which society is regulated.

For example, one school might have rules relating to uniform while another school might have a non-uniform policy.

The law relates to your health and safety at school and applies to every school.

As society has developed over time, the issues that society expects the legal system to help resolve have become more complex, involving the reconciliation of different views about what fairness or justice are and increasing our awareness and understanding of issues of **discrimination**. In recent years, a number of

Legislation against discrimination

- Equal Pay Act 1970
- Sex Discrimination Act 1975
- Race Relations Act 1976
- Disability Discrimination Act 1995
- Employment Equality (Religion or Belief) Regulations 2003
- Employment Equality (Sexual Orientation) Regulations 2003
- Employment Equality (Age) Regulations 2006
- Equality Act (Part 2) 2006
- Equality Act (Sexual Orientation) Regulations 2007

pieces of legislation have been enacted, for example to counter discrimination. Many of the examples of legislation listed in the box below have now been consolidated into the Equality Act 2010.

Society has also developed areas of law relating to the rights of the citizen.

See Table 11.1 on page 95 for further examples of changes to individual rights and equality issues in the UK.

Discussion point

Today there are still areas of contention about fairness, justice and discrimination. Here are some of the complex issues about which the legal system is called upon to make a judgment.

> Earl Daren Rodney was jailed for taking part in ransacking shops during the 2011 London riots. He was not deported back to Jamaica because he had fathered children in the UK.

- Should the fact that a person has children in the UK overrule their deportation after they have served a prison sentence?

> Paralysed former builder Paul Lamb lost his case in the European Court of Human Rights. He had requested the right to die. This was the culmination of a campaign to allow disabled people the right to die with dignity. The case went to the European Court after the Supreme Court of the UK rejected the case by a 7:2 vote of the judges. In September 2015, in a free vote in the House of Commons, MPs voted by 118 votes to 330 against plans to allow some terminally ill adults to end their lives with medical supervision.

- Should there be a right to supervised death if that is the patient's wish?

> NHS staff who blow the whistle on substandard and dangerous practices are being ignored and bullied and work within 'a climate of fear', according to a report written by Sir Robert Francis.

- How should whistleblowers be protected if they report unsafe and dangerous practices?

Rights in local to global situations

Spec coverage
- Rights in local to global situations where there is a conflict and rights and responsibilities need to be balanced.

Different societies, cultures and countries have differing views on some legal issues. For example, the death penalty was abolished in the UK while it is still used in other countries. In the USA, it is fairly easy to obtain a gun legally, and the country has a very high death rate from gun violence, whereas in the UK there are very tight controls over gun ownership.

Following the end of the Second World War in 1945 and the establishment of the United Nations, it was decided to try to establish agreement on common human rights for all people. This led to the **Universal Declaration of Human Rights** being drafted. It was added to and in 1976 gained the standing of International Law. Currently 192 countries have signed the Declaration.

The Council of Europe further devised the European Convention on Human Rights. The UK played a major part in its drafting and was one of the original signatories in 1950. Currently 47 countries have signed the Convention. Many members of the Council incorporated the Convention into their constitutions.

The Equality and Human Rights Commission is a government body that oversees and regulates the **Equality Act 2010**, which brought together over 116 separate pieces of legislation into one single Act. The Act aims to provide a framework to protect individuals from unfair treatment and promote a fair and more equal society.

Increasingly, where there are complex issues – especially those involving international disputes – bodies have been established to allow countries to resolve issues peacefully rather than by taking action. The International Criminal Court is one example. The World Trade Organization helps resolve trade disputes.

Rights and differences of view internationally can also have an impact upon individuals.

The **European Arrest Warrant** is a European Union agreement that allows a police force in one member country to ask a police force in another to arrest someone. It has assisted in bringing many people to justice.

In 2019/20 the UK received 14,533 requests from other countries to trace and arrest people. Countries can send requests to every member country if they do not know where the person is living. In 2019/20 the UK arrested 1168 wanted persons who were subject to EAWs. In the same year, the UK made 228 requests to other countries. Since leaving the EU, the UK no longer has access to the EAW system and must apply through Interpol for assistance.

Many cases of rights across borders affect individual citizens. In the following case studies, what course of action would you have taken? What is the balance between rights and responsibilities?

Case study
School launches campaign to stop deportation

Schools across Ireland have been asked to support a secondary school in Cork that is fighting to stop the deportation of four brothers, three of whom attend the school.

Hamsa, Zubair, Umair and Mutjuba Khan came to Ireland with their parents in 2017.

They have all been refused asylum. The oldest brother left the school in 2019 and is now studying computer sciences. Their parents fled from Pakistan to Saudi Arabia in 1982, to escape persecution. All of their children were born in Saudi Arabia and the family lived there until 2015, when new tax laws were introduced that favoured Saudi citizens, and led to the family facing deportation to Pakistan. The Khans fled Saudi Arabia and are now facing deportation to the United Kingdom as that was their first landing point in Europe.

(Source: **www.rte.ie/news/2020/0113/1106183-cork-students-deportation**)

Different viewpoint
How can issues surrounding the Khan family be fairly and justly resolved?

Websites
The Equality and Human Rights Commission: www.equalityhumanrights.com

European Court of Human Rights: www.coe.int/t/democracy/migration/bodies/echr_en.asp

Universal Declaration of Human Rights: www.un.org/en/universal-declaration-human-rights

European Convention on Human Rights: www.echr.coe.int/Documents/Convention_ENG.pdf

Activity
Consider the scenario on page 46 about the group of people living on the desert island. What do you think are the ten most important laws or rules that they should all agree? Organise a class or group discussion to arrive at your decisions.

Review questions

1 When was the UNDHR devised?
2 Where does the European Court of Human Rights meet?
3 What was the aim of the 2010 Equality Act?
4 Which body in the UK is responsible for promoting anti-discrimination policies?

Learning review points

● What are the basic principles of law?
● What do you understand by 'justice' and 'fairness'?
● What laws has the UK introduced to outlaw discrimination?
● Why is the UNDHR important?

EXAM PRACTICE

1 Explain what is meant by the phrase 'equality before the law'. (AO1) [1 mark]
2 Using the information on page 48, describe using other examples how rules differ from laws. (AO2) [4 marks]
3 Justify the case for **or** against all non-UK citizens who serve a prison sentence in the UK being deported back to their own country after their release from prison. (AO3) [8 marks]

Chapter 7: Rights and responsibilities within the legal system

Key question

- What are a citizen's rights and responsibilities within the legal system?

The operation of the justice system

Spec coverage

- The operation of the justice system:
  - the role and powers of the police
  - the role and powers of the judiciary
  - the roles of legal representatives
  - how the different criminal and civil courts work
  - tribunals and other means of dispute resolution.

The justice system in the UK is made up of distinct interlocking parts that are independent of each other. The nature of the justice system varies slightly in the different parts of the United Kingdom, mainly for historical reasons.

The role and powers of the police

The part of the justice system that we are most likely to encounter is the police. While other countries have national police forces accountable to a government department and minister, in the UK the police are organised on a regional basis. Figure 7.1 shows the boundaries of the 43 distinct police forces in England and Wales. The former regional police forces in Scotland have just merged into a single force called Police Scotland and there is a single police force in Northern Ireland called the PSNI (Police Service of Northern Ireland).

In the capital city, London, there are two police forces. The City of London Police just operates within the old historical boundaries of the city, sometimes called the 'Square Mile'. It is the smallest police force in the UK. The Metropolitan Police Service covers over 600 square miles and a population of over 8 million, and is the largest police force in the UK. It employs over 44,000 people.

Figure 7.1 Boundaries of the 43 police forces

Roles within the police

In 2012, the role of Police and Crime Commissioner was established. These Commissioners are in charge of the workings of local police forces. They are directly elected by, and accountable to, the public.

Candidates for this role can stand independently or with the support of a political party.

In the 2012 elections for the 41 posts (the two forces in London do not have Police and Crime Commissioners), the Conservatives won 16, Labour 13 and 12 were won by Independents. The average turnout was 15 per cent. The elections are now held at the same time as local government elections, which has improved the voter turnout. The 2016 elections for 40 posts resulted in the election of 20 Conservative, 15 Labour, 3 Independent and 2 Plaid Cymru Commissioners.

Each force is also headed by an appointed chief constable, a serving police officer who is responsible for the day-to-day management of the police force.

The police force is organised by a ranking system that progresses from police constable to **chief constable**. Table 7.1 shows that the force is predominately made up of police constables. **Police community support officers** are uniformed staff whose role is to support the work of police officers within the community, acting as the eyes and ears on the streets. **Special constables** (specials) are members of the public who volunteer to undertake police functions on a part-time basis. A special's main role is to conduct local, intelligence-based patrols and to take part in crime prevention initiatives, often targeted at specific problem areas.

Table 7.1 Police workforce in 2020, England and Wales

Association of Chief Police Officers ranks	231
Chief superintendents	315
Superintendents	937
Chief inspectors	1732
Inspectors	5654
Sergeants	18,826
Constables	101,415
Police community support officers	9180
Special constabulary	9571

The role of the police is to: maintain law and order; protect members of the public and their property; prevent, detect and investigate crime.

Policing powers

The police have been granted many powers by Parliament over the years in order to keep the peace and protect the general public, but there are also limits on police powers and behaviour.

The powers the police use most commonly relate to:

1 stop and search
2 power to arrest
3 entry, search and seizure.

Stop and search

- A police officer may stop and search any person or vehicle for stolen items or prohibited articles.
- A police officer must have reasonable grounds for suspecting that they will find stolen items or prohibited articles. A police officer cannot simply stop and search anybody they want without reasonable grounds.

> **Discussion point**
> Why are 'stop and search' powers controversial?

Power to arrest

- The police have the statutory power to arrest someone as long as the individual is involved in committing or attempting to commit a criminal offence.
- The arrest is subject to strict provisions. The individual must be informed that they are under restraint and the police must only use the reasonable force necessary to arrest the individual. The suspect must then be told why they are being arrested.

Entry, search and seizure

- A police officer will normally have to obtain a warrant (court order) in order to enter and search premises. This will be awarded provided there are reasonable grounds for believing either a criminal offence has been committed or that there is material on the premises likely to be valuable to a criminal investigation.

In 1986, the **Crown Prosecution Service** (CPS) was established as a body independent from both the police and government to prosecute criminal cases in England and Wales. The CPS works closely with the police who make the initial arrest and the CPS decides whether the evidence is sufficient to charge the accused and what the charge should be. CPS prosecutors prepare cases for court hearings and represent the state in Magistrates' Courts and higher courts. The head of the CPS is the **Director of Public Prosecutions** (DPP). The work of the CPS is overseen by the Attorney General, a government minister who is accountable to Parliament for the work of the CPS.

Discussion point

Why is it important that we have an independent body like the CPS to decide who is charged with a crime rather than leaving it to the police?

The role and powers of the judiciary

The term the **judiciary** means 'the system of judges'. Table 7.2 describes the different roles that exist within the judiciary.

In the UK, there are three distinct legal systems (one each for England and Wales, Scotland, and Northern Ireland). Our membership of the Council of Europe means that UK citizens can take some cases to the European Court of Human Rights, based in Strasbourg, after they have exhausted all the avenues of appeal available in UK courts.

The judiciary is a section of the state that is responsible for the settlement of legal issues. The judiciary examines issues and cases where the citizen is accused of breaking the law and has to make a judgment as to whether or not they have. If a determination of guilt is made, the judiciary determines the sentence to be given. On points of law or appeals against sentencing, it determines the outcome. At each stage of a court case the outcome can be appealed to a higher court. The role of the judiciary is to enforce the law and interpret the law as it stands. The judiciary is politically neutral and should show no form of bias. Judges are in control of the trial in court. They can: grant adjournments, encourage cooperation between the sides, hear evidence to help decide a case, and they have the power to direct a jury on the evidence they have heard in regard to the law.

Unlike some countries, the UK ensures that the judiciary is independent and neutral through the appointment structure and the tenure of office that judges are given and the salaries awarded. Members of the judiciary have normally worked in a legal profession for many years before they are appointed to a full-time judicial post.

Discussion point

Why do you think it is important that judges are not politically appointed and are independent of government?

Table 7.2 The different roles within the hierarchy of the judiciary (see Figure 7.2 on page 56 for the court structure in England and Wales)

Lord Chief Justice: The most senior judge in the UK: the head of an independent judiciary
President of the Supreme Court: Head of the UK's highest domestic appeal court
Justices of the Supreme Court: Judges who hear civil and criminal appeals in the UK's most senior court
Senior President of Tribunals: The head of the judges in the UK Tribunal Service
Master of the Rolls: President of the Court of Appeal (Civil Division)
Chancellor of the High Court: The head of the Chancery Division of the High Court
President of the Family Division: Head of Family Justice
President of the Queen's Bench Division: Also the Deputy Head of Criminal Justice
Lord Justices of Appeal: These judges hear appeal cases in the civil and criminal divisions of the Court of Appeal
High Court Judges: These judges may hear trial and appeal cases in the High Court, sit on some appeals in the Court of Appeal and judge serious cases in Crown Court trials
Circuit judges: These judges hear criminal cases in Crown Courts and civil cases in the County Courts
Recorders: These judges work part-time hearing criminal cases in the Crown Court and civil cases in County Courts. These judges are qualified barristers or solicitors
District judge: These judges hear the bulk of civil cases in the county courts
District judge (Magistrates' Court): These judges deal with the most complex cases in a Magistrates' Court
Tribunal judges: These judges deal with most cases brought before tribunal hearings; they often sit with **lay members**
Magistrates: Magistrates are volunteers from the local communities who agree to sit and dispense justice in Magistrates' Courts. They are also referred to as Justices of the Peace (JPs). They receive training and are supported by legal advice in the courtroom. They normally sit as a 'bench' of three magistrates. In 2014, there were 22,214 magistrates.

The roles of legal representatives

Many citizens only occasionally encounter members of the legal professions. This may be in connection with buying a house, making a will or being involved in a dispute or divorce. This will involve talking to and taking advice from a local solicitor. Many people, especially those with limited means and if the issue is a civil dispute, will visit their local **Citizens Advice office** and seek free legal advice.

The three main branches of the legal profession are: **legal executives**, **solicitors** and **barristers**. A way of recalling their roles is to think about your health: the legal executive is the paramedic, the solicitor is the GP, and the barrister is the hospital consultant.

- **Legal executives** are legally qualified professionals employed largely by solicitors and they normally specialise in a given area of law. They are regulated by the Institute of Legal Executives.

- **Solicitors** undertake most of the work in Magistrates' Courts and County Courts, including both the preparation of the case and its advocacy. They also deal with a large amount of commercial work, land and building issues and the sale of houses, making wills and advising on tax matters. Many are graduates with a law degree. They must undertake professional training of a one-year legal practice course and then two years training in a solicitor's practice. They are regulated by the Law Society.

- **Barristers'** traditional work has been **advocacy**. They present cases in court. A barrister is briefed (employed) by a solicitor to work on the solicitor's client's behalf. Barristers are independent of the solicitor and pursue their own judgement about how to proceed with the case. They can work in a Magistrates' Court, but they mainly work in Crown Courts, the High Court or in the appeal court. They are normally specialists in a specific area of law, either civil or criminal. Most barristers are law graduates and they have to undergo training by undertaking the Bar Vocational Course and then pupillage (on-the-job training) with a qualified barrister. Most senior barristers apply to become **Queen's Counsel (QCs)**. Barristers work for themselves, but often share premises, known as chambers, with other barristers.

How the different criminal and civil courts work

Our legal system distinguishes between **civil law** and **criminal law** and has distinct legal pathways for resolving the differing cases. Criminal cases are brought on behalf of the state against a citizen for breaking the law of the land. Civil cases relate to disputes between individuals or organisations and are resolved by the award of damages. The differences between these two branches of the law are discussed more fully later in the chapter.

Civil law

In a civil court, the vast majority of cases do not involve a jury (libel and slander trials are the main exceptions). Most civil cases are dealt with by County Courts. This includes small claims cases (up to £5000). If the case is more serious it will be forwarded to the High Court. Civil courts deal with personal injury claims, breaches of contract and other matters that arise between individuals or companies.

Criminal law

In a criminal law case the trial is held in a Magistrates' Court for minor matters or the Crown Court for more serious offences. The CPS brings criminal cases.

In a civil case, the claimant – the person seeking damages – must provide proof and the judge decides the outcome 'on the basis of probability'. If the judge decides that the claim is genuine, they will make an award in the claimant's favour. In a criminal case, the charges must be proved beyond reasonable doubt, which means that the court must be absolutely sure of the guilt of the accused to be able to return a guilty verdict.

Tribunals and other means of dispute resolution

Tribunals are officially established bodies that can determine a resolution of a dispute and have similar powers to a court. The government has also established ombudsmen relating to government services. These can make recommendations and publish reports but their findings are not binding. For details of tribunals and ombudsmen, see Table 7.3 on page 57. Many civil disputes and disagreements are settled without a formal court hearing taking place. In recent years, governments have encouraged claimants to use other methods than court hearings, as these can be very expensive and use up a lot of court time, often on minor disputes.

Alternate Dispute Resolution (ADR) refers to the following methods of resolving a dispute: negotiation, mediation, conciliation and arbitration (see Table 7.4 on page 57). Agreements reached in this way can then be lodged with a Court. In October 2015 the government introduced regulations that require traders to provide information on the availability of Alternative Dispute Resolution when customers are still in dispute after using the traders' dispute processes.

The Structure of the Courts

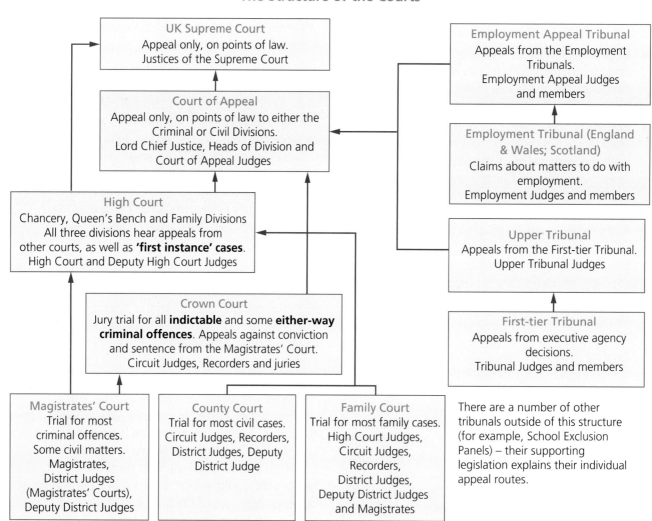

Figure 7.2 The court structure in England and Wales

Table 7.3 Advantages and disadvantages of tribunals and ombudsmen

	DETAILS	ADVANTAGES	DISADVANTAGES	EXAMPLES
Tribunals	Tribunals are inferior courts. They deal with a large number of cases each year. A variety of subjects are dealt with by specialised tribunals. These include employment, health and social care, pensions and finance, and commerce.	Can deal with specialised issues. Simple and informal procedure. Can be cheaper than conventional courts. Can be quicker than the court system.	Applicants who pay legal professionals to represent them tend to be more successful, which possibly results in inequality for those who cannot afford this option. Reasons for decisions reached are not always clear.	Employment Tribunal: **www.gov. uk/courts-tribunals/employment-tribunal** Special Educational Needs and Disability Tribunal: **www.gov. uk/courts-tribunals/first-tier-tribunal-special-educational-needs-and-disability** Special Immigration Appeals Commission: **www.gov.uk/ guidance/appeal-to-the-special-immigration-appeals-commission**
Ombudsmen	An ombudsman is an official who is appointed to check on government activity on behalf of an individual citizen and to investigate complaints that are made. This can be in a range of areas, e.g. health service, local government, legal services and housing. Ombudsmen also operate within the private sector.	The problem may be solved. Can lead to recommended changes made to government agencies or public bodies.	Their powers are constrained by the fact that they cannot deal with matters that could be dealt with by the courts. Complaints must be made through an elected representative and so this can be a barrier to citizens wishing to scrutinise government actions.	**Public sector** Parliamentary and Health Service Ombudsman: **www.ombudsman. org.uk** Prisons and Probation Ombudsman: **www.ppo.gov.uk** **Private sector** Financial Services Ombudsman: **www.financial-ombudsman.org. uk** Rail Ombudsman: **www. railombudsman.org**

Table 7.4 Different methods of dispute resolution

TYPE OF ALTERNATIVE DISPUTE RESOLUTION	DETAILS	ADVANTAGES	DISADVANTAGES
Negotiation	Parties involved discuss issues and compromise or make a decision about how the issues can be resolved.	Very informal No cost Private	The parties involved may not be able to make a decision or compromise.
Mediation	Parties discuss disputes with a neutral third party known as a mediator. The mediator does not disclose their own opinion but instead acts as a facilitator who helps the parties reach their own agreement.	Much cheaper than courts. Parties reach their own agreement, so likely to last longer than settlements that are forced on them.	The process may not lead to a settlement. The process is not binding.
Conciliation	A conciliator is used to help to resolve disputes but plays a more active role than a mediator, e.g. they might suggest grounds for a possible compromise.	It is much cheaper than other forms of legal action. It is entirely private. It has a good success rate.	Process may not lead to a settlement and so parties may have to litigate anyway. Can put pressure on claimants to settle in employment cases and mean that they might accept a lesser settlement than a tribunal would award.
Arbitration	Arbitration is the process whereby parties agree to have their dispute heard by a private arbitrator who will make a binding decision. Many commercial contracts contain clauses that say the parties will use arbitration to settle any disputes.	Can be cheaper than courts. Decisions are binding and can be enforced by courts. Parties can choose their own arbitrator. Quicker than court proceedings.	No state funding for arbitration. Professional arbitrators' fees can be high, so may be as expensive as courts. Using professional arbitrators and lawyers might cause delays similar to those experienced in the court system.

Rights and legal entitlements of citizens at differing ages

Spec coverage

- Rights and legal entitlements of citizens at differing ages: the age of criminal responsibility and other legal ages when young people become legally responsible for their actions (drive, marry, vote, join the armed forces).

Discussion point

Table 7.5 lists your rights at different ages. Why don't we get all our rights by the time we are 16?

Table 7.5 Some examples of the rights of young people at different ages. These legal rights have developed over time

AGE	RIGHTS
8	Age of criminal responsibility in Scotland
10	You are able to decide your own religion Age of criminal responsibility in England and Wales
12	You can watch a 12 or 12A film or play a 12-category computer game You can be remanded into a secure unit or secure training facility for persistent offending Age of criminal prosecution in Scotland
13	You can have a part-time job, with some restrictions You can have an account on a social networking site such as Facebook or Twitter
14	You can enter a pub if the landlord allows it, but you cannot buy or drink alcohol
15	You may be remanded to a prison to await trial You can be fined up to £1000 and sentenced to prison time if you are convicted of a criminal offence
16	You can work full-time if you have left school, have a National Insurance number and the job has accredited training You can give consent and have sex You can be married or live together, with a parent's permission You can be prosecuted for having sex with someone who is under 16 You are able to apply for your own passport, with a parent's consent
17	You can hold a driving licence and apply for a motorcycle licence You can be interviewed by the police without an appropriate adult being present
18	You have reached the age of majority (that is, you are an adult!) You can have a tattoo or body piercing You can watch an 18 film or play an 18 computer game National minimum wage entitlement increases You can get a debit card and credit card You are able to change your name You can vote and be called for jury service You can buy and drink alcohol in a bar You can get married, enter a civil partnership or live together without parental consent You are able to stand as an MP or a local councillor
21	You can drive certain types of larger vehicles such as lorries or buses (with the appropriate licence) You are entitled to full national minimum wage You are able to apply to adopt a child You can get certain types of jobs, for example become a driving instructor You can apply for a licence to fly commercial transport, aeroplanes, helicopters, gyroplanes and airships

Civil law cases involving divorce affect a number of young people because of the issues that arise about where the young person will live. Increasingly, the wishes of the young people are taken into account when such decisions are made. In recent years, there have been campaigns relating to the rights of young people in regard to sexuality and voting. Others have argued for better harmonisation of rights at either 16 or 18.

How civil law differs from criminal law

> ## Spec coverage
> - How civil law differs from criminal law.

Civil law deals with disputes between individuals, groups or organisations where they wish to use the law through the courts to seek redress of wrongs or for damage done and to seek compensation. For example, a tenant refuses to pay their rent and the landlord takes the tenant to court. The tenant claims they have withheld the rent because of issues with the property. The landlord states that the tenant has caused the problems at the property because the issues were not identified when the tenant moved into the property. The judge has to decide based upon the evidence presented.

- If the judge finds in favour of the landlord, they are likely to order the tenant to pay the outstanding rent, the repair costs at the property and the legal costs of the landlord in bringing the case.

- If the judge finds in favour of the tenant, they are likely to order that the repairs be carried out within a stated time, that the outstanding rent be paid, but that the landlord pay their own legal costs and pay any legal costs of the tenant.

In a criminal case, the main object of the law is to punish the wrongdoer. The sentence given acts as a warning to others, an inducement not to commit further crime and to satisfy the public that justice has been administered. Examples of criminal law cases include assault, **battery** and cases of murder. Different courts deal with civil and criminal cases. Most civil cases commence in a County Court while most criminal cases start in a Magistrates' Court.

How the legal systems differ within the UK

> ## Spec coverage
> - How the legal systems differ within the UK:
>   - England and Wales
>   - Northern Ireland
>   - Scotland.

Within the UK there are currently three legal jurisdictions: England and Wales; Scotland; and Northern Ireland. Each jurisdiction has its own court system and legal profession.

Table 7.6 Some of the differences between civil and criminal law and their application

ISSUE	CIVIL LAW	CRIMINAL LAW
Case brought by	Individual or group or organisation	CPS on behalf of the state
Decision	Defendant found liable or not liable in regard to the issue.	Defendant is convicted if guilty or acquitted if not guilty. Decided by a jury or magistrates.
Proof required	Extensive range of evidence; evidence must be produced to support the claim.	Beyond reasonable doubt
Burden of proof	The claimant must give proof of the claim.	The accused is innocent until proven guilty. The prosecution must prove its case; the accused does not have to prove their innocence.
Punishment	Damages, compensation or an injunction (an order to stop taking an action)	Non-custodial or custodial sentence if found guilty.
Appeal	Either party can appeal a court's decision.	The defendant may appeal a court's verdict in regard to either the verdict or the sentence. It is now possible for the state to ask for the sentence to be reviewed.

Until 1707 Scotland was an independent country, and its legal tradition and background is therefore different to that of the rest of the UK. Since the union it has maintained its distinct judicial system, which is based upon Roman law, where the law gave people rights but in return they had certain duties. In England, law developed using the decisions of judges in specific cases; this is called 'Common Law' (see page 64). The structure that has developed in Northern Ireland relates to a 1978 Act of Parliament, which established its court structure.

Today, while decisions are made in slightly different systems, much of the law is the same.

Scotland

Scotland has a distinct criminal and civil law court structure.

Criminal courts in Scotl and

- Justices of the Peace Court – operates in a similar way to those in England and Wales.
- Sheriff Court – cases are heard by a Sheriff and a 15-person jury. Cases may also be heard by a Sheriff without a jury.
- Sheriff Appeal Court – decides appeals against lower courts' decisions.
- High Court of Justiciary – decides appeals against decisions of the Sheriff Appeal Court.
- Supreme Court of Scotland – the ultimate appeal court in the Scottish system.

The civil court structure is similar to that for criminal cases except that cases start in the Sheriff Court civil branch. Appeals go to the Sheriff Appeal Court and can be further heard in the Court of Session.

Northern Ireland

Northern Ireland has its own judicial system, which is headed by the Lord Chief Justice of Northern Ireland (see Table 7.7). The Department of Justice is responsible for the administration of the courts.

Table 7.7 Court structure of Northern Ireland

NORTHERN IRELAND COURT STRUCTURE	WHAT THE COURT DOES
UK Supreme Court	Hears appeals on points of law in cases of major public importance
The Court of Appeal	Hears appeals on points of law in criminal and civil cases from all courts
The High Court	Hears complex or important civil cases and appeals from county court
County Courts	Hear a wide range of civil actions including Small Claims and family cases
The Crown Court	Hears all serious criminal cases
Magistrates' Courts (including Youth Courts and Family Proceedings)	Hear less serious criminal cases, cases involving juveniles, and civil and family cases
Coroners' Courts	Investigate unexplained deaths
The Enforcement of Judgments Office	Enforces civil judgments

Websites

Scottish Government: www.gov.scot

Courts and Tribunals Judiciary: www.judiciary.gov.uk

Crown Prosecution Service: www.cps.gov.uk

Police.UK: www.police.uk

nidirect government services: www.nidirect.gov.uk/articles/introduction-justice-system

The Law Society: www.lawsociety.org.uk

Chartered Institute of Legal Executives: www.cilex.org.uk

Review questions

1 What is the title of the most senior police officer in each local police force?
2 What is the function of the CPS?
3 Which type of legal case would award you damages?
4 At what age can you have your own passport without a parent's consent?

Activity

Outside London, every police force is held to account for its actions by an elected Police and Crime Commissioner. In London, the Mayor has similar responsibilities. Write to your local commissioner and request an interview.

Investigate the work, the budget and the performance of your local police force and prepare a series of questions for an interview with your local commissioner or their representative.

Remember when preparing your questions to ensure you have your own facts about the question so that you can agree, counter or further pursue the answer you get.

If you cannot get a face-to-face meeting, send in your questions so that you can discuss the reply you receive.

Learning review points

- What are the powers of the police?
- Why are judges important?
- How does criminal law differ from civil law?
- What are my rights at different ages?
- How does the legal system differ in different parts of the UK?

EXAM PRACTICE

1 Which of the following determines the sentence in a Magistrates' Court? (AO1) [1 mark]
   A Solicitor
   B Court usher
   C Justice of the Peace
   D Appeal Judge
   E Barrister

2 Referring to Table 7.6 (page 59), discuss why a divorce case is a matter of civil law and an armed robbery is a matter for criminal law. (AO2) [4 marks]

3 Examine why a person charged with a criminal offence may prefer to have the matter dealt with in a Magistrates Court rather than a Crown Court. (AO3) [8 marks]

Key question

- How has the law developed over time, and how does the law protect the citizen and deal with criminals?

How citizens' rights have changed and developed over time

Spec coverage

- How citizens' rights have changed and developed over time, from the importance of Magna Carta (1215) to today and the Human Rights Act (1998).

Magna Carta

As early as 1215, the rights of individuals and the right to justice and a fair trial have been embedded in English law. In that year, the English Barons forced King John to sign **Magna Carta** (or Great Charter). This document stated that everyone, even the King, was subject to the law:

No free man shall be taken or imprisoned, or dispossessed or outlawed or exiled or in any way ruined, nor will we go or send against him except by the lawful judgement of his peers or by the law of the land.

Over the centuries, as the rights of individuals have developed (see Figure 8.2 on page 63), Magna Carta has remained at the heart of our legal system and any conflicting statutes have been ruled invalid.

In 1965 the Law Commission, which was reviewing the repeal of out-of-date laws, decided that eight chapters of Magna Carta were of no practical use today or had been superseded by more recent legislation. Legislation passed in 1970 stated that four chapters of the original Magna Carta were still enforceable:

- A chapter promising freedom for the English Church.
- A guarantee of the City of London's ancient liberties and free customs.

Figure 8.1 Extract from Magna Carta

- Powers to curb the powers of the Crown to pursue individuals beyond the law.
- A clause maintaining the perpetuity of Magna Carta's liberties.

Magna Carta played a central role in the seventeenth century during the conflict between the King and Parliament. In eighteenth-century America, Magna Carta and its principles played an important part in the rebellion against the British and the subsequent founding of the Constitution of the federal United States.

The Human Rights Act

In 1998, Parliament passed the **Human Rights Act (HRA)**. This is seen as a major **codification** of the law relating to human rights. While it did not extend existing human rights, it did ensure that they were embraced within a single Act.

From Magna Carta in 1215 there began the development of basic **legal rights:**
- The right to a free trial
- The use of juries
- Not being arrested without reason.

From this grew a call for **political rights**, with major changes taking place in the nineteenth and twentieth centuries with the right to vote. It was not until 1918 that some women got the right to vote, and all women got the vote at 21 in 1928. The voting age was lowered from 21 to 18 in 1971.

Campaigns regarding **religious rights** continued into the nineteenth century. Male Roman Catholics were only given the vote in 1829, and in 1832 the first major reform of who could vote and the size and distribution of parliamentary seats took place.

As the UK became an industrial society in the nineteenth century, campaigns took place to develop **economic rights** – for example, the right to form and join a trade union. In 1834, some farm labourers from Dorset, known as the Tolpuddle Martyrs, were sent as convict prisoners to Australia because they swore an illegal oath on joining an agricultural workers' trade union.

In the twentieth century, the idea of **welfare rights** developed in the UK. Citizens now have an expectation that certain services and benefits are provided for everyone – for example education, health care, pensions and unemployment benefit.

In recent years, **rights** relating to a citizen's **personal** life have become the basis for changes in law – for example equal opportunities legislation, equal pay and issues relating to sexuality, such as the decriminalisation of same-sex (homosexual) relationships and the concept of civil partnership and equal marriage rights.

There are currently growing calls in regard to rights concerning **global issues**.

Figure 8.2 How rights have developed since Magna Carta

Case study
Campaigning for LGBTQ rights

Stonewall is a campaign group set up in 1989 to seek to overturn Section 28 of the Local Government Act, which aimed to prevent the 'promotion' of homosexuality in schools. It sought to create a professional lobbying group to overturn the legislation and promote the cause of equality. The work it has undertaken is an example of how attitudes on issues can change over time.

The following timeline shows how rights regarding LGBTQ issues have changed over time:

1533 – The Buggery Act: Conviction of a homosexual act was punishable by death

1861 – Offences Against the Person Act: The death penalty was replaced by a minimum 10 years in prison.

1885 – Criminal Law Amendment Act: Removed the requirement for a witness statement, so acts carried out in private could be prosecuted. A letter expressing affection between two men could be sufficient for a prosecution. The case of Oscar Wilde is an example of the impact of this law.

1921 – First mention of female homosexuality in regard to any legislation. This reference was removed from the final legislation.

1957 – Wolfenden Report: This report to the government recommended that 'homosexual behaviour between consenting adults in private should no longer be a criminal offence'.

1967 – Sexual Offences Act: Passed into law the Wolfenden recommendations. Legalised in the UK same-sex acts conducted in private between men aged 21 and over.

1988 – Section 28 of the Local Government Act: Prohibited local authorities from 'promoting homosexuality' or 'pretended family relationships' (non-traditional family structures).

2003 – Section 28 repealed.

2004 – Civil Partnership Act: Allowed same-sex couples to enter into a legal partnership recognised by the state.

2004 – Gender Recognition Act: Gave trans people full legal recognition, allowing them to acquire new birth certificates.

2010 – Equality Act: Gave LGBT employees protection from discrimination, harassment and victimisation at work.

2013 – Marriage (Same Sex Couples) Act allowed same-sex couples to marry. This law applied to Scotland from 2014 and Northern Ireland from September 2020.

Different viewpoint

Why does changing the law regarding people's rights about their personal lives so often take years to achieve? A starting point for research is the website of Stonewall – www.stonewall.org.uk

This Act also ensured that the European Convention on Human Rights was embedded in UK law. This meant that UK citizens could bring cases before UK Courts and have them resolved without having to go to the Court in Strasbourg. It also meant that UK courts had to abide by and take account of decisions of the Court in Strasbourg when arriving at their own decisions. It also stated that UK public bodies had to abide by the Convention. The nature of the HRA and its impact and call for changes are discussed more fully in Chapter 9.

Discussion point

What area of rights do you think will be developed or enhanced in the next 20 years?

Common law and legislation

Spec coverage
- Common law, legislation and how they differ.

In earlier times, **common law** originated in the King's Court and from the King's judges as they travelled around the country adopting what they considered the best legal rules. The common law has developed through judicial decisions in cases and is linked to legal principles and rules. Common law is, therefore, constantly evolving to deal with ever-changing situations in society. English law works on a common law basis. Judges create common law by delivering written judgments about the case before them.

Statute law or **legislation** is law passed by Parliament. For example, a road traffic Act might define speed limits and punishments relating to speeding. When considering a case brought in regard to this Act, a judge would work within the exact wording of the

law. If other judges have already ruled on the same matter, the judge would follow their written guidance. If matters are unclear or ill-defined, the judge's decision in their written judgment would revise the common law. This revised common law would then be used by other judges in their decision-making.

If the judgment is challenged in a Court of Appeal and the judgment is overruled, the Appeal Court ruling becomes the new common law on this issue. Parliament may decide to look at the matter again and pass re-drafted legislation that clarifies the issue, so nullifying the existing common law.

When preparing cases, a solicitor or barrister may need to research a point of law about the case. They will check any relevant statutes and then look at recent case law decisions of the higher courts to see if there is any guidance to assist them. So while statute law provides a legal framework for society, common law enables statute law to be applied in differing situations and to be updated as required.

The right to representation

Spec coverage
- The right to representation; the role and history of trade unions in supporting and representing workers; the role of employers' associations.

Trade unions are groups of workers who have joined together in order to protect their rights and to have an organisation to speak and negotiate on their behalf with employers in regard to:
- pay and conditions
- consultation on major workplace changes, such as workers being made redundant

- their members' concerns with employers
- supporting members in disciplinary and grievance meetings
- providing members with legal and financial advice.

Most trade unions in the UK date from the end of the nineteenth century or the early part of the twentieth century. Initially the members of trade unions belonged to specialist skilled trades like the Amalgamated Society of Engineers (ASE) formed in 1851, and they could afford to pay a reasonable membership fee. The **Trades Union Congress (TUC)** – a body that brought a variety of unions together to discuss and promote the rights of trade unions – was formed in 1868. Unions were formally legalised in 1871, following a Royal Commission that agreed there were advantages to both employers and employees in the existence of trade unions.

The Match Workers' Strike in 1888 was an early example of action being taken by a largely female union membership. The Trades Dispute Act of 1906 exempted trade union funds from being taken in compensation by employers and others as a result of their union actions.

In 1926, the TUC organised a General Strike, calling all unions belonging to the TUC to bring their workers out on **strike**. More recently, the 1970s was a period of large-scale industrial unrest and union action. During the 1970s, 21.9 million working days were lost each year to strike action. The phrase 'Winter of Discontent' was used in 1979 to describe the impact of union action. During the 1980s, Conservative governments under Margaret Thatcher passed legislation to curb the power of trade unions and the impact of their actions. In 1984, a miners' strike was called and the government, which owned the coal mines at that time, was determined that the strike would not succeed. The government prevailed and the miners were forced back to work.

The trade unions formally established the Labour Party in 1900. Today, many unions have political funds and donate money to support the party. The unions are the Labour Party's largest source of income. For many years, the trade unions were a major political force in the UK, but since 1979 their political influence has been in decline.

Trade union membership in the UK peaked in 1979 at 13 million. It now stands at just over 7 million. In recent years, the number of unions has declined as many have merged to form larger bodies.

Figure 8.3 Unison campaigning in Scotland for workers' rights

Figure 8.4 University and college lecturers campaigning about the gender pay gap

Discussion point

Is it important that employees have the right to belong to a trade union?

The unions have more members in the public sector than in the private sector. In the UK, most trade unions belong to the Trades Union Congress.

There are some unions that do not belong to the TUC, such as the Royal College of Nursing (RCN) with over 435,000 members, and the British Medical Association (BMA) which represents doctors and has 159,000 members. Laws regulate the action unions can take in support of their members. For example, if they wish to strike, the members must vote for the action in a secret ballot. One group of workers cannot take strike action to support another group of workers already on strike. This is called **secondary action** and was outlawed by the Employment Act of 1990.

People join trade unions for a variety of reasons. Many people join a union for protection, to safeguard their rights and to have someone to turn to and speak on their behalf. Union membership can also give members social and financial benefits. On joining a union, a member has to pay a regular subscription. At some places of work, the employer has agreed that the workforce can only join one union. This is called a Single Union Agreement and ensures that the employer has only one union with which to negotiate.

The role of employers' associations

In the same way that workers in particular industries and types of employment needed to work together to achieve their objectives with regard to pay and conditions at work, so did groups of employers. The two **employers' associations** best known to the public in the UK are the Confederation of British Industry (CBI) and the Institute of Directors (IoD), which are often quoted in the media on economic and industrial issues, but most employer associations relate to specific industries or are regionally based.

Many UK employers' associations belong to international bodies, so that they can lobby and influence debate and decisions. An example of such a body is Pearle, which is a transnational body that was founded in 1991 as an umbrella organisation to represent the interests of those involved in the performing arts.

Case study

Trade union action: Equal pay for women

Before 1970, it was common for women in the UK, especially in the private sector, to receive lower rates of pay than men, regardless of their skill levels. In 1968, women sewing machinists at Ford's Dagenham factory went on strike demanding equal pay. This led to a number of other equal pay strikes and the start of a national campaign led by the trade unions. A massive equal pay demonstration took place in May 1969.

The Equal Pay Act of 1970 permitted equal pay claims to be made by women in the public and private sector if their work was deemed the same as, or broadly similar to, the work of their male equivalents.

Different viewpoint

To what extent do you consider that trade unions have been crucial in improving the working life of ordinary workers since 1970? A starting point for research is the website of the TUC – www.tuc.org.uk

Case study

Make UK: The Manufacturers' Organisation

www.makeuk.org

This is a national body that is the largest sector employers' association in the UK. It has regional offices throughout the country. It was set up in 1896. It aims to provide its member businesses with advice, guidance and support on employment law, employee relations, health and safety issues, and information and research about occupational health issues. It also acts as a lobbying body on behalf of its members, having offices in London and Brussels where it can talk to MPs, the government, MEPs and European institutions.

Different viewpoint

How do employer groups help their members?

Examples of employers' associations

Use these web links to find out more about regional, national and transnational employers' bodies and the work they undertake.

Association of British Orchestras: www.abo.org.uk

British Amusement and Gaming Trades Association: www.bacta.org.uk

Construction Plant-hire Association: www.cpa.uk.net

Federation of Master Builders: www.fmb.org.uk

Lancashire Textile Manufacturers' Association: www.ltma.co.uk

Malt Distillers Association of Scotland: www.bfbi.org.uk/members/malt-distillers-association-of-scotland

National Farmers' Union: www.nfuonline.com

Pearle: www.pearle.eu

Retail Motor Industry Federation Limited: www.rmif.co.uk

Scottish Decorators' Federation: www.scottishdecorators.co.uk

Road Haulage Association: www.rha.uk.net

University and Colleges Employers Association: www.ucea.ac.uk

The nature of criminality in the UK today

Spec coverage
- The nature of criminality in the UK today:
  - differing types of crimes
  - profile of criminality in the UK
  - factors affecting crime rates in society and strategies to reduce crime.

Differing types of crimes

Table 8.1 on page 68, published by the Home Office, shows the number of recorded offences from April 2018 until March 2019. Two issues arise from looking at data and surveys relating to criminality. Firstly, the data in Table 8.1 relates to 'recorded crime', which is those crimes that each regional police force records. Policy on which crimes to record, especially for less serious crimes, can vary from force to force.

Secondly, there is a need to see these figures in the context of society as a whole, where the likelihood of crimes impinging upon ordinary citizens can vary according to a range of factors, such as age, gender, where you live, ethnicity, time of day, lifestyle, etc. The Crime Survey for England and Wales (CSEW) surveys and records people's experiences of crime using the following categories:

- **Violent crime** – violence against the person, which can range from murder, manslaughter or knife attack to common assault.
- **Sexual offences and intimate personal violence**
  - these are recorded as two groups:
  - Rape
  - Other sexual offences
- **Robbery offences** – an offence in which force or the threat of force is used either during or immediately prior to theft or attempted theft.
- **Theft offences** – involve burglary, offences against vehicles, theft from the person, bicycle theft, shoplifting and all other theft offences.
- **Criminal damage and arson** – defined as intentional or malicious damage to the home, other property or vehicle.
- **Fraud and computer misuse offences** – an act of deception intended for personal gain or to cause a loss to another party. It includes offences like using another's credit card and internet and insurance deception. Computer misuse may relate to issues such as identify theft and downloading and distributing illegal material.
- **Other crimes against society** – may include such actions as antisocial behaviour – including nuisance, rowdy or inconsiderate neighbours, vandalism, graffiti and fly-posting, street drinking – and those actions defined as hate crimes: any criminal offence that is perceived by the victim or any person to be motivated by hostility or prejudice, based upon race, religion/faith, sexual orientation, disability or gender.

Table 8.1 Police reported crime, April 2018–March 2019

TYPE OF OFFENCE	NUMBER OF RECORDED OFFENCES, APRIL 2018–MARCH 2019	PERCENTAGE CHANGE, APRIL 2018–MARCH 2019
Victim-based crime	4,508,380	7
Violence against the person	1,671,039	20
Sexual offences	162,030	7
Robbery	85,736	11
Theft	2,015,998	0
Criminal damage and arson	573,577	-3
Total fraud and computer misuse offences	693,418	9
Other crimes against society	748,701	14
Total recorded crime – all offences including fraud and computer misuse	5,950,499	8

The Crime Survey for England and Wales

The Office for National Statistics (ONS) describes the Crime Survey for England and Wales (CSEW) as follows:

'The CSEW is a face-to-face survey asking people in England and Wales about their experiences of a range of crimes in the past year. The survey interviews both adults and children. The survey started in 1982.

The CSEW provides a better reflection of the extent of crime than police recorded figures, as the survey asks about crimes that are not reported to or recorded by the police. The survey is also unaffected by changes in police recording practices or levels of public reporting to the police, so it provides a more consistent measure over time.

It also provides crucial information on the nature of crime, such as a demographic profile of victims, location and time of day of the incident. The findings from the survey help inform the policy and operational response to crime.'

(ONS 2015)

The categorisation of crime can differ between different organisations, although the government has been trying to improve the way crime data from different sources relate to each other. The CSEW tends to use broader categories than the police use for '**recorded crime**'. For example, in regard to the category 'Violence' used by the CSEW, the police use the following categories:

CSEW	POLICE
Violence	Assault with intent to cause serious harm
	Assault with injury
	Racially or religiously aggravated assault with injury
	Assault with injury on a constable
	Assault without injury on a constable
	Assault without injury
	Racially or religiously aggravated assault without injury

The CSEW measures the public's perception of crime. Its numbers, shown in Figure 8.5 (on page 69), differ from the number of crimes recorded by the police. Since 2016 a new category of crime has been added to the survey, that of fraud and computer misuse.

Profile of criminality in the UK

The nature of differing crimes and recent crime statistics were included on page 67 and on this page. But what do we know about the nature of people who commit crimes? There are two aspects to a profile of criminality: the type, range and number of crimes committed and the nature of the people who commit these crimes.

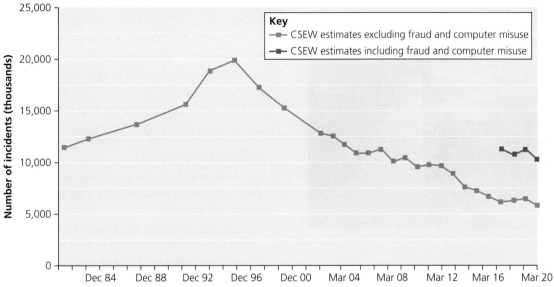

Figure 8.5 Crime Survey for England and Wales from 1981 to 2020 (Source: Office for National Statistics – Crime Survey for England and Wales)

Many studies have been carried out to look at the factors that might influence whether or not a person will commit a crime, such as gender, age, class, employment status, region, etc.

> ## Discussion point
> What image of the nature of burglary does the information on ITCC Locksmiths' website present (see box below)?

Burglary facts and stats

- A burglary takes place every 40 seconds in the UK.
- Around 75% of burglars use a door, of which 3% were open.
- Every year around 1 million burglaries and attempted burglaries are reported, meaning there are probably many more that were never reported.
- According to a Victim Support survey, 1 in 4 victims has been burgled more than once.
- 56% of burglaries happen during the night.
- The majority of burglaries are not planned and are committed by opportunistic thieves.
- Approximately 57% of burglaries occur when the home is occupied.
- A Halifax survey found that around a third of people who have an alarm rarely activate it.
- According to *The Sun*, the police solve fewer than 1 in 10 burglaries.

Who is burgled?
- The biggest victims of burglaries are single-parent families living in urban areas.
- The second biggest victims of burglaries are the elderly.

Who burgles?
- 88% of burglars are male and 6% of burglars are females.

- Approximately half of burglars are known to the victim.
- The demographic of the average burglar is between 16 and 24, with 16% being of school age.
- Many burglars have drug addictions and steal to gain money to feed their addiction.

How much it costs

The average cost of a burglary is estimated to be nearly £3000. This includes fixing any damage and replacing the stolen items.

The most stolen items are:
- Cash
- Jewellery
- Electronics such as TVs, radios and game consoles
- Power tools, such as drills, chainsaws, hedge trimmers or grinders, as they are relatively expensive items and fairly easy to sell on.
- Alcohol and prescription drugs – many burglars have drug addictions and steal to feed their habit.
- Your identity – burglars are increasingly looking to steal your identity, which can enable them to purchase items online or take out loans, all in your name.

Source: **https://itcclocksmiths.co.uk/burglary-facts**

Case study

The riots in London in August 2011

In August 2011 riots broke out across several cities in the UK. There was widespread looting and buildings were set alight. Many were left homeless after a night of riots on the streets of Tottenham after a peaceful demonstration on 6 August over the death of a man who was shot by police turned violent. Figure 8.6 relates to those who were arrested by the police in London.

Different viewpoint

If you had to write a newspaper article based upon this information, what would be your main headline and supporting points?

You may wish to invite in the editor or a journalist from a local paper or radio station to discuss how the media present news items and compare your response to theirs.

Key statistics

1,984 Before courts

13% Involved in gangs

26% Juveniles (age 10–17)

2,584 Businesses attacked

664 People robbed/injured

231 Homes targeted

Education

66% 10–17-year-olds charged have special educational needs

21.3% Average for all pupils in maintained secondary schools

Poverty

42% 10–17-year-olds charged claim free school meals

16% Average for all pupils in maintained secondary schools

Figure 8.6 Statistics of the August riots

Case study

Criminal statistics

By studying the data and research regarding criminality it is possible to draw conclusions about the nature of criminal activity, those who commit crime, how the criminal justice system deals with them and the extent to which the system changes their behaviour.

Statistics published in 2020 for England and Wales show that in regard to those in prison:

- 27 per cent of prisoners are from a minority ethnic group.
- There is a clear association between ethnic group and the odds of receiving a custodial sentence.
- 34 per cent of prisoners assessed reported that they had a learning disability or difficulties.

- Women make up 5 per cent of the total prison population.
- Women tend to commit less serious offences, many serving sentences of 12 months or less.

When thinking about children and criminality, the latest data, from 2020, indicates:

- Around 21,700 children received a caution or sentence.
- The proportion of black children given a caution or sentence is almost three times greater than the proportion of black children in the general 10–17-year-old population.
- There were just over 60,200 arrests of children.
- Black children were over four times more likely than white children to be arrested.
- Boys make up 82 per cent of the total youth offenders, while making up 51 per cent of the general 10–17-year-old population.

- The number of female young offenders is 2100.
- 4500 knife and offensive weapon offences were committed by children.
- The average custodial sentence given to children has increased to 17.7 months.
- 38.4 per cent of children and young people re-offended.

(Source: **Youth Justice Board/Ministry of Justice, published 30 January 2020**)

Different viewpoint

The way in which facts and figures are presented by the media and others about crime can influence the views of the public.

Looking at the source of the statistics given here at https://bit.ly/3cnJHZe, to what extent do you believe the points in the case study present a selective or partial version of the facts?

What amendments do you think are needed to the content of the case study?

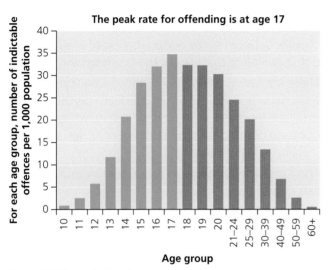

Figure 8.7 Age of offending

Figure 8.7 relates to the age of offenders and it shows that the peak age for offending is 17 and the bulk of crime is committed by those within the 14–30-year-old age range.

Discussion point

What possible links, based on actual evidence, can you find between criminality and associated factors (such as prisoners' backgrounds)?

Factors affecting crime rates in society and strategies to reduce crime

A range of factors can influence crime rates and strategies to lower crime. The following are examples of factors that can influence crime rates:

- **The nature of law** – if certain laws didn't exist, or the nature of the crime was redefined, or the sentencing provision changed, this would impact on measurable crime figures. Recent examples of debates about

changes in the law indicate that if the law was changed, this would impact upon crime rates.

The use of and powers associated with 'stop and search', the legalisation of certain drugs and making non-payment of the television licence a civil debt rather than a criminal offence, are all examples of this.

- **Sentencing policy** – the length of sentences has increased over the years. If more community sentencing was used rather than prison, would that impact upon the crime rate?
- **The function of prison** – is the function of prison to punish or to rehabilitate? Is enough support given to those leaving prison to ensure that they do not become repeat offenders?
- **Strategies to reduce crime in the community** – different policies can have effects on the crime rates. For example:
  - Should there be more Neighbourhood Watch schemes to encourage residents in the local community to watch out for each other and assist the police?
  - Would a return to community policing assist in lowering crime, where the police actually live and work within the local community?
  - Would a zero-tolerance strategy like the one used in New York in the 1980s work? This involved the following-up of minor offences in order to reduce the number of serious offences.
  - Should local authorities be encouraged to create more CCTV schemes? Do they discourage crime or are they a threat to one's civil liberties?
- **The state of the economy** – one of the major factors that appears to influence the crime rate is the overall state of the economy. In times of prosperity, high employment and high wages, the crime rate decreases. When there is high unemployment and economic recession, the crime rate rises.

How we deal with those who commit crime

Spec coverage

- How we deal with those who commit crime:
  - differing forms of punishment available in the UK
  - the purposes of sentencing
  - the effectiveness of differing types of sentence
  - how the youth justice system operates.

The purposes of sentencing

The Criminal Justice Act of 2003 stated that there were five purposes of sentencing:

1 **Punishing** the offender.
2 **Deterrence** – trying to reduce crime.
3 **Rehabilitation** of the offender – trying to reform their behaviour.
4 **Protection** for the community.
5 **Reparations** by the offender – a form of compensation to those affected by the offending.

When a court sentences someone, it takes into account a combination of several of these elements.

Differing forms of punishment available in the UK

The Criminal Justice Act 2003 also stated that the Sentencing Council had responsibility for:

- developing sentencing guidelines and monitoring their use
- assessing the impact of guidelines on sentencing practice
- promoting awareness among the public regarding the sentencing issues.

Sentences given by criminal courts fall into two broad categories: **custodial** and **non-custodial**. The term 'custodial' means any form of imprisonment.

Custodial sentences

- **Imprisonment** is the most severe sentence available to the courts and is reserved for the most serious offences. It is imposed where it is felt that the public needs to be protected. The length of

sentence depends upon the seriousness of the crime and the maximum penalty laid down in the legislation. For some serious offences, Parliament has laid down minimum sentences:

- – Seven years for some drug offences
- – Three years for a third burglary offence
- – Five years for some firearms offences.

Some countries in the world still use capital punishment for some crimes. This involves the state carrying out the death penalty on the prisoner. A law was passed in 1965 that abolished the death penalty in the UK. The death penalty was carried out by hanging in this country. Other countries use or have used a gas chamber, shooting, the administration of a lethal drug or the guillotine to carry out the death penalty.

There are strong views held by those who support and those who oppose the use of the death penalty. Those in favour see it as the ultimate deterrent, while those opposed point to past miscarriages of justice and the inability to right a wrong.

There are different types of prison sentences available to a court:

- **Life sentences** – Parliament has decided that judges must give a life sentence to all offenders found guilty of murder. The judge will set a minimum term before the offender can be considered for release by the Parole Board. The 2003 Act laid out a schedule regarding sentencing; for example, for murder involving a knife or other weapon the starting point is 25 years. Some are sentenced to a whole-life order, which means they should never be released from prison. There are currently about 65 people who are serving whole-life sentences in the UK. They include Rosemary West and Jeremy Bamber. There are other offences where the maximum sentence is life imprisonment, such as rape or robbery, but this is only applied in the most serious cases.
- **Extended sentences** – this sentence was introduced to provide extra public protection, where the public may need protection from the individual after their release. So the person serves a prison sentence and then can be on a licence for up to a further eight years. Being released on licence means that you are released from custody and serve the remainder of your sentence in the community. You agree to abide by the terms of your licence. The prison sentence and the licence period cannot go beyond the maximum sentence for the offence. In 2017, 575 offenders were given extended sentences.

- **Determinate sentences** – this the most common type of prison sentence. In 2017, 85,913 offenders were given determinate sentences. Prisoners serve half of their sentence in prison and the remainder on licence. If they are serving a prison sentence of two years or less they are then subject to post-sentence supervision.

SENTENCE IMPOSED BY COURT	PERIOD IN CUSTODY BEFORE RELEASE	ARRANGEMENTS ON RELEASE
6-month sentence	3 months	3 months' licence and 9 months' post-sentence supervision Total supervision: 12 months
6-year sentence	3 years	3 years' licence

- **Suspended sentences** – if the court imposes a custodial sentence of between 14 days and two years, the judge can decide to suspend the sentence for up to two years. The court will require the offender to undertake other tasks such as:
  - doing unpaid work
  - being subject to a curfew
  - undertaking treatment regarding drugs or alcohol abuse
  - being subject to a supervision order.

  If the offender does not comply or commits another offence, the earlier offence is taken into account when sentencing. In 2017, 53,148 offenders were given a custodial sentence, about 8 per cent of all court sentences.

Non-custodial sentences

- **Fines** – monetary fines are the most common type of sentence. In 2017, 75 per cent of all offenders received a fine, 896,611 in total. Since March 2015, both Magistrates' Courts and Crown Courts have powers to set unlimited fine levels.
- **Community sentences** – these sentences combine punishment with activity. The offender may be required to meet any of 12 requirements:
  - Up to 300 hours' unpaid work
  - Attending appointments
  - Attending a programme about their behaviour
  - Being prohibited from doing some activities
  - Keeping to a curfew
  - Being excluded from certain places or areas

  - Being required to be resident at a certain address
  - No foreign travel being allowed
  - Mental health treatment
  - Drug treatment
  - Alcohol treatment
  - If under 25, attending a specific centre.

  In 2017, 95,112 offenders were sentenced to community sentences.
- **Ancillary orders** – in addition to any of the above sentences, a court may apply additional orders. These aim to redress the harm caused by the offender: for example, a compensation order. In the case of death by dangerous driving, the offender must also be disqualified from driving for at least two years. There are a variety of these orders available to a court:
  - Compensation orders
  - Confiscation orders
  - Criminal behaviour orders
  - Deprivation orders
  - Disqualification from being a company director
  - Disqualification from driving
  - Drink banning orders
  - Financial reporting order
  - Football banning order
  - Forfeiture order
  - Parenting order
  - Restitution order
  - Restraining order
  - Serious crime prevention order
  - Sexual harm prevention order.
- **Discharge** – these are given for less serious offences such as minor theft. The court can give an absolute discharge, where no punishment is required, or a conditional discharge, which means if another crime is committed the offender can be sentenced for both the first and the new offence. In 2017, 53,104 people were given a discharge.

The effectiveness of differing types of sentence

How can we assess the effectiveness of sentencing? One way is to look at the behaviour of offenders once they are released from prison. Figure 8.8 shows the percentage of offenders who are arrested for offences after their release. For example, of those released after serving less than 12 months 59 per cent re-offend, which means 41 per cent do not re-offend.

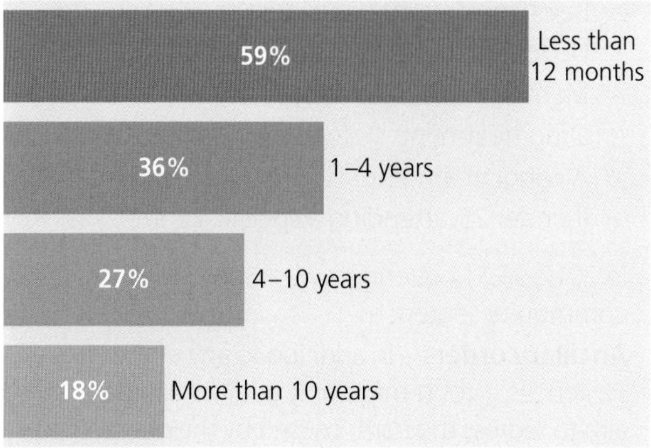

Figure 8.8 Re-offending rates by length of prison sentence

Recent figures show that one in four criminals re-offend within a year, committing 500,000 offences between them. Over half of these offences were committed by people who had 11 or more previous convictions. 50,000 of the offences were committed by people who had been in prison at least 11 times.

Recently a think-tank, Civitas, argued that lengthening prison sentences for burglary and fraud would reduce offending. **NACRO**, a prison reform group, said in response that longer sentences just delay the re-offending. It argues that the state needs to rethink its approach. If a burglar is sentenced to prison for 12 months, the cost to the taxpayer is more than £40,000. NACRO argues that a community-based programme with 80 hours' unpaid work would cost £4200. It says that sending someone to prison also has an impact on their employment and their family. It points out that more than 70 per cent of male prisoners suffer from two or more mental health issues and two-thirds of male prisoners have a reading age of 11 years or lower.

Case study
The Prison Reform Trust

The Prison Reform Trust (PRT) is a UK charity working to create a just, humane and effective penal system.

PRT was founded in 1981 to inform and influence public debate on prison conditions and the treatment of prisoners. At the time it was concerned about a projected prison population of 48,000 by 1984. With the prison population in England and Wales now exceeding 82,000 and projected to rise to 86,400 by 2023, the charity remains as relevant as ever.

We are willing and equipped to hold the state to account for its treatment of vulnerable people in prison. Our reputation, built on almost four decades of knowledgeable, reliable analysis and presentation of the facts, gives us influence behind the scenes.

Our main objectives are:

1 reducing unnecessary imprisonment and promoting community solutions to crime
2 improving treatment and conditions for prisoners and their families
3 promoting equality and human rights in the justice system.

We do this by inquiring into the workings of the system; informing prisoners, staff and the wider public; and by influencing Parliament, government and officials towards reform.

(Source: **www.prisonreformtrust.org.uk/WhoWeAre**)

Different viewpoint

Should government listen more to the victims of crime or to those who want to reform how we deal with those who commit crime? What should government do to ensure that all sides in the debate on criminal justice are heard?

So what is the best way to achieve the aims of sentencing as set out in the 2003 Act:

- making more use of prison
- using more community orders
- dealing with the reasons why the offender offends
- or making prison a place where behaviour can be changed as well as a place of punishment and protection for the community?

Discussion point

Do you think the ideas put forward by NACRO and the Prison Reform Trust are the best ways to stop re-offending?

How the youth justice system operates

Youth Courts are a special type of Magistrates' Court for people aged 10 to 17. The age of criminal responsibility in England is 10 years. A Youth Court is made up of either three magistrates or a district judge who hear the case. There is no jury in a Youth Court. Parents or guardians must attend if the young person is under 16. Youth Courts are less formal than adult courts. People before the court are addressed by their first names and members of the public are not allowed unless they get prior permission. The Youth Court deals with less serious offences like theft, antisocial behaviour and drug offences. More serious crimes start in the Youth Court but are transferred to a Crown Court.

The court can give a range of community sentences or Detention and Training Orders, which are served in secure centres for young people:

- **Absolute or conditional discharge:** The offence does not warrant a formal punishment, or conditions are attached, i.e. no further offence for 12 months. If one occurs the person is then punished for both offences.

- **Binding over the offender's parents:** The parents have to agree to control their child for a set period. If this doesn't work, they can be brought before the court.

- **Fines up to £1000:** Monetary payment to the court. If not paid, the person is taken back to court for further sentencing.

- **Youth Community Orders:** A set number of hours undertaking community activity under supervision.

- **Reparation Orders:** Payments and/or actions that mitigate the damage that might have occurred. For example, for vandalism, the person is forced to repair damage.

- **Referral Orders:** If the young offender pleads guilty to an offence or it is their first offence, they can be referred to a panel of two trained community volunteers and a member of the youth offending team. It can be for a minimum of three months and a maximum of 12 months.

- **Detention Training Orders:** Custodial sentence of between four and 24 months; 12–14-year-olds are sent to Secure Training Units and 15–17-year-olds are sent to Youth Offender Institutions.

- **Ancillary orders:** An additional punishment available to the court on top of any other punishment. It may be a payment order of compensation or an order to carry out voluntary work.

The sentence given will take into account:

- the age of the offender
- the seriousness of the crime
- whether the offender has a criminal record
- whether the offender pleaded guilty or not guilty.

The court takes into account any **aggravating** or **mitigating circumstances** before it passes sentence. The press are allowed to report the case but not the name of the accused, their address or school, or information relating to any other young person involved in the case.

A Witness	**E** Defendant
B Magistrates	**F** Parent
C Clerk of the court	**G** Youth offending team worker
D Lawyers for the prosecution and defence	**H** Usher

Figure 8.9 A Youth Court in session

Once a young person commits an offence, they become involved with the Youth Justice System. This was set up as a result of the Crime and Disorder Act 1998. Its aim is to prevent young people offending and re-offending.

The Act required local councils, education and children's services, the police, the probation service and health services to set up youth offending teams (YOTs).

There are 157 YOTs in England and Wales and each relates to a local authority area.

They are multi-disciplinary bodies, involving social workers, probation officers, the police, educational staff, health workers, substance abuse specialists and in some areas specialist accommodation workers. The system is monitored and supported nationally by the Youth Justice Board.

Websites

Trades Union Congress: www.tuc.org.uk

Unite: www.unitetheunion.org

Office for National Statistics: www.ons.gov.uk

Sentencing Council: www.sentencingcouncil.org.uk

Youth Justice Board for England and Wales: www.gov.uk/government/organisations/youth-justice-board-for-england-and-wales/about

NACRO (National Association for the Care and Resettlement of Offenders): www.nacro.org.uk

Review questions

1 Besides the UK, what other country has made the ideas of Magna Carta central to the way the country is run?
2 Who makes common law?
3 What is a trade union?
4 Give an example of a custodial sentence.

Learning review points

- How have human rights developed and changed?
- What do we mean by the right to representation?
- How do we define different crimes?
- What is the profile of criminality in the UK?
- What factors affect crime rates?
- How does society deal with criminality?
- How are young people treated in the justice system?

Activity

Report back to your class about the level of crime in an area nearby. Use the website links on **www.police.uk** or **www.adt.co.uk/crime-in-my-area** and study the data available to present a report to your class.

EXAM PRACTICE

1 Why is Magna Carta seen as an important document? (AO1) [2 marks]
2 Referring to Figure 8.5 (page 69), identify a trend from the data and offer an explanation. (AO2) [4 marks]
3 Examine the case made for dealing with young offenders through the Youth Courts system. (AO3) [8 marks]

The importance of key international agreement and treaties

Spec coverage
- The importance of key international agreement and treaties in regard to human rights:
  - the UN Universal Declaration of Human Rights
  - the European Convention on Human Rights
  - the UN Convention on the Rights of the Child
  - the Human Rights Act (1998)

In Chapter 4, pages 24 to 27, we studied the UK's involvement with a number of international organisations. In this section about the law, we consider the implications of various international agreements the UK has agreed to.

The Universal Declaration of Human Rights

At the end of the Second World War, the United Nations (UN) was formed. Its aim was to rebuild a world on the values of peace, freedom and justice. In 1948, the UN approved the Universal Declaration of Human Rights (UDHR), which was drawn up by a committee headed by Eleanor Roosevelt (the wife of US President Franklin D. Roosevelt). The Declaration sets out the fundamental human rights of all citizens and was built upon existing human rights declarations: Magna Carta of 1215; the **Petition of Right 1628**; the **US Declaration of Independence 1789**; and the **Declaration of the Rights of Man and of the Citizen 1789**. Today, 193 nations are signed up to the UDHR.

But what is a **human right**? It is the fundamental right that someone is entitled to have, to be or to do. Figure 9.1 on page 78 shows the main points of the UDHR.

The Declaration is now over 70 years old and some feel that it now needs to be updated. It is based upon the values of its time rather than of today. Issues relating to sexuality, gender and our relationship to the environment are not mentioned. Later human rights conventions and Acts do attempt to cover some of these points.

The European Convention on Human Rights

The European Convention on Human Rights and Fundamental Freedoms (ECHR) is an international agreement adopted in 1950, which came into force in 1953. The UK was one of the original signatory countries and played a large part in the drafting of the agreement.

The Council of Europe created the agreement. The Council is an inter-governmental body that was set up after the Second World War to protect human rights and the rule of law and help promote democracy. Countries that sign up to the ECHR make a legal agreement to protect the basic rights of all people within their country as set out in the agreement. The agreement also led to the establishment of the **European Court of Human Rights** to oversee whether governments were meeting their obligations under the ECHR.

Figure 9.1 The Universal Declaration of Human Rights (Source: **www.thinglink.com/scene/885518633164341250**)

Figure 9.2 The European Court of Human Rights building in Strasbourg

Figure 9.3 The European Court of Human Rights in session

The Council of Europe and the European Court of Human Rights are based in Strasbourg in France. Neither the Council, the European Convention nor the Court is in any way connected to the working or the institutions of the European Union, although the European Parliament of the European Union also meets in Strasbourg.

All members of the Council of Europe must sign up to the ECHR and must respect the Articles shown in the box below.

Over time, as societies have developed, the ECHR has developed via Protocols. These have included rights relating to property, education and the abolition of the death penalty.

Articles of the European Convention on Human Rights

Article 1: Obligation to respect human rights

Article 2: Right to life

Article 3: Prohibition of torture, inhuman and degrading treatment

Article 4: Prohibition of slavery and forced labour

Article 5: Right to liberty and security

Article 6: Right to a fair trial

Article 7: No punishment without law

Article 8: Right to respect for private and family life, home and correspondence

Article 9: Freedom of thought, conscience and religion

Article 10: Freedom of expression

Article 11: Freedom of assembly and association

Article 12: Right to marry

Article 13: Right to an effective remedy

Article 14: Prohibition of discrimination.

The ECHR has also been instrumental in the Council of Europe developing other treaties and agreements on human rights, such as the European Convention for the Prevention of Torture and Inhuman or Degrading Treatment or Punishment, the Convention on the Exercise of Children's Rights and the Convention on Preventing and Combating Violence against Women.

Many in the media and some politicians in the UK criticise the decisions of the ECHR and say it is over-reaching itself, thereby compelling member countries to undertake actions that they did not initiate or agree with. The court is made up of judges drawn from member countries, and some in the UK are concerned about the quality of some of the judgments.

In 2015, the Conservative Party proposed that if it returned to government, it would introduce a British Bill of Rights that would involve the following:

- Repeal the existing Human Rights Act 1998
- Write the original Convention rights into UK law
- Clarify the Convention rights to give a balance between rights and responsibilities
- Break the link between UK courts and the European Court
- End the ability of the European Court to oblige the UK to change its laws
- Stop UK law being 're-written' by the European Court
- Limit the use of human rights laws to the most serious examples.

The Conservative Party has been in government since 2015, and there have been two general elections since the proposal was made, but as yet the government has not introduced a British Bill of Rights.

Discussion point

What would be your main proposals to include in a new British Bill of Rights?

Here are examples of UK cases heard before the ECHR Court that have caused some controversy in the UK.

Case study
Votes for prisoners

In 2005, the Court said that rules banning all prisoners from voting in the UK and other countries were a breach of their human rights and therefore unlawful. The UK Parliament refused to accept the ruling and voted against giving any prisoners the vote.

Different viewpoint
Is there a case for giving some or all prisoners the vote?

Case study
Abu Qatada

Abu Qatada was a radical cleric whom the UK government had wanted to deport. In 2012, the European Court of Human Rights blocked his deportation to Jordan, believing that evidence that might be used against him in Jordan had been obtained by using torture. This ruling was based on the right to a fair trial. The UK government was forced to agree a new treaty with Jordan that guaranteed a free and fair trial. This new treaty eventually convinced the European Court of Human Rights and he was deported in July 2013.

Different viewpoint
Is it right that the European Court of Human Rights can overrule a decision of a British Home Secretary?

Case study
Whole-life prison sentences

Three multiple murderers took the UK government to the Court over the issue that whole-life sentences did not allow for any form of review or therefore a possible release date. The Court ruled that a whole-life sentence breached Article 3 of the Convention, which prohibits torture, because a whole-life sentence was deemed to be a form of torture.

Different viewpoint
Should a life sentence mean life or should there be a review process to allow for possible release?

The United Nations Convention on the Rights of the Child

The Convention on the Rights of the Child came into force in September 1990 and by 2020, 196 countries had agreed to abide by the Convention. The one major exception is the United States of America. The Convention places a duty on governments in regard to the following areas in relation to children:

- The right to life
- The right to their own name and identity
- The right to be protected from abuse or exploitation
- The right to an education
- The right to have their privacy protected
- The right to be raised by, or have a relationship with, their parents
- The right to express their opinions and have these listened to and, where appropriate, acted upon
- The right to play and enjoy culture and art in safety.

In total, there are 54 articles in the Convention. All the rights are connected and all are seen as equally important.

The rights of the child in many ways mirror those that are included in the UDHR and the ECHR.

The Human Rights Act (1998)

In 1998, the Human Rights Act (HRA) was passed by the UK Parliament; it came into force in 2000. This Act means you can defend your rights in UK courts and that public bodies such as the government, the police and local councils must treat everyone equally, with fairness, dignity and respect. This Act protects everyone in the UK, whether they are young or old, rich or poor. The provisions of the Act can be called upon by everyone resident in the UK. It is not limited to British citizens. Organisations and companies can also use it. The Act formally incorporated the European Convention on Human Rights into UK law. The UK government signed the Convention in 1950 and it was taken into account when drafting laws and in court judgments. But often cases had to be taken to the Court in Strasbourg for final clarification, which could then lead to the UK Parliament amending or introducing legislation to ensure the UK complied with the Court ruling. What the HRA did was make sure that judges in the UK ensure that the Convention is upheld and that public bodies do not act in any way that is incompatible with a Convention right.

Articles 1 and 13 of the ECHR appear in the HRA. This is because, by creating the Human Rights Act, the UK has fulfilled these rights.

- Article 1 says that states must secure the rights of the Convention in their own jurisdiction. The Human Rights Act is the main way of doing this for the UK.

- Article 13 makes sure that if people's rights are violated they are able to access effective remedy. This means they can take their case to court to seek a judgment. The Human Rights Act is designed to make sure this happens.

What rights does the Human Rights Act protect?
- The right to life
- Prohibition of torture and inhuman treatment
- Protection against slavery and forced labour
- The right to liberty and freedom
- The right to a fair trial
- No punishment without law
- Respect for your privacy and family life
- Freedom of thought, religion and belief
- Freedom of expression
- The right to education
- The right to participate in free elections
- The right to marry and start a family
- Freedom of assembly and association
- No discrimination: everyone's rights are equal
- Protection of property.

As an individual, if you think a public body has interfered with your rights:
- You can contact the body and remind it of its legal obligations in the HRA.
- If the matter goes to a court and it finds in your favour, the public body must remedy the situation.
- If a court finds that a section of law is contrary to the Convention, it can make a declaration to that effect. This encourages Parliament to amend or repeal that section of the law.

The role of international law in conflict situations

Spec coverage
- The role of international law in conflict situations:
  - to protect victims of conflict
  - how International Humanitarian Law helps establish the rules of war.

International Humanitarian Law

Through history, warfare has always had its own customs and principles that each side follows. During the nineteenth century, however, these customs were set down as a set of rules, known as **International Humanitarian Law (IHL)**. The aims of IHL are to:
- protect people who are not involved or are no longer involved in hostilities: the sick and wounded, prisoners and civilians
- set out the rights and obligations of those involved in the armed conflict.

IHL applies to both sides of a conflict, as soon as the fighting begins. Its main points are contained within the **Geneva Conventions** of 1949 and the **Hague Convention** of 1899 (and 1907). Nearly every state in the world is bound by these Conventions.

Protecting victims of conflict and establishing rules of war

Born out of the suffering of the Second World War, the Geneva Conventions of 1949 set out to protect soldiers on land and at sea, prisoners of war and civilians caught up in the fighting.

Further additions to the Geneva Conventions were made in 1977 and 2005 to cover areas such as conventional weapons, biological and chemical weapons, landmines, and the protection of children in armed conflicts.

In 1980, a Hague Convention was agreed relating to children due to issues of child trafficking and abduction often relating to countries involved in wars or civil wars. The Civil Aspects of International Child Abduction protects children from the harmful effects of abduction across international borders and provides for a procedure to bring about their prompt return.

The International Committee of the Red Cross is regarded as the 'guardian of the Geneva Conventions' and the various other treaties that constitute International Humanitarian Law.

The International Criminal Court

For the IHL to be respected, it is important that, if laws are broken during conflicts, the individuals or groups who break them are brought to justice. Examples of this taking place include:

- In 1946, the Nuremberg International Military Tribunal used these conventions as a basis for holding a series of trials of those who had committed war crimes during the Second World War.
- In 1993, the International Criminal Tribunal for the former Yugoslavia was set up to try those charged with crimes of genocide and crimes against humanity.

In 1998, an international conference led to the establishment of the **International Criminal Court** (ICC), an independent intergovernmental organisation based in The Hague in the Netherlands. This court is the first permanent court with jurisdiction to prosecute individuals for international crimes of genocide, crimes against humanity, war crimes and crimes of aggression. At the end of 2019, 123 states had agreed to work with the ICC.

War crimes

The Treaty establishing the International Criminal Court also established what was meant by a war crime. It involves any of the following:

- Wilful killing
- Torture or inhuman treatment, including biological experiments
- Wilfully causing great suffering, or serious injury to body or health

- Extensive destruction and appropriation of property, not justified by military necessity and carried out unlawfully and wantonly
- Compelling a prisoner of war or other protected person to serve in the forces of a hostile power
- Wilfully depriving a prisoner of war or other protected person of the rights to fair and regular trial
- Unlawful deportation or transfer, or unlawful confinement
- Taking of hostages.

Criticisms of the ICC

Since it was established, the ICC has come in for some criticism. Some countries have failed to sign up to the Treaty, including the USA, China, India, Iraq, Libya, Yemen, Qatar and Israel. Not having either the USA or China as members hinders its international standing.

The ICC has dealt with cases relating to the wars that followed the break-up of the former Yugoslavia. In recent years the cases it has pursued have related to crimes alleged to be committed in Africa. Many countries in Africa see the Court as being biased against them.

Discussion point

Why do you think the International Criminal Court may be a better way forward than leaving individual countries to deal with those who commit war crimes?

Case study

Joseph Kony – child kidnapper and warlord

Joseph Kony has been wanted by the International Criminal Court since 2005 on 12 counts of crimes against humanity and 21 of war crimes.

He led a group called the Lord's Resistance Army (LRA) in Uganda, South Sudan, Democratic Republic of Congo and Central African Republic. In 2012, he became the focus of an international social media campaign that used the hashtag #Kony2012.

Millions supported the social media campaign and the USA sent troops to Africa to find him. However, he has still not been found and arrested.

Different viewpoint

In 2012, three Americans launched a social media campaign to make Joseph Kony the most infamous person in the world. To what extent where they successful?

Search 'Kony2012' on the internet to gauge their success.

Activity

Refer to the Universal Declaration of Human Rights and present a case to your class for the Declaration to be updated or amended to include further rights.

Websites

British Institute of Human Rights: www.bihr.org.uk

United Nations: www.un.org/en/universal-declaration-human-rights/index.html

UNICEF: www.unicef.org

UN Office of the High Commissioner: www.ohchr.org

Liberty: www.libertyhumanrights.org.uk

Human Rights Investigations: https://humanrightsinvestigations.org

International Committee of the Red Cross: www.icrc.org

Equality and Human Rights Commission: www.equalityhumanrights.com

International Criminal Court: www.icc-cpi.int

Review questions

1 Name the Court of the Council of Europe and the Court of the European Union.
2 What is a human right?
3 What do the initials HRA stand for?
4 What types of offences does the International Criminal Court deal with?

Learning review points

- Why are the UDHR and the ECHR important?
- What are the Rights of the Child?
- Why is the Human Rights Act 1998 important?
- Why is international law important?

EXAM PRACTICE

1 In which year was the Human Rights Act approved in the UK? (AO1) [1 mark]
   - **A** 1970
   - **B** 1990
   - **C** 1998
   - **D** 2000
2 The box on page 81 indicates rights protected under the Human Rights Act. Explain what is meant by 'The right to a fair trial' and 'No punishment without law'. (AO2) [4 marks]
3 Assess the criticisms made by some in the UK of the European Court of Human Rights. (AO3) [8 marks]

Chapter 10: Bringing about change in the legal system

Key question

- How do citizens play a part to bring about change in the legal system?

The role of the citizen within the legal system

Spec coverage

- Students, through research, investigations or interaction with members of the community, should understand the roles undertaken by citizens within the legal system and how the role of the citizen has been seen to be pivotal to our justice system. Students should understand the responsibilities and roles of citizens in the legal system: as a juror, a witness, a victim of crime, a magistrate, a special constable, a police commissioner or a member of a tribunal hearing.

Central to any justice system within a democracy are the support and involvement of its citizenry. There has been a long tradition of citizen involvement in the justice system in the various parts of the United Kingdom. Citizens can take part in the justice system in numerous ways:

- By carrying out **jury service**
- As members of tribunals, resolving issues
- By becoming special constables, working alongside their local police force
- As magistrates, dispensing justice locally
- By standing for election as a Police and Crime Commissioner
- By becoming a member of a Neighbourhood Watch scheme.

Those who witness a crime or are a victim of crime also have a role to play to ensure the justice system operates fairly and justly.

Jury service

Juries are groups of 12 citizens, randomly selected from the local electoral register. They have been shortlisted to hear a case in a court located in their own area. They jointly determine the verdict of the case, making a decision based on the facts and evidence, in consultation with the judge on rules of law. Juries are normally expected to reach a unanimous verdict, but judges can allow them to reach a majority verdict with one or two jurors disagreeing with the majority.

One of the jurors is appointed the foreman of the jury. This person chairs the meeting in the jury room and reads out the verdict of the jury to the court. A jury only announces the verdict. The judge determines the sentence to be given.

Figure 10.1 Jury members listening to the evidence

A Ministry of Justice spokesperson said: 'Jury service is one of the most important civic duties that anyone can be asked to perform. It has served us well for hundreds of years and continues to deliver justice across the country every day.'

Each year about 178,000 people are called to serve on juries. Being called does not necessarily mean that you will sit on a jury. Sometimes the offender changes their plea, so a jury is not required. More people are called than are needed, so you may not be required. It is also possible for lawyers in the court to object to an individual being on a jury, often due to the gender or age balance of those put forward.

Some people are not eligible to serve on a jury:

- Those under 18 or over 75 at present
- Most criminals and those on bail
- Those who do not meet certain residency qualifications
- People who have certain jobs are excluded.

It is possible to apply to the court to be exempt from serving.

You can claim some loss of earnings and child-minding costs. However, if you are called for jury service and you fail to turn up, you will be fined £1000.

There have been concerns in recent years about those called for jury service trying to opt out for a range of reasons. The government has now tightened up both the reasons why some groups of people can be excluded and a person's ability to try to not take part if called for jury service.

In recent years many experts and politicians have challenged the need to keep trial by jury. They state that there is often a problem in getting a balanced section of the community to serve. Many cases now are so technical and last such a long time that it is difficult for lay members of the public to follow the evidence. In cases that have gained publicity and notoriety it is often difficult for the jury to remain impartial.

> **Discussion point**
> Can you make a case for retaining trial by jury?

Member of a tribunal

Citizens can apply to become members of official tribunals that deal with specific complaints and issues. One of the best known are Employment Tribunals, which deal with problems relating to work and employment contracts. Tribunals can advertise either for lay members or for those with a specialist background to serve. Local authorities also set up panels to deal with issues like school admission policy and these can invite citizens to become members. There are a number of tribunals, for example:

- Social Security and Child Support
- Criminal Injuries
- Mental Health Review
- Care Standards
- Immigration and Asylum

- Valuation
- War Pensions and Armed Forces Compensation
- Employment.

Special constables

Figure 10.2 Many people choose to volunteer as special constables, supporting the work of their local police force

The special constable is a trained volunteer who works with and supports their local police. Special constables can come from any walk of life. They volunteer for a minimum of four hours a week with their local police force.

Once they have completed their training, they have the same powers as regular police officers and wear a similar uniform.

Traditionally, special constables have not received payment for their work. However, a small number of forces have a system under which special constables are given an allowance in return for specific commitments. The uniform is provided free, and expenses are paid. In 2018 there were over 11,000 special constables in the UK.

Magistrates

Magistrates are also referred to as Justices of the Peace (JPs). They are citizens from the local community who volunteer to administer justice in their local Magistrates' Court. They do not have to have a legal background as training is provided once they are selected. Advertisements appear in the local press for people to apply to become magistrates. They sit as a 'bench' made up of three magistrates. They can also sit alongside a district judge.

All criminal cases start in a Magistrates' Court. The most serious cases are referred to the Crown Court.

Over 90 per cent of all cases start in and are dealt with in a Magistrates' Court. Magistrates deal with crimes such as minor assaults, motoring offences, theft and handling stolen goods. They can give out fines of up to £5000 per offence and community orders, and can send an offender to prison for six months, or twelve months for more than one crime. They also deal with some civil law cases such as: unpaid council tax, TV licence non-payment, child custody and adoption cases, and cases involving taking children into care. Cases involving the care of young people can only be heard by magistrates who have had specialist training.

Magistrates have existed for over 600 years. There are currently 14,000 lay magistrates, and almost half are women. When hearing a case, magistrates are supported by a professional legal adviser called the Court Clerk Legal Adviser.

Police and Crime Commissioners

Police and Crime Commissioners are elected by the public for each regional police force. While the Chief Constable maintains day-to-day operational control, the Police Commissioner controls the policy priorities for the force and the allocation of funds. They are also funded to set up their own private office to support their work.

Most of these Commissioners are elected on a political platform, representing either the Conservative or Labour Party. Those who support the idea of directly elected commissioners believe that, by being elected, they are accountable for their actions to the public and in that way the police are more responsive to local needs.

Prior to Police Commissioners, there was an appointed local police committee made up of local councillors and magistrates, who elected their own Chair and oversaw the work of the police.

In 2012, elections were held for the first time for Police and Crime Commissioners for each regional police force. These elections were not well advertised or funded and those elected were elected on a very low turnout. The average turnout was less than 15 per cent. In total 192 candidates stood for the 41 posts in England and Wales. (London does not have elected Police and Crime Commissioners. That function forms a part of the duties of the Mayor of London.) Elections for Police and Crime Commissioners are now held on the same day as local elections, which has led to an increase in voter turnout.

These posts were contested by the political parties and by independent candidates.

The results in 2016 were:
- Conservative – 20
- Labour – 15
- Independents – 3
- Plaid Cymru – 2

Case study

A Police and Crime Commissioner – a profile

Meet the Commissioner for Sussex (Conservative): Katy Bourne, elected in 2012 and re-elected in 2016

The Sussex Police and Crime Commissioner is responsible for policing and crime in its totality across the county.

Katy lives in Sussex with husband Kevin and two grown-up sons.

She is a graduate of Aberystwyth University, a School Governor at Oriel High, Crawley and was a Mid Sussex District Councillor from 2011 to 2013.

Katy has been described as a 'serial business builder', having had either direct ownership or indirect interests in the success of several businesses, including her own leisure company, which was successfully sold to her main competitor.

Following the sale in 2005, she re-invested some of the proceeds in start-up projects including a music and dance broadcasting business and a low-carbon economy financial modelling company.

Katy has recently been appointed a Director of the Board of the College of Policing.

Case study
A Police and Crime Commissioner – a profile

Meet the Commissioner for the West Midlands (Labour): David Jamieson, elected in 2012 and re-elected in 2016

David Jamieson was born and bred in the West Midlands.

He qualified as a teacher from St Peter's C of E College, Saltley, Birmingham and has taught in schools across the Midlands. David served as an MP from 1992 to 2005. From 1997 to 2005 he was a government minister.

David is vastly experienced in issues relating to community safety and policing from his roles as an MP, local councillor in Solihull and as a former member of the West Midlands Police and Crime Panel. As a Transport Minister, David worked closely with the police on road safety issues, and was instrumental in giving police the powers to seize uninsured vehicles and making it illegal to drive while using a handheld mobile phone.

David lives in Solihull with his wife, Patricia.

www.apccs.police.uk

> ### Different viewpoint
> Many people feel too many ex-politicians are Police and Crime Commissioners. Looking at the two PCCs, what CV would you construct for someone you would support as a PCC?

New elections were due to be held in 2020, but were postponed until 2021 due to the Covid-19 pandemic.

What do they do?

The role of Police and Crime Commissioner includes:
- meeting the public to listen to their views about policing
- producing a police and crime plan and setting out police priorities
- deciding how the budget should be spent
- appointing chief constables and dismissing them if necessary.

Neighbourhood Watch

The government and local police forces encourage local residents to work together with them in monitoring what is happening in the local community.

Many areas have established **Neighbourhood Watch** schemes. Household and motor insurance companies often give discounts to people who live in Neighbourhood Watch areas. People living in an area form a committee, work with their local police force and are encouraged to report any concerns to the police. The police also attend Neighbourhood Watch committee meetings and report back on crime in the area. Together they often publish newsletters, so the community is aware of the crime or lack of crime in the area.

Witnesses and victims

Witnesses and victims may not appear at first sight either to be volunteers or people trying to make a difference, but both groups are vital to the operation of the justice system in the UK.

- A **witness** to a crime is vital to the police, the Crown Prosecution Service and the defence team of any person accused of an offence. As a witness, giving your version of events means that you can contribute to the process of justice, and potentially prevent a case of injustice. You may have to appear in court and recount the evidence you have already given, which will be in a written format and/or recorded. The lawyers on both sides of the case will take you through your evidence to clarify points to support the arguments they are putting forward. The judge is there to support you to ensure the questioning is not unfair. In some very serious cases a witness's anonymity is protected or they are given witness protection.

- A **victim of crime** – it is important if you are a victim of a crime that the matter is reported to the police so an investigation can be undertaken. Once you have reported a crime to the police you have the right to be told about the progress of the case. You are also notified about any arrest and court cases. You should also receive: information about Victim Support; notification about the outcome of the case; information about any entitlement to claim for compensation; and support from a family liaison police officer if required.

Roles played by different groups

Spec coverage

- The roles played by pressure and interest groups, trade unions, charities and voluntary groups, public institutions and public services in providing a voice and support for different groups in society campaigning to bring about a legal change or to fight an injustice.

The case studies in this section illustrate the role played by groups of citizens campaigning regarding changing the law or legal processes.

Many such groups are formed as a result of the impact of the law upon the lives of the campaigners.

Many have specific issues they want resolved, and may continue in existence broadening the issues about which they campaign.

Case study
INQUEST – Truth, Justice & Accountability

TRUTH, JUSTICE AND ACCOUNTABILITY

Stand with INQUEST, bereaved families & lawyers in our pursuit of truth, justice, & accountability

INQUEST are working to end deaths caused by unsafe systems of detention, a lack of care, the use of force and by institutional failures.

We are campaigning for

1. Legal Aid for Inquests: Automatic non means tested legal aid funding for families' specialist legal representation immediately following a state related death to cover preparation and representation at the inquest and other legal processes. #LegalAidforInquests

2. A National Oversight Mechanism: A new, independent, public body with a duty to collate, analyse and monitor recommendations and their implementation arising from post death investigations, inquiries and inquests.

3. The Public Authority (Accountability) Bill: Re-introduce 'Hillsborough Law' to Parliament to establish a duty of candour on state authorities and officers and private entities whose activities impact on public safety.

**Learn more and sign up to our newsletter:
WWW.INQUEST.ORG.UK**

INQUEST is a campaign group that actively supports individuals and families who find themselves before an inquest hearing investigating a death that has involved the state, i.e. a death in police custody. For almost 40 years it has fought to improve the inquest and investigation process.

The INQUEST campaign has formal backing from numerous organisations, such as Liberty, Grenfell United, Mind, Bar Council, Women in Prison, Legal Aid Practitioners Group, Runnymede Trust, Criminal Justice Alliance, Operation Black Vote, National Autistic Society and many others.

Different viewpoint

Why is it important to support those involved in inquest cases where the government is involved?

Case study
The Guildford Four

The case of the Guildford Four relates to four people who were arrested in 1974 and accused of being involved in an IRA bombing in Guildford in which five people were killed. Gerry Conlon, a Belfast-born 20-year-old at the time, was one of those arrested. He was sentenced to life imprisonment on the basis of false confessions made after days of mistreatment by the police. In 1989, the Court of Appeal overturned the convictions when the court was told that evidence showing that the police knew he had an alibi was not given to his defence team. There was also evidence of police collusion in fabricating the statements that formed the only evidence produced against them at the original trial.

On his release, Gerry Conlon stood outside the High Court in London and promised to fight to clear others who had been wrongly accused. In 1993, a film *In the Name of the Father* told his story. In 1991, he and others formed a pressure group to fight against miscarriages of justice, called the Miscarriages of Justice Organisation (Mojo). In 1997, he was given £546,000 in compensation. In 2005, the Prime Minister Tony Blair gave him a personal apology. Conlon said:

> Back then it was the Irish, now it's Muslims. But nobody is safe. One of the Guildford Four was English. Everyone thinks this happens to other people, but it's closer than you think. Who's to say you're not going to be next.

Different viewpoint
Do you think cases like the Guildford Four could still occur today?

Case study
The Equal Partnership campaign

In June 2018, the Supreme Court gave a ruling in favour of allowing mixed-sex couples to enter into a civil partnership.

This ruling was the result of four years of campaigning by Rebecca Steinfeld and Charles Keidan. They argued that while legislation passed in 2004 and 2013 allowed same-sex couples either to have a civil partnership or to be married, for mixed-sex couples only marriage was an option. This meant that the 3.3 million co-habiting mixed-sex couples in the UK did not have the same legal protection or rights as those who had entered into a same-sex civil partnership. Steinfeld and Keidan argued that this was incompatible with the European Convention on Human Rights.

At the head of the Equal Civil Partnership group, Steinfeld and Keidan set up an online petition that attracted 130,000 signatures, and worked with MPs to change the law. In March 2019, a Private Member's Bill, sponsored by Tim Loughton MP, passed all its stages in Parliament. It was given the royal assent and became law.

Different viewpoint
On which human rights issues would you campaign and why?

Case study
The Hillsborough disaster

On 15 April 1989, 96 Liverpool football fans were crushed to death and hundreds more were injured at the Sheffield Wednesday stadium, which was hosting an FA Cup semi-final match.

In the same year, an inquiry into the disaster led by Lord Chief Justice Taylor established that the main cause was a failure of police crowd control. Crowd behaviour and violence were also blamed.

Relatives, friends and supporters of those who died did not believe that the full facts about what happened that day had been brought to the public's attention and campaigned for more information.

In April 2009, 20 years after the tragedy, the Home Secretary requested South Yorkshire Police release all the files it had containing detailed evidence.

In December that year, the Hillsborough Independent Panel was set up by the Home Secretary to oversee a 'full public disclosure of relevant government and local information'.

In September 2012, the panel reported that the police had deliberately altered more than 160 witness statements in an attempt to blame Liverpool fans for the fatal crush.

It found that crowd safety was 'compromised at every level' and that 41 of the 96 who died could have survived, prompting calls for fresh inquests.

The disclosures prompted apologies from the Prime Minister and the former editor of *The Sun* newspaper over comments that had been made about the fans who died.

Following public pressure, in December 2012 the High Court quashed the original inquest verdicts, and the Home Secretary ordered a fresh police inquiry into the disaster.

The fresh inquiry into the deaths commenced in March 2014. In April 2016 the inquest jury decided that the

96 who died at Hillsborough had been unlawfully killed.

In 2019 David Duckenfield, aged 75, who was the police commander when the Hillsborough disaster took place, was put on trial for the negligent manslaughter of the 95 Liverpool fans. On 28 November, the jury returned a verdict of not guilty.

Christine Burke, whose father Henry Burke was killed in the disaster, stood in the public gallery and addressed the judge after the verdict was read out:

> With all due respect, my lord, 96 people were found unlawfully killed to a criminal standard. I would like to know who is responsible for my father's death, because someone is.

This case study shows how a group of concerned citizens, together with media and political support, can eventually seek out the truth and use the legal system in order to try to achieve justice.

Different viewpoints

In what ways do you think this could be claimed to be a successful campaign?

Why do you think some of the campaigners feel they have not achieved justice?

Different forms of democratic and citizenship actions

Spec coverage

- Students should be aware of the different forms of democratic and citizenship actions people can take to bring about change and hold those in positions of power to account in regard to issues relating to human rights and the justice system: joining an interest group; campaigning; advocacy; lobbying; petitions; joining a demonstration; volunteering.

As was outlined in the case studies in the previous section, there are many methods that can be employed to bring about change when confronting issues relating to human rights and the justice system. Some of the methods such as lobbying, protests and petitions can relate to any type of campaign, but others link more closely to campaigns related to human rights. The legal system itself can be used to right an injustice. Citizens can use both the court system in the UK and the European Court of Human Rights.

Case study
The Grenfell Tower fire

On Wednesday 14 June 2017 at 00:54, a fire was reported in the Grenfell 24-storey residential tower block in North Kensington, London. With 40 fire engines and 200 firefighters attending the blaze, it took nearly 24 hours to get the fire under control. Seventy-six people died and hundreds were made homeless. The youngest victim was six months old and the oldest was 84.

In the immediate aftermath of the tragedy, the local community rallied together to offer food, accommodation and support to those affected. As more information about the blaze became known, questions were raised about how the fire started and spread, the material used for the cladding of the building, whether building regulations were adequate, and the response of the fire brigade as well as of central and local government. The government launched a formal public inquiry into the fire and reviews of cladding on other high-rise tower blocks throughout the country were carried out.

The local community has formed action groups to ensure both that those responsible are held to account and that a similar tragedy does not happen elsewhere. One such group is Grenfell United: **www.grenfellunited. org.uk**, which supports those impacted and the wider community, by campaigning for justice and change. Other campaign groups have been inspired by this tragic event – see page 37 and page 88.

Different viewpoint

Do you think the Grenfell fire campaign will lead to major changes in housing policy?

Consider inviting a local councillor or your local MP to your school to discuss this issue before reaching your own conclusion to the question.

Case study
Hidden Housing Scandal

The Hidden Housing Scandal campaign is being led by the *Sunday Times* newspaper. It is using its influence to try to bring about change. As a result of the Grenfell fire (see previous case study) there has been a call to ensure that all housing, especially high-rise flats, is safe. Not only do 20,000 homes still have the cladding involved in the 2017 Grenfell fire, 186,000 flats in 3000 high-rise schemes have other flammable cladding.

This has led banks and building societies, which lend mortgages to buyers, to demand that all properties they think are at risk have an EWS1 certificate (which states the building's walls are not combustible) before they will lend money against the property. The newspaper claims that 1.5 million modern flats could be unmortgageable for many years as owners can't prove they are safe.

The campaign already has a long list of supporters. Its five aims are:

1 Additional government funding needed to cover all the costs of the works, which should then be claimed back from the original builders, not from the people living in the flats.
2 Plans to make flats safe to be extended to fix all private and social housing blocks, not only those above 18 metres.
3 A national effort to strip all unsafe cladding from buildings by June 2022.
4 To replace the EWS1 with a fairer, faster process.
5 To change the law so residents are not liable for historic defects.

Different viewpoint

Do you think this campaign is likely to succeed?

Design a grid sheet of the campaigning methods the group could use and think about the degree of influence of each before reaching a response to the question.

Websites

Jury Service: www.gov.uk/jury-service/overview
Police Specials: https://recruit.college.police.uk/Special/Pages/default.aspx
The Association of Police and Crime Commissioners: www.apccs.police.uk
The Bar Council: www.barcouncil.org.uk
Neighbourhood Watch: www.ourwatch.org.uk
Miscarriages of Justice UK: www.miscarriagesofjustice.org

Activity

What would your policing priorities be for your community? Carry out some online research regarding crime in your community. Study the Police and Crime Commissioner's policing plan for your region. Invite a representative from the police to come into school and carry out a class Q&A based on your research.

Review questions

1 How many people serve on a jury?
2 What do the initials PCC stand for?
3 What is a Neighbourhood Watch scheme?

- How does the citizen participate in the legal system?
- How have citizens tried to make a difference to change the law or seek legal redress?

EXAM PRACTICE

1 Identify one benefit to a community of Neighbourhood Watch schemes. (AO1) [2 marks]
2 Referring to the INQUEST case study on page 88, consider two arguments you could put forward to support its aims. (AO2) [4 marks]
3 Analyse the arguments put forward by those who wish to abolish trial by jury. (AO3) [8 marks]

Chapter 11: Political power in the UK

- Where does political power reside in the UK and how is it controlled?

The concept of democracy

Spec coverage
- The concept of democracy and different forms of democracy, including representative democracy.

In basic terms, **democracy** is a type of government based upon the principle that all people are equal and collectively hold power. The term derives from the ancient Greek words *demos* meaning people and *kratos* meaning strength/power, hence the link to the expression 'people power'. In ancient Greece, all free men gathered together and debated and decided issues affecting their city state. This form of democracy is called **direct democracy**, where those involved directly determine the outcome.

As societies became larger and more complex, it became impossible for all the citizens to meet together to make decisions. So a system developed whereby groups of citizens appointed or elected a person or persons to represent their views; hence the term **representative democracy**. In the UK, there are elections to local, regional and national bodies to elect a local representative on behalf of a group of electors. These representatives make decisions on behalf of their communities and are held to account when they next stand for election.

Modern-day democracies

The UK is described as a **liberal democracy**, which is a name given to a system of democracy through which certain freedoms of the individual are upheld and citizens are protected from excessive government power. The extent of these freedoms and rights can vary within countries that describe themselves as liberal democracies.

Today, in the UK, we associate the following elements and freedoms with a modern-day democracy:

- Regular, fair and open elections to public bodies
- An electoral system that allows all voters to participate, where there is a secret ballot and an accountable results system, and where the result reflects the views of the electorate
- The ability of citizens to be able to stand for elections without unfair impediment
- A government that is accountable and faces regular elections
- A system where all candidates can campaign equally and no person can bribe or intimidate the electors
- A system where the media can freely report upon the work of government
- A system where the judiciary is separate from government and citizens can use the legal process to hold government to account.

The elements that we recognise as a democracy today developed and evolved over many years. For example, the secret ballot was not introduced until 1870. Women were not given the vote at the same age as men until 1928. More recently, political power has been devolved to the nations of the United Kingdom.

Still today people campaign for changes to our democracy. Some want the voting age to be lowered to 16, or the way we vote to be changed so that Parliament is more representative of how the electors have voted. Others want to abolish our second parliamentary chamber, the House of Lords, or make it elected.

Referendums

Citizens in the twenty-first century are increasingly seeking more direct democracy. There has been an increase in the use of referendums in the UK since the first national referendum in 1975, which was on UK membership of the European Economic Community (EEC), now known as the European Union (EU). A referendum is a vote on a single issue, normally with a 'Yes' or 'No' response required. A national referendum was held in 2016 on our continued membership of the European Union (EU). In recent years, there have also been referendums on Scottish independence, changing the electoral system, and the Good Friday Agreement in Northern Ireland.

There are concerns expressed by many about the growth in the use of referendums. It is claimed that they undermine representative democracy and the power of Parliament. Those in favour of referendums state that there are some issues that are of such importance they should be made by a referendum and not by our elected representatives.

Winston Churchill famously said:

Democracy is the worst form of government, except all those other forms which have been tried from time to time.

Discussion point

What do you think of Churchill's view on democracy?

Different forms of government

Democracy is just one form of government. There are many others, for example:

- **Dictatorship** – Rule by one person or group, which is all-powerful. Often associated with a military takeover of a state, for example Nazi Germany.
- **One-party state** – A state where only one political party exists and runs the country. Often associated with a communist form of government, for example North Korea.
- **Theocracy** – Where religious leaders run the state. An example is Iran.
- **Monarchy** – A form of government where political power is held by a family and that power passes down through the generations. An 'absolute monarchy' is where all power is held by the monarch; an example of an absolute monarchy is Saudi Arabia. The UK is a 'constitutional monarchy', where almost all of the power normally held by a monarch has been transferred to the elected government.

It is also possible to have a situation in which **anarchy** exists – this is where no government operates. This occurs when there is a total breakdown in society, for example after a civil war.

Discussion point

Match each photo below to the type of government it represents. Use the descriptions in the box to help you.

Can you name any other states that are examples of these systems?

The values underpinning democracy

Spec coverage

- The values underpinning democracy: rights, responsibilities, freedoms, equality and the rule of law.

Democracy does not stand in isolation. As a concept it is supported by a range of other concepts, principles and values that over time have enabled the UK to establish a liberal democracy. Within a democracy citizens have certain rights, but alongside rights come responsibilities. The state in a democracy ensures that there is a range of freedoms. For example, governments have, through their actions, attempted to ensure that society is based upon the concept of **equality**.

The rule of law is vital in a democracy, as citizens must know that the legal system is not controlled by government or politicians and is impartial and treats all citizens fairly and equally.

Rights, responsibilities, freedoms, equalities and the rule of law

- **Rights** are the legal, social and ethical entitlements that are considered the building blocks of a society. All citizens within our society enjoy them equally. The idea of freedom of speech is an essential part of our way of life, but society does limit that right where your right conflicts with other rights. Rights within a society structure the way government operates, the content of laws and the morality of society. Rights are often grouped together, and debates take place about human rights, children's rights or prisoner's rights, for example.

- **Responsibilities** relate to those duties placed upon its citizens by a society. For example, you are expected to pay your taxes, obey the law and take part in the judicial system as a jury member if required. These responsibilities are not optional and are often enshrined in law.

- **Freedoms** – the power or right to speak and act or think as one wants. We often explain freedom in relation to a context. Expressions like 'freedom of choice', 'the freedom of the press' and 'freedom of movement' relate to some basic beliefs in our society.

- **Equality** is about ensuring that every individual, irrespective of their background, has an equal opportunity to make the most of their life and talents. No one should have poorer life chances because of where they are born, what they believe or whether they have a disability. This concept is often linked to the phrase 'equality of opportunity' and within the legal system refers to everyone being treated equally.

- **The rule of law** is a doctrine that states that every person, no matter who they are, must obey the law. There can be no different treatment before the law or leniency because of title, background, wealth, religion or sex, for example.

In Britain, we do not have a formal written constitution that acts as a fixed reference point for our laws, rights, responsibilities and individual liberties. So changes to shared values, beliefs, rights and responsibilities normally take place after a lengthy public debate where a consensus develops in favour of a change. Table 11.1 indicates how, through the passage of new laws, often after lengthy public campaigns, a new consensus about life in modern Britain has arisen.

Table 11.1 Examples of changes to individual rights and equality issues in the UK

ISSUE	LEGISLATIVE CHANGES
Rights of women	Representation of the People Act 1928
	Equal Pay Act 1970
	Sex Discrimination Acts 1975, 1986
	Employment and Equality Regulations 2003 and 2006
	Equality Acts 2006 and 2010
Racial equality	Race Relations Acts 1965, 1968, 1976 and 2000
Rights of the child	The United Nations Convention on the Rights of the Child came into force in 1992. Every child in the UK is entitled to over 40 specific rights.
Sexual rights	The Sexual Offences Act 1967
	Sexual Offences Act 2003
	The Gender Recognition Act 2004
	Civil Partnerships Act 2005
	Marriage (Same Sex Couples) Act 2013
Disability rights	Disability Discrimination Act 1995 and 2005
	Special Needs and Disability Act 2001
The Equality Act of 2010 brought together all the laws shown above into a single new law.	

Discussion point

In what ways has the legislation in Table 11.1 made the UK a fairer and more just society?

The institutions of the British constitution

Spec coverage

● The institutions of the British constitution: the power of government, the Prime Minister and Cabinet; the sovereignty of Parliament; the roles of the legislature, the Opposition, political parties, the monarch, citizens, the judiciary, the police and the civil service.

The institutions of the British constitution are similar to a jigsaw puzzle: they need to interlink in order for us to understand the nature and complexity of the constitutional, political and legal structures that exist in the United Kingdom.

The power of government

Government can appear all-powerful within the UK system, but it can only act with the authority it is given by Parliament. The recent pandemic has seen government take powers to control many aspects of everyday life – from closing shops and enforcing national lockdown, to providing financial support to many individuals and businesses. None of this could have been undertaken unless Parliament had granted permission. Parliament can delegate powers to government and ministers to be able to act without gaining parliamentary prior permission.

It is only in recent years that the power to declare war or take military action has involved Parliament. Government can appear very powerful but it does have restraints in the form of parliamentary accountability, the courts regarding legality, and the media and public opinion.

Discussion point

Many people say Prime Ministers today have become more 'Presidential' rather than appearing to lead a team of ministers. What evidence is there for this view? See also pages 138–139.

The Prime Minister and Cabinet

The **Prime Minister** is the Head of Government not the Head of State in the UK; Head of State is the role of the monarch. In some countries like France and the USA, the elected President holds both posts.

Normally the Prime Minister is the elected leader of the largest party in the House of Commons. Today the Prime Minister is a Member of Parliament (MP), but in the past Prime Ministers have been members of the House of Lords. The last Prime Minister who was a member of the House of Lords was Lord Home in 1963. On becoming Prime Minister, he stood for election as an MP.

The Cabinet are the most senior members of the government appointed by the Prime Minister and they head up government departments like Health and Education. The four most senior members are the Chancellor of the Exchequer, the Foreign Secretary, the Home Secretary and the Minister of Defence. The phrase 'cabinet government' is often used to describe our system of government, whereby decisions of government are made collectively and all ministers agree to abide by these decisions. Hence the phrase about the Prime Minister being 'first among equals' and the Cabinet having 'collective responsibility'.

Under Tony Blair the phrase 'sofa government' was used, whereby policy decisions were made by him and a few advisers. Other have described how the role of Prime Minister has become more 'Presidential'.

Figure 11.1 A decade of Prime Ministers – David Cameron (Con) 2010–16 and Deputy Prime Minister Nick Clegg (Lib Dem) 2010–15; Theresa May (Con) 2016–19; and Boris Johnson (Con) 2019–

Sovereignty of Parliament

Parliament is sovereign so therefore can pass any laws it wishes. This is an important political concept. Only Parliament in the UK can pass laws and only Parliament can repeal or change them. The Supreme Court has been given powers to state whether government laws/actions are compatible with human rights legislation.

There can be issues when a government has a large majority and therefore can easily pass legislation. But the power of the House of Lords to delay, the role of opposition parties to scrutinise and the ability of the media to discuss, means that there are checks and balances within the system, and eventually all governments have to face the electorate at a General Election.

Role of the legislature

The **legislature** is another name for Parliament, the body that can pass and amend laws. In the case of the UK, this can be done through the House of Commons or the House of Lords.

The House of Commons is an elected body currently made up of 650 MPs, who each represent a parliamentary constituency. They are elected at a General Election and remain in office until the next General Election, when most stand for re-election. For the past 150 years the Commons has been the more dominant of the two Houses. The House of Lords is made up of hereditary peers and appointed life peers, all of whom remain in office until they decide to retire or die. The UK has what is known as a **bicameral** Parliament (meaning it is made up of two parts, the Commons and the Lords).

The role of both bodies is to pass legislation and hold the government to account. The Commons is the more powerful of the two Houses in that the Lords recognises that the government is elected and has a manifesto to deliver.

Work of the House of Lords

The Lords has three main roles:

- Making laws
- In-depth consideration of public policy
- Holding government to account.

The House of Commons also carries out these tasks, but it is the more powerful of the two Houses as it is elected and can overturn the decisions of the House of Lords.

It can be questioned whether the legislature or the government is more powerful, as governments with large majorities can normally pass all their legislation with ease. The unelected House of Lords can often act as a check on a powerful government as its members are appointed for life and are not accountable like elected MPs.

The opposition

The title the Official Opposition is given to the largest party not in government. It sits opposite the government in the House of Commons. The phrase 'opposition' relates to all those Members of Parliament who represent parties that are not in the government. The role of the opposition is to hold the government to account for its action and to oppose policies it disagrees with. Her Majesty's Official Opposition is formally recognised within our system of government and the leader of the opposition and the opposition chief whip receive salaries equivalent to that of a government Cabinet minister.

If a government has a large majority, the power of the opposition is often very limited. While it may not defeat the government in votes, its task is to hold the government to account and try to promote its own policies.

Political parties

Political plurality in a democratic system means that the electorate has a range of political parties from which to choose at elections. A political party is a voluntary group of people who share a common ideology and political beliefs and who wish to win elections in order to carry out their ideas. At a General Election each party publishes a **manifesto**, a document outlining the policies it would like to introduce if it wins power. Political parties can either be UK-based or based in parts of the UK. For many years the UK had what was called a two-party system, whereby the House of Commons was made up almost entirely of members from two parties. Up until the early part of the twentieth century the two parties were the Conservatives and the Liberals; from the 1920s onwards the two parties were the Conservatives and the Labour Party. Since the 1970s three-party politics has developed, with the Liberal Democrats emerging strongly at some elections. A more apt description for the UK currently is that it has a multi-party system, due to the growth of regionally based parties in Northern Ireland, Wales and Scotland. These political parties also contest elections to local authorities, the devolved bodies and Police and Crime Commissioners.

The monarchy

Figure 11.2 Queen Elizabeth II

The monarch's role is described as follows:

The sovereign is the head of state of the UK, providing stability, continuity and a national focus. By convention, the sovereign does not become publicly involved in the party politics of government, although he or she is entitled to be informed and consulted, and to advise, encourage and warn ministers.

For this reason, there is a convention of confidentiality surrounding the sovereign's communications with his or her ministers. The sovereign retains prerogative powers but, by constitutional convention, the majority of these powers are exercised by, or on the advice of, his or her responsible ministers, save in a few exceptional instances (the 'reserve powers').

(Source: taken from the *Cabinet Manual 2011*)

The present monarch, Queen Elizabeth II, has reigned longer than any other monarch, having come to the throne following her father's death in 1952. The next monarch will be her eldest son, Charles, the Prince of Wales. If Charles dies before the Queen, the throne will pass to his eldest son, Prince William, the Duke of Cambridge. After William, the line of succession has been changed to the eldest *child*, ending the automatic line of male succession. The Queen is our monarch as her father and mother only had two daughters and she was the elder of the two.

Citizens

Within this vast array of constitutional arrangements, what is the role of the citizen? Many freedoms and rights are contained within the various components of our constitution. In the last resort, the citizen has the power through the ballot to change the government and replace it with another or stand for election themselves to put forward their ideas for government.

The judiciary

'The judiciary' is the term used to describe the judges who operate in the courts of the United Kingdom. Within our constitutional arrangements they are free of all forms of interference and are appointed by a selection panel and serve until their retirement age. Unlike in some other countries, they neither stand for election nor are political appointees.

The police

Policing in this country is decentralised, being based upon a number of regional forces. There is no national police force in the UK. These forces are accountable to elected Police and Crime Commissioners. The London Metropolitan Force is responsible to the London Mayor. The National Crime Agency provides specialist support to regional forces. The police in the UK are non-political and are effectively servants of the Crown.

The civil service

The term 'the **civil service**' refers to all those employed by central government to administer its policies. The most senior civil servants work alongside government ministers and offer advice. Three principles apply to the operation of the civil service:

1 **Impartiality** – Civil servants serve the Crown, not a specific government. They cannot be members of political parties.

2 **Anonymity** – Civil servants are anonymous individuals who should not be identified or associated with specific policies.

3 **Permanence** – Civil servants stay in their posts when a government leaves office; they are expected to serve governments irrespective of their composition.

The relationships between the institutions

Spec coverage

- How the relationships between the institutions form an uncodified British constitution and examples of how this is changing.

As with any organisation, club or team, there has to be a set of rules by which the organisation is run. In relation to a state, this set of rules is called a constitution. Often when the phrase is used, people think about the American Constitution, which is a written document dating from the eighteenth century that is still the working document for how America is governed today. A major debate in the USA relates to gun ownership, which is written into the second amendments to the Constitution and the Bill of Rights:

'A well-regulated militia, being necessary to the security of a free State, the right of the people to keep and bear arms, shall not be infringed'

(5 December 1791)

From the Declaration of Independence, USA, 4 July 1776:

We hold these truths to be self-evident, that all men are created equal, that they are endowed by their Creator with certain unalienable Rights, that among these are Life, Liberty and the pursuit of Happiness. — That to secure these rights, Governments are instituted among Men, deriving their just powers from the consent of the governed, — That whenever any Form of Government becomes destructive of these ends, it is the Right of the People to alter or to abolish it, and to institute new Government, laying its foundations on such principles and organizing its powers in such form, as to them shall seem most likely to effect their Safety and Happiness.

As can be seen from the two examples from the Declaration of Independence, a written constitution can clearly lay out the rights of citizens and the powers of government, but it is not easy to change if issues arise.

The British Constitution

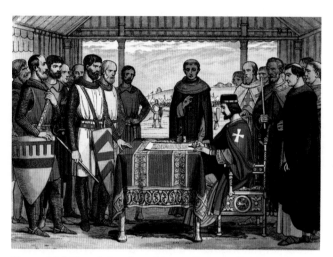

Figure 11.3 King John signs Magna Carta at Runnymede in 1215

Discussion point

Do you think the UK would be better governed if it had a written constitution?

In 1215 at Runnymede, the barons of England forced King John to sign Magna Carta, a document that many see as a precursor to many modern constitutions. It clearly set out the powers of the King in relation to his subjects.

The phrase the 'British Constitution' is often used, but no such formal document exists. The United Kingdom has what is known as an unwritten, uncodified constitution. Unlike, for example, the USA, there is no single document that is called the Constitution. In the UK, many laws, court precedents and conventions make up what others would call a constitution. Being uncodified means that there is no set text divided into chapters or sections. This means that the UK constitution is flexible. Parts can be changed or amended as circumstances change.

There are no formal procedures for changing elements of the constitution, unlike in other countries where formal national votes have to take place. So changing the voting age or giving devolved powers to parts of the UK or allowing same-sex marriages, is brought about in the same way as any other change in the law. In the UK, one of the key principles of our parliamentary system is the supremacy of Parliament to make decisions and laws.

One of the key elements of the British constitution is the 'separation of powers' whereby each part of government – the legislature (those who discuss and agree laws – Parliament), the executive (government and the civil service) and the judiciary (the judges) – should be separate (see Figure 11.4), with checks against one element trying to exercise power over another.

In practice, there is an overlap between the three elements. A government emerges from a Parliament. Judges are appointed in the monarch's name but following a formal process. Parliament as a body often takes on the role of ensuring that a government does not become overbearing, that judges do not interfere with its work, and that the civil service maintains its impartiality and neutrality.

A country belonging to a multi-national organisation will often have to transfer sovereignty or power to, or share power with, others in the organisation. This can have an impact on the role of its Parliament to make laws in regard to some policy areas. By being a signatory to the European Convention on Human Rights, the UK agreed that the European Court of Human Rights had legal authority with regard to UK citizens and that the UK Parliament could not pass laws that contravened the European Human Rights Convention.

In 2005, Parliament passed the Constitutional Reform Act, which established a Supreme Court in the United Kingdom to ensure that judicial decisions were separated from those of Parliament and government. Previously the Law Lords sat as Members of the House of Lords and heard legal cases in the House of Lords.

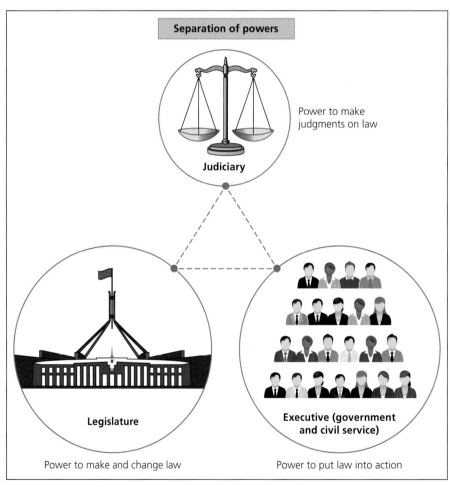

Figure 11.4 Judiciary, legislature and executive – the separation of powers

Websites

Parliament: www.parliament.uk

Prime Minister's Office: www.gov.uk/government/
organisations/prime-ministers-office-10-downing-street

Ministerial Code: www.gov.uk/government/publications/
ministerial-code

Magna Carta: www.bl.uk/magna-carta

Review questions

1 What is an absolute monarchy?
2 Identify one modern form of direct democracy.
3 What is a manifesto?
4 What is separated when one discusses the idea of separation of powers?

Activity

Draft a report drawing up criteria for countries to be considered democratic. First, you need to define what you mean by democratic. Second, list your criteria that say a country is democratic. Third, research a number of countries that claim to be democratic and see how they measure up against your criteria.

Learning review points

- What is meant by the term 'democracy'?
- How does direct democracy differ from representative democracy?
- What other forms of government exist beside democracy?
- What values underpin democracy?
- How would you describe the UK constitution?

EXAM PRACTICE

1 Explain the difference between an absolute monarch and a constitutional monarch. (AO1) [2 marks]
2 Referring to the separation of powers diagram on page 100, describe what this term means in a UK context. (AO2) [4 marks]
3 Examine the advantages of an unwritten constitution. (AO3) [8 marks]

Key question

- What are the powers of local and devolved government and how can citizens participate?

The role and structure of elected local government

Spec coverage

- The role and structure of elected local government.
- The services provided by local government for citizens in local communities.
- Roles and accountability of councillors.

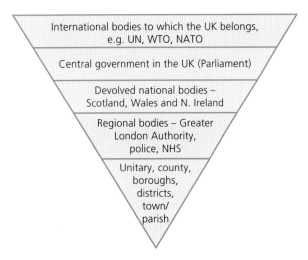

Figure 12.1 The government of the UK operates at several levels. These levels of government are often referred to as tiers

Within the United Kingdom, political power is divided between these different **tiers** of government. Unlike the American system, where the powers of each level are clearly defined and built into the Constitution, in the United Kingdom ultimate political power resides with the Parliament in Westminster. All the other tiers of government have their powers decided by Parliament. The UK Parliament could abolish local government, give more powers to a devolved assembly, or take powers away. The central government of the UK Parliament decides whether to join or leave tiers above the UK Parliament.

All other tiers of government exist at the will of the UK Parliament.

Over the centuries it has been agreed that some services are better delivered by national government and others by local councils.

Discussion point

Consider the services below. Which do you think are most effectively run by local councils and which by national government?

- Collecting your rubbish bins
- Nuclear deterrent
- Services for disabled people
- Planning for new houses
- Foreign affairs
- Taxation policy
- Car parking policy

In the UK, political power is held by **central government**. It determines the nature of political power that is devolved to other bodies within the UK, for example national assemblies/parliaments or local authorities.

These other bodies cannot act beyond the powers they have been granted by central government. If they do so, they can be held accountable for their actions and individual councillors will be held to account by the justice system.

Central government is able to control local government spending through setting limits to how it may raise income and the funding it receives from central government.

Since 1997, there has been a restructuring of powers and responsibilities within the UK. There have been moves towards greater **devolution**, attempts at regional government and various strategies to invigorate local government. Changing attitudes have also influenced the way central government has organised and structured bodies like the NHS and the police (for example, the introduction of directly elected Police and Crime Commissioners that mirror **directly elected mayors** for local councils).

The structure of local government

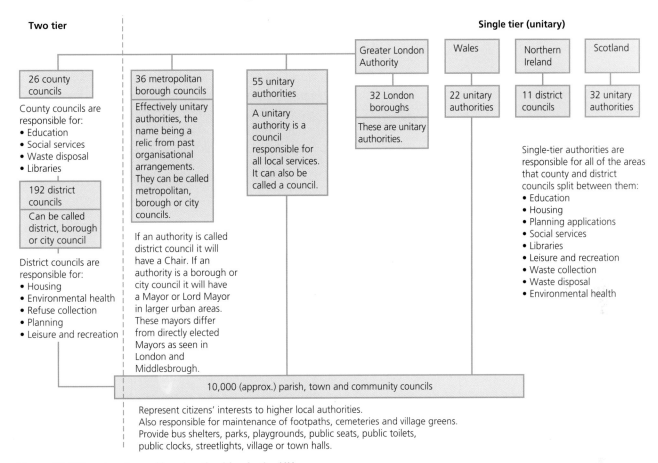

Two tier

Single tier (unitary)

26 county councils

County councils are responsible for:
• Education
• Social services
• Waste disposal
• Libraries

192 district councils

Can be called district, borough or city council

District councils are responsible for:
• Housing
• Environmental health
• Refuse collection
• Planning
• Leisure and recreation

36 metropolitan borough councils

Effectively unitary authorities, the name being a relic from past organisational arrangements. They can be called metropolitan, borough or city councils.

If an authority is called district council it will have a Chair. If an authority is a borough or city council it will have a Mayor or Lord Mayor in larger urban areas. These mayors differ from directly elected Mayors as seen in London and Middlesbrough.

55 unitary authorities

A unitary authority is a council responsible for all local services. It can also be called a council.

Greater London Authority

32 London boroughs

These are unitary authorities.

Wales

22 unitary authorities

Northern Ireland

11 district councils

Scotland

32 unitary authorities

Single-tier authorities are responsible for all of the areas that county and district councils split between them:
• Education
• Housing
• Planning applications
• Social services
• Libraries
• Leisure and recreation
• Waste collection
• Waste disposal
• Environmental health

10,000 (approx.) parish, town and community councils

Represent citizens' interests to higher local authorities.
Also responsible for maintenance of footpaths, cemeteries and village greens.
Provide bus shelters, parks, playgrounds, public seats, public toilets, public clocks, streetlights, village or town halls.

Figure 12.2 The structure of local authorities in the UK

The United Kingdom is divided into local authority areas (see Figure 12.2). Some have very large populations; others have smaller populations: for example, compare London with 8.6 million and Merthyr Tydfil with 58,800. Over the years, there have been many re-organisations of local government to make councils larger so they can provide a wider range of services. Local government is differently organised within each nation of the UK.

In total, there are five possible types of local authority in England. These are:

● **County councils** cover the whole county and provide 80 per cent of services in these areas, including children's services and adult social care.

● **District councils** cover a smaller area, providing more local services (such as housing, local planning, waste and leisure, but not children's services or adult social care). They can be called district, borough or city councils.

● **Unitary authorities** – in some areas there is just one level of local government responsible for all local services. They can be called a council (e.g. Medway Council), a city council (e.g. Nottingham City Council) or a borough council (e.g. Reading Borough Council).

● **London boroughs** – each of the 32 London boroughs is a unitary authority.

● **Metropolitan districts** are also unitary authorities. The name comes from the 1973 re-organisation of local councils. They can be called metropolitan, borough or city councils.

Many parts of England have two tiers of local government:

1 County councils

2 District, borough or city councils.

In other parts of the country, there is just one (unitary) tier of local government providing all the local services.

103

The lowest tier of local council is a parish, community or town council. These function at a level below district and borough councils and, in some cases, unitary authorities. They are elected but have a limited range of powers and finance. They are responsible for:

- allotments
- public clocks
- bus shelters
- community centres
- play areas and play equipment
- grants to help local organisations
- consultation on neighbourhood planning.

Services provided by local government

Table 12.1 shows the responsibilities of each local council.

Table 12.1 The services provided by local councils

	UNITARY AUTHORITIES	COUNTY COUNCILS	DISTRICT COUNCILS	METROPOLITAN DISTRICTS	LONDON BOROUGHS	GREATER LONDON AUTHORITY
Education	✓	✓		✓	✓	
Highways	✓	✓		✓	✓	✓
Transport planning	✓	✓		✓	✓	✓
Passenger transport	✓	✓				✓
Social care	✓	✓		✓	✓	
Housing	✓	✓	✓	✓	✓	
Libraries	✓	✓		✓	✓	
Leisure and recreation	✓		✓	✓	✓	
Environmental health	✓		✓	✓	✓	
Waste collection	✓		✓	✓	✓	
Waste disposal	✓	✓		✓	✓	
Planning applications	✓		✓	✓	✓	
Strategic planning	✓	✓		✓	✓	✓
Local tax collection	✓		✓	✓	✓	

Wales

In Wales, there are 22 unitary local councils. There are also 735 community and town councils that cover 70 per cent of the population and 94 per cent of the land area.

Scotland

Local government in Scotland is made up of 32 unitary local councils, responsible for the provision of a range of public services.

Combined authorities

Since the establishment of the Greater Manchester authority in 2011, groups of councils have formed combined authorities in some areas of England. These combined authorities – currently in and around Manchester, Sheffield, the North East, Liverpool and West Yorkshire – receive additional powers and funding from central government. They are particularly important for transport and economic policy across the regions in which they are based.

Northern Ireland

From 1 April 2015, 11 new councils took over from the previous 26 and are in effect unitary authorities.

London

London has a different structure of local government from that in the rest of the UK.

The Greater London Authority (GLA) is an elected strategic authority made up of two parts: an elected

Mayor and an assembly consisting of 25 elected members who hold the Mayor to account.

Greater London Assembly (GLA) results 2016

- Labour 12 seats
- Conservative 8 seats
- Green 2 seats
- UK Independence Party 2 seats
- Liberal Democrats 1 seat

Much of the actual work of the GLA is undertaken by four bodies: Transport for London (TfL), the Mayor's Office for Policing and Crime (MOPC) and the London Fire and Emergency Planning Authority (LFEPA). The GLA spends about £17 billion a year.

London also comprises 32 borough councils and the City of London Authority, which are responsible for most of the day-to-day services. These are in many ways unitary authorities. Together they spend more than £12 billion a year, including £7 billion on children's services and education and £2 billion on adult social services.

Council budgeting

Discussion point

Councils raise their income from three main sources: council tax; revenues from services and charges; and central government support. Do you think there is a better way for local councils to be funded? Look at the council's spending in Figure 12.3. If you were in charge, what changes would you make and why?

How councils operate

Decisions about local services are made by elected local councillors. Councillors are elected to represent people in a local area (ward) for a term of four years. Councillors have to balance the needs and interests of the local community, voters, their political party and the policy of the council. Councillors decide on the overall direction of policy. Council officers then implement these policy initiatives and are responsible for delivering services on a daily basis.

- **Full council** – The full council is made up of all elected councillors. The full council debates and decides upon policy based on reports from the various committees.
- **Committees** – Councillors on committees monitor the council's performance and decision-making process and hold it to account for its actions. In councils without a cabinet, these committees have more power as they vote and decide upon council policy.

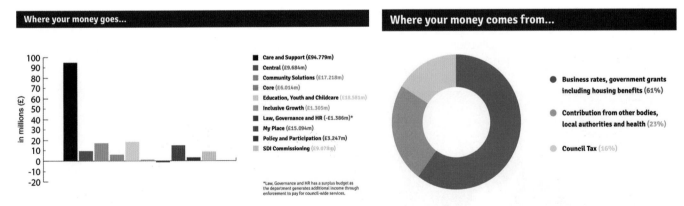

Figure 12.3 The income and expenditure of the London Borough of Barking and Dagenham (Source: **www.lbbd.gov.uk/what-your-council-tax-pays-for**)

- **Cabinet** – Like central government where the Prime Minister appoints members of the Cabinet who are then responsible for departments (e.g. education), the same concept has been introduced into local government. The party or group that has a majority on the council appoints a leader of the council who works with a small group of councillors who are each responsible for a service area. On many councils they use the terms Portfolio Holder and Executive Committee rather than cabinet and cabinet member. Since 2011, the government has allowed local councils to move back to the old committee system, where groups of councillors are responsible for a particular service.

Leader or directly elected mayor

Traditionally most councils had a mayor as the ceremonial head of the council, normally serving for one year. The party or group with the majority of seats on the council ran the council, appointing one of their members to chair each of the committees, and each party had a group leader on the council. Now councils formally have a leader of the council: the leader of the largest group of councillors or a directly elected mayor who appoints their own cabinet. Many councils still keep the role of a ceremonial mayor. The councillors who accept these more important roles or who are directly elected mayors receive a much higher level of payment than ordinary councillors.

Of late, governments have encouraged local councils to have directly elected mayors and recently it was made a condition of giving local councils more powers. The most well known directly elected mayor is the one for London.

Figure 12.4 Sadiq Khan, Mayor of London, elected in 2016

In May 2016 Sadiq Khan (Labour Party) was elected, replacing Boris Johnson (Conservative Party). Also, in 2016 in a local referendum the electors of Torbay in Devon decided to abolish their directly elected mayor and bring back the former leader and committee structure.

> **Discussion point**
> What is the case for having more directly elected mayors?

Accountability

All councillors are accountable for their actions. If they agree to the council working outside its powers (**ultra vires**), they can be held personally responsible. Most councils adopt a code of conduct that ensures councillors declare any financial interests that might relate to their council duties. The government has made it a criminal offence to fail to declare any outside interest. The role of the local media can be important in holding councils and councillors to account. The media attend council meetings and report on local government activity. In the last resort, councillors are accountable to their electors, who decide whether or not to re-elect them.

The nature and organisation of regional and devolved government

> ## Spec coverage
> - The nature and organisation of regional and devolved government: Scotland, Wales, Northern Ireland and England.

The term '**devolved government**' is used to describe the concept of devolution. This is the transfer of power from one body to another; normally from the centre to the locality. From 1997, the momentum for devolution in the UK increased. In 1998, a referendum was held and Scotland voted for a Scottish Parliament with the authority to have tax-varying and law-making powers. The Welsh people also voted for an Assembly and power over policy areas. The Good Friday Agreement in Northern Ireland was followed by a referendum in 1998 that re-established devolved government in Northern Ireland.

Devolution in the UK created a National Parliament in Scotland, a National Assembly in Wales and a

Northern Ireland Assembly. This process transferred, and continues to transfer, varying levels of power from the UK Parliament to the UK's nations. The UK Parliament still has the ultimate authority and could if it wished abolish or amend the current arrangements.

Devolved and reserved powers

Devolved powers are decisions that the UK Parliament controlled in the past, but that are now handed over to the devolved bodies, like the Scottish Parliament.

Reserved powers are those still taken by the UK Parliament on behalf of all parts of the United Kingdom: for example, defence and foreign policy.

Transfer of powers

The Scottish Parliament and the National Assembly for Wales took responsibility for their devolved powers on 1 July 1999. The Northern Ireland Assembly followed on 2 December 1999. The Northern Ireland Assembly was suspended at midnight on 14 October 2002. Power was restored to the Northern Ireland Assembly on 8 May 2007. The assembly was again suspended from January 2017 until January 2020 due to disagreements between the parties that make up the executive.

Since the original transfer of powers, new legislation has seen additional powers devolved to Scotland, Wales and Northern Ireland.

Scotland

The Scottish Parliament, also known by the name 'Holyrood', is in Edinburgh. It is a democratically elected body of 129 members (Members of the Scottish Parliament – MSPs) who are elected for a four-year term. The Scottish Parliament has the powers to pass legislation within its areas of devolved powers. The Scotland Act 2016 gave the Scottish government greater powers relating to taxation and welfare. The majority party, or a coalition of parties if there is no majority, forms a government under the First Minister and operates under a cabinet system.

Wales

The National Assembly in Wales became known as the Welsh Parliament in 2020. It is based in Cardiff. There are 60 elected members of the Welsh Parliament. The majority party, or a coalition of parties if no single party wins a majority of the seats, forms a government. The First Minister and his or her government ministers run the devolved services in Wales as ministers do in the Westminster Parliament.

Northern Ireland

The Northern Ireland Assembly consists of 108 elected members – six elected from each of the 18 Westminster constituencies. Their role is to scrutinise and make decisions on the issues dealt with by government departments and make legislation.

A First Minister and a Deputy First Minister are elected to lead the Executive Committee of Ministers (Cabinet). They must stand for election jointly and to be elected they must have cross-community support by the parallel consent formula, which means that a majority of both the members who have designated themselves Nationalists and those who have designated themselves Unionists, and a majority of the whole Assembly, must vote in favour.

The First Minister and Deputy First Minister, acting jointly, determine the total number of ministers in the Executive.

The parties elected to the Assembly choose ministerial portfolios and select ministers in proportion to their party strength. Due to the divided nature of Northern Ireland society and 'the Troubles' that took place prior to the Good Friday Agreement, the parliamentary system is both proportional and needs representatives of both community traditions to work together, so that all decisions are jointly made.

The Northern Ireland Executive is made up of the First Minister and Deputy First Minister, who are nominated respectively by the largest party and the second-largest political designations in the Assembly. One represents the Unionist tradition, the other the Nationalist tradition. Ministers of the Executive, with the exception of the Minister of Justice, are nominated by the political parties in the Northern Ireland Assembly. The number of ministers that a party can nominate is determined by its share of seats in the Assembly.

England

Devolution to English regions has been put to local referendums, but no region has voted for the devolved powers on offer. As we have seen, London is in effect a devolved regional authority under the GLA. Currently, the move towards more devolved power in England has centred around councils agreeing to work together under a directly elected mayor. If this is agreed with central government, some government funds and decision-making – mainly about economic development and infrastructure – are transferred to the new combined authority.

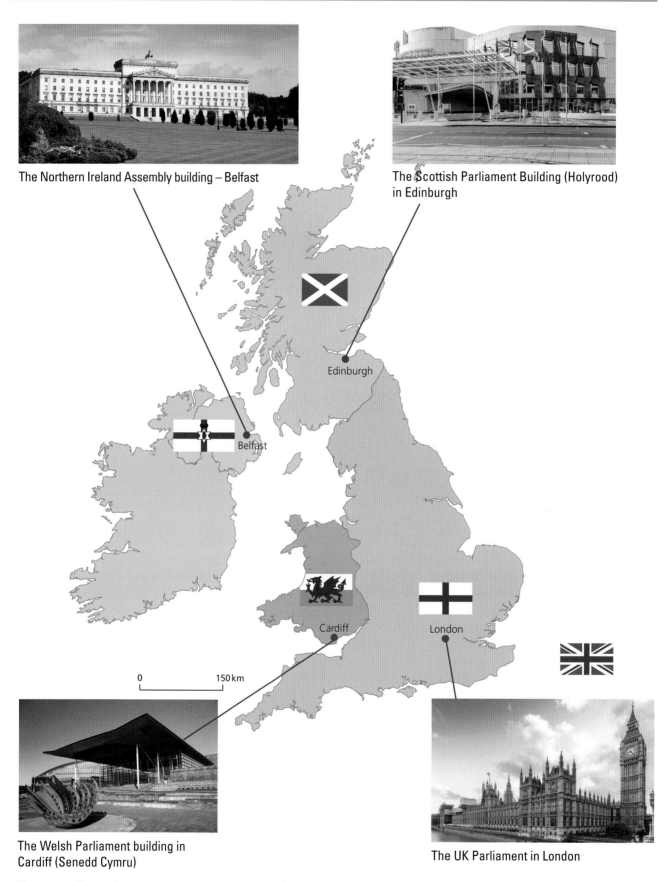

The Northern Ireland Assembly building – Belfast

The Scottish Parliament Building (Holyrood) in Edinburgh

Edinburgh

Belfast

Cardiff

London

0   150 km

The Welsh Parliament building in Cardiff (Senedd Cymru)

The UK Parliament in London

Figure 12.5 Devolution within the UK

In recent years, Cornwall, a sparsely populated rural county, decided to form itself into a unitary authority, abolishing all its district councils and now working through the county council structure. This has enabled it to gain further government funding.

How powers are organised

Spec coverage
- How powers are organised between the Westminster Parliament and the devolved administrations in Northern Ireland, Scotland and Wales.
- How relations are changing between England, Scotland, Wales and Northern Ireland.
- The debate about 'English votes for English laws'.

Each of the devolved bodies has differing powers due to the degree of devolution they were granted by the Westminster Parliament (see Table 12.2). There had been a Northern Ireland Parliament from 1921 until 1972, when direct rule by Westminster was introduced, so it had a tradition of devolved powers. Scotland voted in its referendum for a Parliament and tax-raising powers so it has been granted a high degree of devolution and the ability to pass laws.

The Welsh Assembly was given the fewest powers, but these have been increased. The majority in Wales for devolution was very small.

English votes for English laws

At times, there have been tensions in the UK Parliament on the ability, especially of Scottish Westminster MPs, to vote on English issues, for example education or health. English MPs are unable to vote on the way similar policies may have an impact on Scottish people because these are policy areas that are devolved to the Scottish Parliament. This has led many MPs to call for English votes for English laws. This has proved very controversial because MPs representing Scottish seats claim they are now second-class MPs in the House of Commons.

After the 2015 **General Election**, the Conservative government introduced new stages to the discussion of English-only legislation in an attempt to resolve the 'English votes for English laws' issue.

Table 12.2 Powers devolved to Scotland, Wales and Northern Ireland

POWERS DEVOLVED TO ALL THREE NATIONS	ADDITIONAL POWERS DEVOLVED TO NORTHERN IRELAND	ADDITIONAL POWERS DEVOLVED TO SCOTLAND	ADDITIONAL POWERS DEVOLVED TO WALES
Health and social services	Justice and policing	Justice and policing	Welsh language
Education, training and skills	Charity law	Charity law	Some income tax
Local government	Energy	Stamp duty land tax	Stamp duty land tax
Housing	Employment law	Licensing of onshore oil and gas extraction	Landfill tax
Economic development	Social security, child support, pensions	Some income tax	Road signs and speed limits
Agriculture, forestry and fisheries	NI Civil Service	Equal opportunities in relation to public bodies in Scotland	Equal opportunities in relation to public bodies in Wales
Environment and planning	Equal opportunities	Tax on carriage of passengers by air	Licensing of onshore oil and gas extraction
Transport	Time	Abortion	Assembly and local government elections
Tourism, sport, culture and heritage	Long-haul rates of Air Passenger Duty	Landfill tax	
Fire and rescue services		Some social security elements	
Water and flood defence		Customer advocacy and advice	
		Scottish Parliament and local government elections	

In October 2015, the House of Commons changed its standing orders (internal rules) to resolve the issue of allowing MPs from Scotland to vote on proposals for laws that don't impact upon Scotland. The change introduced the concept of English votes for English laws (EVEL).

Under the new process, the Speaker of the House of Commons, on advice, has to decide whether any proposed government legislation is English 'only'. The proposals are discussed in the normal way, but at committee stage only MPs representing English constituencies can serve on the committee, and voting on the proposed legislation can involve only English constituency MPs.

Who can stand for election and how candidates are selected

If you want to be a candidate in a **local election** in the UK you must be at least 18 years old and a British citizen or an eligible Commonwealth citizen.

You must also meet one of the following four qualifications:

1 You are a registered elector for the local council area for which you wish to stand.

2 You have occupied as owner or tenant any land or other premises within the local council area for at least 12 months prior to handing in your election nomination papers.

3 Your place of work during the past 12 months has been in the local council area.

4 You have lived in the local council area during the whole of the 12 months before the day your election papers have to be handed in.

There are certain people who are disqualified from standing for election:

- If you are employed by the local authority
- If you hold a politically restricted post
- If you are the subject of a bankruptcy restrictions order
- If you have been sentenced to a term of imprisonment of three months or more, including a suspended sentence, during the past five years
- If you have been disqualified under the Representation of the People Act 1983 (which covers corrupt or illegal electoral practices and offences relating to donations).

If you want to become an MP at Westminster, the requirements are:

- You must be at least 18 years old.
- You must be either a British citizen, a citizen of the Republic of Ireland or an eligible Commonwealth citizen.

There is no requirement in law for you to be a registered elector in the UK.

You cannot stand in more than one constituency at the same UK Parliamentary General Election.

Citizens of other countries (with the exception of the Republic of Ireland, Cyprus and Malta) are not eligible to become a member of the UK Parliament.

The following are disqualified from standing:

- Civil servants
- Members of police forces
- Members of the armed forces
- Government-nominated directors of commercial companies
- Judges
- Members of the legislature of any country or territory outside the Commonwealth
- Peers who sit in and can vote in the House of Lords
- Bishops of the Church of England (known as the Lords Spiritual) who are entitled to sit and vote in the House of Lords.

Candidate selection

Each political party has its own methods of selecting candidates and this may vary depending on the type of election a person is being selected for. When selecting a candidate to stand for a parliamentary election, a local party will advertise in a party journal for those interested to apply. They normally have to be on the list of candidates approved by the national party before they can put their names forward. A selected group of local party workers will draw up a shortlist after interviewing a number of candidates to put to the local party membership. A 'returning officer', a trained member from another local party branch who represents the national party, normally oversees the whole process. The potential candidates are invited to attend a meeting of party members. They address the meeting and answer questions. Through the returning officer they also send a leaflet to all party members asking for their vote.

Some parties have experimented with what are called 'open primaries' where any local resident can vote at a meeting, not just party members. This is often a very expensive exercise. People vote by post or at the meeting and the returning officer is responsible for counting the votes and declaring a winner.

Political parties are also able to run 'women only' shortlists when selecting candidates. This has been done to encourage local parties to select more female candidates and thereby increase the number of women MPs. Political parties are able to do this through an exemption in equality legislation.

Who can and cannot vote in elections and why

> **Spec coverage**
> - Who can and cannot vote in elections and why.
> - Debates about the voting age.

General Elections

To vote in a UK General Election a person must be registered to vote and also:

- 18 or over
- a British citizen, a qualifying Commonwealth citizen or a citizen of the Republic of Ireland
- not subject to any legal incapacity to vote.

The following cannot vote in a UK General Election:

- Members of the House of Lords (although they can vote at elections to local authorities and devolved legislatures)
- EU citizens resident in the UK (although they can vote at elections to local authorities and devolved legislatures) (this forms a part of the negotiations with the EU following the UK decision to leave the EU in June 2016)
- Anyone other than British, Irish and qualifying Commonwealth citizens
- Convicted persons in prison (though remand prisoners – unconvicted prisoners – can vote if they are on the electoral register)
- Anyone found guilty within the previous five years of corrupt or illegal practices in connection with an election
- Those who have been detained under certain sections of the Mental Health Act.

In England, Northern Ireland and Wales, you can register to vote when you are 17. However, you can only vote when you are 18. In Scotland, you can register to vote when you are 15. You can vote in local and Scottish Parliament elections when you are 16 and UK Parliamentary elections when you are 18.

Discussion point

Do you think prisoners should be able to vote? The European Court of Human Rights ruled in 2005 that the ban on prisoners voting contravened the European Convention on Human Rights (ECHR).

In 2017, the UK government announced a compromise, allowing those prisoners released on licence to vote. The ECHR accepted this compromise.

Local elections

To vote in a local council election you must be on the electoral register and also one of the following:

- Of voting age on the day of the election
- A British citizen, a qualifying Commonwealth citizen or a citizen of a country with which the UK has an agreement.

EU residents and voting in the UK, post-Brexit

Voting rights for EU citizens did not form a part of the UK's EU Withdrawal Agreement. The UK intends that any future agreements will be on a country-by-country basis. So far agreements have been reached with Spain, Luxembourg, Portugal and Poland, allowing their citizens to stand and vote in local and regional elections. Irish citizens can vote in all UK elections. Maltese and Cypriot citizens similarly enjoy voting rights on the basis of their status as Commonwealth citizens.

The debate about the voting age

During the twentieth century, there were many debates about who could vote and at what age. Women were first given the vote in General Elections in 1918, but they had to be 30 years old. Men could vote at 21. In 1928, women were given the vote at 21. In 1970, the voting age for all was lowered to 18.

In the vote in the referendum on Scottish independence the voting age was 16. In Scotland 16-year-olds are allowed to vote in elections to their councils and Parliament. Many people now argue that the voting age should be lowered to 16 for all parts of the UK and all elections.

Discussion point

Can you make a case for lowering the voting age to 16?

Issues relating to voting

Spec coverage

- Issues relating to voter turnout, voter apathy and suggestions for increasing voter turnout at elections.

Turnout relates to the number of people who vote as a percentage of the number of people who could vote. For a number of years, politicians have been concerned about the turnout at various elections in the UK. This was one of the factors behind introducing Citizenship as a National Curriculum subject in schools. Table 12.3 shows the turnout in recent General Elections in the UK. Many argue that this low turnout is due to political **apathy**; people not being interested in politics. But the counter-argument is that the number of those involved in single-interest groups and pressure groups is increasing, so is the problem the way we do politics in the UK, the politicians themselves or just lack of interest from many citizens?

Table 12.3 Turnout in recent UK General Elections

ELECTION YEAR	UK PERCENTAGE TURNOUT (%)
2019	67.3
2017	68.8
2015	66.1
2010	65.1
2005	61.4
2001	59.4
1997	71.4
1992	77.7
1987	75.3
1983	72.7
1979	76

When one considers a range of different elections, the picture is even bleaker, with Parliamentary elections topping the poll in regard to turnout. Table 12.4 (on page 113) shows turnout at various elections since 2012. The lowest ebb came with the new Police and Crime Commissioner election in 2012, with a turnout of 15 per cent. Since this was the average, turnout in some areas was much lower.

Table 12.4 Turnout in different elections

YEAR	TYPE OF ELECTION	PERCENTAGE TURNOUT (%)
2019	General Election	67.3
2019	EU Parliamentary	36.9
2018	Local election (average)	35.0
2017	N. Ireland Assembly	64.0
2016	EU Referendum	72.0
2016	Scottish Parliament	55.6
2016	Welsh Assembly	45.5
2016	London Mayor	45.3
2014	Scottish Referendum	84.6
2012	Police and Crime Commissioners	15.0

Discussion point

Why do you think referendums have a higher turnout than other elections?

In 2015 the referendum on Scottish independence, which included 16- and 17-year-old voters, saw an 84.6 per cent turnout. So is it the nature of the issue and thereby the importance of your vote that motivates people to vote? Some countries have compulsory voting, which resolves the turnout issue. But many in the UK believe that it is as much a right not to vote as a right to vote.

The Electoral Commission has published reports looking at changes that might encourage more people to vote. A number have been tried out in some local elections. These included:

- allowing weekend voting
- changing polling hours
- opening polling stations in different locations
- encouraging postal voting and early voting.

Others have suggested online voting or telephone voting.

These are all system changes to get people more interested and involved in politics. But is it politics and the way we do politics that have to change?

In 2015, the Recall of MPs Act introduced a new concept into our political system: the idea that an MP could lose their seat in the House of Commons if there was a petition signed by sufficient electors in their constituency. If a petition is successful, a by-election is held to elect a new Member of Parliament.

This gives a legal dimension to the concept of an MP's accountability to their local electorate.

The Act sets out the criteria that must be met before a recall petition can be triggered and the rules that govern how any petition campaign is organised. A petition can take place in the following circumstances:

- If an MP is convicted of an offence and receives a custodial sentence (including a suspended sentence).
- If an MP is barred from the House of Commons for ten sitting days or 14 calendar days.
- If an MP is convicted of providing false or misleading information regarding their parliamentary allowances.

How public taxes are raised and spent by government

Spec coverage

- How public taxes are raised and spent by government locally and nationally.

One of the major ways in which governments are judged is in regard to their management of the economy. If the economy appears to be successful and voters feel their lives are improving, governments are normally re-elected.

There are several key questions relating to the economy and government income and spending that are at the heart of politics in the UK:

1 How much of the nation's wealth should a government spend?
2 In what ways should a government raise its income?
3 What services should a government provide?
4 How should government services be paid for?

These four key questions have divided political parties and the public for the past 50 years.

How much should a government spend?

The wealth or economic output of a country is measured using the term GDP (Gross Domestic Product). More recently, a measure called GNI (Gross National Income) has been used. The more the state wishes to spend on services for its citizens, the larger percentage of GDP the state consumes and the less is left for individuals and companies to spend.

Figure 12.6 indicates how much as a percentage the state has taken of GDP in recent years. The consensus for many years was that about 40 per cent of GDP should be spent by government. The more a government spends, the higher it has to raise taxes or increase government borrowing. A lower percentage of GDP spending means it can reduce taxes or the national debt.

As well as the percentage of a country's wealth, there is also the consideration of the actual amount of money the government spends. Figure 12.7 shows the pattern of **real government spending** from 2006 to 2020. It indicates that government spending has increased. As the GDP of a country increases, a government can spend more and cut the percentage of GDP it consumes. It is even possible to lower taxes and for the government to raise more income when there is growth in the economy as consumers and companies spend more money. Issues arise when the GDP of the country slows or declines, as was the case after the financial crisis in 2007/08.

As Figure 12.8 on page 115 shows, GDP was rising prior to the financial crisis in 2007/08 and then there was a rapid decline. The Covid-19 pandemic, like the financial crisis, impacted the economy as government income declined and at the same time the government had to spend vast amounts of additional money supporting the economy and public services.

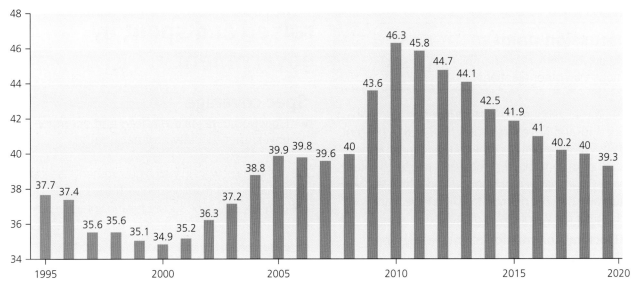

Figure 12.6 Government spending as percentage of GDP (%)

(Source: **https://tradingeconomics.com/united-kingdom/government-spending-to-gdp** and **https://obr.uk/docs/dlm_uploads/Brief_guide_to_the_public_finances_March_2019.pdf**)

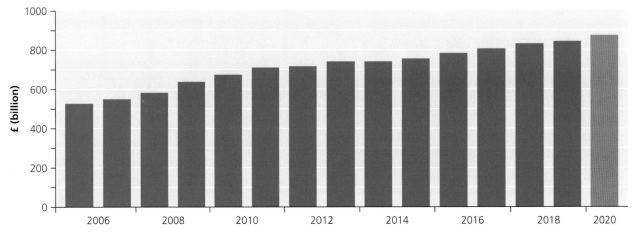

Figure 12.7 Change in UK public spending, 2006–2020

(Source: **www.ukpublicspending.co.uk**)

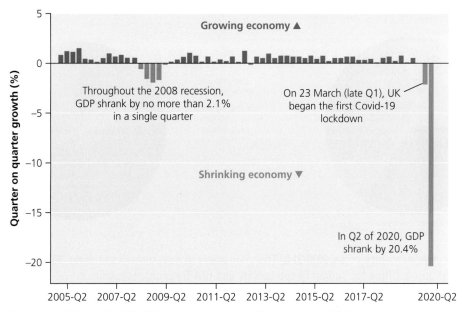

Figure 12.8 Change in UK GDP from 2005 to 2020 (Q = quarter, which means every three months; there are four quarters in a year: Jan–Mar; April–Jun; July–Sept; and Oct–Dec) (Source: Office for National Statistics)

How does a government raise its income?

The government can either raise income through differing forms of taxation or borrow money to balance its yearly budget. Each year, the Chancellor of the Exchequer delivers an annual **budget**. Since 2017, the government has decided to present a single autumn budget to allow for greater parliamentary scrutiny. Prior to 2017, there was an Autumn Statement outlining spending for the following year and a Spring Budget announcing tax changes.

Figure 12.9a on page 116 indicates how the government intended to raise its income in 2020/21. The three largest sources are:

- **Income tax** – paid by everyone earning or having an investment or savings income above a set annual level. It is collected mainly through the PAYE system (Pay As You Earn) and is taken directly from your wages before you receive your pay.
- **National Insurance** – paid by everyone aged below 65 who is in employment and earning above a set level, and again is taken directly from your wages before you are paid.
- **Value-added tax (VAT)** – paid on a large range of goods and services. Excise duties relate to additional duties on items such as alcohol.

Corporation tax is paid by companies on their profits. Business rates are paid by businesses based on the value of their properties. Council tax is the annual tax levied by local councils on properties in their area. Local authorities have limited room for raising income. The amount of money raised by council tax is often subject to government pressure to be kept low. The rest of their income comes from charges they make for their services and from direct government grants.

What services should a government provide?

This question is key to the questions posed on page 113. Once a government has a spending programme, it must agree how to raise the money to pay for the services it wishes to provide. It can do this through taxation or by increasing its debts. Figure 12.9b on page 116 indicates the main areas of government spending. Clearly those we would label as welfare-related – personal social services, health, education and social protection – account for a very large part of government spending. Debt interest relates to the interest the government pays on the national debt, which has accumulated over several hundred years.

When it puts its manifesto before the electorate at a General Election, each political party will outline its intentions for public spending and its taxation policy.

From 1945 until 1979, the UK had what is called a **mixed economy**, where the state owned and provided many services alongside the private sector.

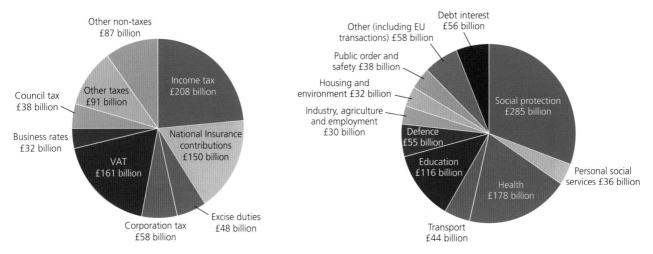

Figure 12.9 a) Sources of government income, 2020/21 **b)** The main areas of government spending, 2020/21. Figures may not sum due to rounding (Source: Office for Budget Responsibility and HM Treasury calculations)

Case study
The cost of Covid

The figures shown in Figures 12.9a and 12.9b have been impacted by the Covid-19 pandemic.
The figures in Table 12.5 have been produced by the Institute for Government.

Table 12.5 The cost of Covid-19 to the UK's public finances in 2020/21 (Source: **www.instituteforgovernment.org.uk/sites/default/files/publications/cost-of-covid19.pdf**)

Support for businesses: £55.8bn	Lower tax revenue: £105.7bn
Support for households: £83.7bn	Higher welfare spending: £24.5bn
Support for public services: £52.8bn	Changes in forecast: -£5.2bn (saving)
Total result of government policy: £192.3bn	**Total result of automatic changes: £125bn**

Different viewpoint

Some people believe the pandemic has shown that it was only dramatic action by government that prevented a greater economic decline. Others are concerned about how the economy can recover for this increased public spending and increased national debt.

What do you consider would have happened during the recent pandemic if the government had not provided the extra financial assistance that it did? Consider aspects such as extra funding for the NHS, local government, paying people's wages, additional benefit payments, support for businesses, and stopping evictions for non-payment of rent.

An economy where the state provides and controls all services is called a **command economy** and is associated with the former communist countries. An economy where the state provides limited services is called a **market economy** and is associated with countries like the USA. Since 1979, governments in the UK have sold off most of the **nationalised** companies that were owned by the government, for example the railways, gas and electricity and water suppliers. They have also allowed tenants to purchase local authority housing stock.

Discussion point

If you had the power to change government income and spending plans, what changes would you make and how would you justify them?

So the question posed about what services a state should provide are at the heart of the political debate. Some want lower taxes and fewer services. Those who want more services, think taxes should be higher to pay for them. Others say it is also about who is best at providing the service: the state or another provider.

Spending on education

This debate can be seen to be at the heart of current education changes. For many years the UK operated a two-track approach to education: approximately 95 per cent of the population attended state-provided schools (including voluntary-aided church schools) free of charge, which came under the control of local councils, and about 5 per cent of the population attended fee-paying private schools. Today schools can be local authority schools, academies which are supported by sponsors and funded directly by the government, free schools funded by the government, or as before a part of the fee-paying private school system.

Government spending

Social protection spending covers areas like housing benefit, pensions and supporting people who are at risk of exclusion from society, such as those on low incomes or refugees. The largest single component is pension provision.

Personal social services is the provision of services such as adult social care that fall outside the remit of the NHS.

Spending on defence

Most political parties agree that the defence of the realm (country) is the first priority of a government, and this appears to be a common thread across whatever economic or political system operates in a country. The question, as before, is how much is reasonable to spend. NATO recommends that its members spend 2 per cent of their GDP each year on defence. The UK government in 2015 made a commitment to maintain UK defence spending at 2 per cent of GDP. The major decision to be made about defence in the next few years is whether the UK continues to maintain a nuclear deterrent, which is very expensive.

Law and order, policing and national security services would also be supported as spending items by most political parties. The other services shown in Figure 12.9b are those that provoke political debate about whether they should or should not be included and, if included, how much they should cost, whether they should be charged for or provided free of charge, and who should provide the service – the state, local council, a private contractor or a voluntary group. There are no right or wrong answers. It all depends upon a person's views about the big economic questions posed on page 113.

The way the government makes decisions about its spending: the factors it takes into account

---

Spec coverage

- The practice of budgeting and managing risk and how it is used by government to manage complex decisions about the allocation of public funding.

The government uses a variety of measures to decide its spending priorities. The initial decisions are based upon the political philosophy of the party in government and whether it is in favour of higher or lower government spending.

The party in power would have made certain commitments in its manifesto at the General Election, so will feel it has to deliver on its political promises. Some decisions will relate to economic factors, such as encouraging economic growth, lowering unemployment and bringing more people back into the workforce. These policies might then have an impact on welfare policy, such as the provision of childcare. Policies in relation to education might relate to improving the skills make-up of the future workforce or increasing university participation.

Some decisions will relate to long-term government spending, such as reviewing pension ages and entitlements and dealing with an ageing population in terms of care and health service provision. Others will emerge once a government is in office and require almost instant decisions about government spending: for example, before 2020, nobody could have predicted that there would be a pandemic that would close down society for long periods of time, both impacting upon government spending to support the NHS and businesses, and leading to a decline in government income due to a massive drop in economic activity.

Irrespective of which party or parties are in power, these are the points they need to consider. Clearly when the economy is growing it is easier for the state to spend more money and actually take a lower percentage of the nation's GDP. Problems arise when there is a crisis or GDP growth stops or goes into reverse. A government is then trapped by greater demands for its services due to increased unemployment as well as lower spending in the

Figure 12.10 Government spending has been dramatically affected by the Covid-19 pandemic

economy cutting its tax revenues. It can also be committed to maintaining the existing levels of provision, which may have become more generous during the years of growth.

In 2015, the government launched an independent National Infrastructure Commission to oversee its £100 billion spending on infrastructure planning.

The Commission advises government on all sectors of economic infrastructure, defined as energy, transport,

Case studies
The future direction of government budgeting

Defence – the replacement of the Trident nuclear programme. The Ministry of Defence (MoD) estimates that the cost will be between £31 billion and £41 billion for a replacement system. The MOD has often had problems in the past bringing large-scale projects in on budget. The Campaign for Nuclear Disarmament (CND), which opposes nuclear weapons, has calculated that replacing Trident, Britain's nuclear weapons system, will end up costing at least £205 billion.

Transport – the HS2 scheme to improve journey times and capacity to the Midlands. The scheme is estimated to cost over £100 billion.

Different viewpoints
1 Are these good investments of taxpayers' money?
2 Which would you support and why?
3 What points would you include in your arguments?
4 Would you wish to amend the existing proposals?
5 Would you spend more or less?

water and wastewater (drainage and sewerage), waste, flood risk management and digital communications. The Commission focuses on three particular areas: connections between cities in the North; London's transport system; and energy.

It is charged with producing a report at the beginning of each Parliament, providing recommendations for spending on infrastructure projects.

Debates about provision for welfare, health, the elderly and education

Spec coverage
- Different viewpoints and debates about how government and other service providers make provision for welfare, health, the elderly and education.

One of the major political debates in the UK is about the future direction of welfare policy. This debate has political, economic, demographic and social dimensions. Figure 12.11 indicates the breakdown of welfare spending in the UK.

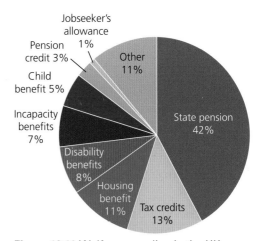

Figure 12.11 Welfare spending in the UK (Source: DWP, HMRC, OBR)

As can be seen from Figure 12.11, decisions made about welfare spending will have an impact on every citizen in the country. If we spend more, where does the money come from: cuts elsewhere or increases in taxation? If we spend less, where do the cuts take place? If we do nothing, the bill will continue to rise due to **inflation** and an ageing population. Consider the following case studies and think through any issues that might arise.

Case study
State pension age

The **state pension age** was raised in 2020, to 66 for both men and women. Previously it was 60 for women and 65 for men. Those in employment have also been encouraged to take up workplace pensions. In the last few years, even those in low-paid employment have been encouraged to join pension schemes.

Different viewpoint

Is it time for the government to consider cutting back on state old-age pension payments?

Should the state provide less or more or just do existing things differently? In many areas, local library services are under threat and increasingly they are being run by volunteers from their local communities. Many services provided locally are now put out to contract to the private sector, leaving the local council just to manage the service rather than provide it. We already have prisons run by the private sector, and hospitals and schools built by private money and leased back by the service providers, which means the government does not have to borrow the money for the building programme which would add to the national debt.

Case study
Housing

Housing benefit is paid by the state to those on low incomes as well as to those who are unemployed. Rents are determined by local demand at the moment. In the past, governments have set rent levels to stop rent being too high and unaffordable.

Different viewpoint

Should the government pay people's housing costs?

What would happen if it stopped? If people become homeless, it becomes the responsibility of local councils to house them and they already have a shortage of houses to rent out.

Case study
The National Health Service

The **National Health Service** is free at the point of delivery for every person in the UK. It is also very expensive to run, and costs are always increasing due to the nature of medical advances. Also an ageing population is putting an increasing strain on the NHS. A limited amount of money is collected via medical prescriptions, but many people are exempt from payment.

Different viewpoint

The NHS is also seen by a large section of the British public as a sort of 'national treasure' that should be protected.

Should people be expected to take out their own private insurance to cover health costs? Many employers offer this to their staff, so they can use private medical provision. Should people be charged for some or all health services?

Case study
Working tax credits

Working tax credits – working people on low pay are supported by the government through the tax credit system, which in effect increases their take-home pay.

Different viewpoint

Is this a role for the government or should employers pay a living wage that means tax credits are not needed?

Would these jobs exist if employers were forced to pay higher wages?

Case study
Child benefit

Child benefit – parents are paid a benefit payment for each of their children. This benefit is means tested for those earning over £50,000 a year. Those earning over £60,000 a year would pay more in tax than they would get by claiming the child benefit.

Different viewpoint

Is it the role of the state to pay benefits for children? Should there be a limit on the number of children that can be claimed for? What issues arise if there is a rise in child poverty?

Case study
University tuition fees

Until 1998, the government met the costs of attending university. The then Labour government introduced annual tuition fees of £1000 per year to be paid by students. This was raised to £3000 a year in 2004. In 2010, the coalition government (Con/Lib Dem) increased the fee level again and it now stands at a maximum of £9250 a year. Students are able to borrow this money and maintenance funding from the Student Loans Company. The loan is then automatically repaid by the student when their income reaches a certain level after they have started work.

As this is a devolved matter in Scotland, the policy is different. Scottish students do not pay tuition fees to attend university.

Different viewpoint

Is it right that students should leave university with massive debts? Instead, should students and parents contribute towards their education or should the government pay for more, or all, of the costs?

Websites

Local Government Association: www.local.gov.uk

The Electoral Commission: www.electoralcommission.org.uk

UK Parliament website: www.parliament.uk

Scottish Parliament: www.parliament.scot

Welsh Parliament: www.assembly.wales/en/Pages/Home.aspx

Northern Ireland Assembly: www.niassembly.gov.uk

Greater London Authority: www.london.gov.uk

UK government: www.gov.uk

Review questions

1 What is meant by the term 'a tier of government'?
2 Which is more powerful: the Westminster or the Scottish Parliament?
3 Identify the two taxes that raise the most revenue in the UK.
4 Which of the three economic systems is associated with the UK?
5 What has happened to the UK's GDP since 2009/10?
6 What is the role of the GLA?
7 Identify one group of UK citizens aged over 18 who cannot vote in a UK General Election.
8 How does the voting age differ in Scotland from that in the rest of the UK?

Activity

Make contact with your local council and ask whether it takes part in local democracy week and ask how you, your class or school can take part.

Ask whether your council has a Youth Council and how students are able to take part. If there is no Youth Council, ask to meet some councillors to suggest that one is formed.

This Activity will help promote a number of skills that could be useful when carrying out your own Investigation.

Learning review points

- What does local government do and how is it organised in the UK?
- How does my local council make decisions?
- What is devolution and how does it work in the UK?
- How can I become a candidate in an election?
- Why is voter apathy an issue?
- How does the government raise and spend its income?

EXAM PRACTICE

1 Identify two possible ways turnout could be improved in local elections in the UK. (AO1) [2 marks]
2 Referring to the state pension age case study on page 119, consider two reasons why it is difficult for governments to increase the pension age. (AO2) [4 marks]
3 'Devolution will lead to the breakup of the United Kingdom.' To what extent can this statement be justified? (AO3) [8 marks]

- Where does political power reside: with the citizen, Parliament or government?

The 'first-past-the-post'

Spec coverage

- The nature of the 'first-past-the-post' system based on parliamentary constituencies.
- The frequency of Westminster elections.

The United Kingdom is a representative democracy where the electorate votes and elects a new Parliament at each **General Election**. The results of recent General Elections are shown in Table 13.1. The election is held on the same day throughout the UK. Currently there are 650 MPs elected, each representing a single-member **constituency**.

All parliamentary boundaries are currently being reviewed and will be finalised in July 2023, with the aim that all constituencies (with the exception of those composed of islands) will consist of around 73,000 electors. Some electorates are smaller and others larger. Each constituency elects one MP using the **first-past-the-post** (FPTP) election system.

Each voter who is registered on the electoral register can vote, either on polling day at a local polling station or via post, or by allowing a **proxy** (another person) to vote on their behalf. Voters exercise their vote by putting an X against the candidate of their choice and then placing their vote in a ballot box. The whole process is what is called a 'secret ballot' because the ballot paper cannot be easily associated with a voter.

The candidate elected under this electoral system is the candidate who has the most votes. There is no requirement to have a certain percentage of the vote or so many votes more than the next candidate or to have the support of a majority of voters or a majority of those who voted. The phrase 'first past the post' is taken from horse racing, where the winner is the first to cross the

Table 13.1 Results of recent General Elections

DATE	RESULT
2019	Conservative majority win
2017	Conservatives largest party, but no majority – make an agreement with the DUP
2015	Conservative majority win
2010	No party wins a majority – coalition of Conservative and Liberal Democrats form a government
2005	Labour majority win
2001	Labour majority win
1997	Labour majority win, defeating a Conservative government
1992	Conservative majority win
1987	Conservative majority win
1983	Conservative majority win
1979	Conservative majority win, defeating a Labour government

finishing line, whether it is by a nose or a mile. A majority of one over the next candidate is enough to win.

Until 2010, it was up to the Prime Minister to decide the date of the next election. Unless forced into calling an election by a vote of no confidence in the House of Commons (this happened in 1979), the Prime Minister would choose a date that suited their party's re-election. A General Election had to be held within five years of the previous election.

In 2011, the Parliament Act fixed the dates of future elections. Under this Act, which was repealed in 2020, the UK had fixed-term parliaments like many other countries. For example, the President of the USA is elected every four years in November, taking office the following January. If the President dies or resigns within that four-year period, the Vice President becomes the President and they choose a replacement Vice President. When an MP dies or resigns, a **by-election** is called. The seat is not left vacant until the next General Election but an election is held in that seat to elect a new MP. In December 2020 the government announced proposals to abolish the Fixed Term Parliament Act of 2011. In future the Sovereign may grant a General Election, on advice from the Prime Minister. An election must be held at the end of a government's five-year term.

Case study

A by-election

Chris Davies was elected as the Conservative MP for Brecon and Radnor in 2015, and held the seat at the 2017 General Election. In February 2019, he was charged with claiming false expenses as an MP. He pleaded guilty, was sentenced to a community order and was fined £1500.

Under the Recall of MPs Act 2015, this conviction triggered a recall petition whereby, if 10 per cent of local residents signed the petition, the MP would have to resign. In this case, 10,005 people signed the petition (19 per cent) and Davies was removed from the seat.

A by-election was called and Chris Davies stood again as the Conservative candidate. Plaid Cymru and the Greens stood down in favour of the Liberal Democrat candidate.

The result on 1 August 2019 is shown in Table 13.2. The Liberal Democrats won the seat, which they had held up until 2015. In the December 2019 General Election, the Conservatives regained the seat with a new candidate.

Table 13.2 The results of the 2019 by-election for Brecon and Radnor (Source: Powys County Council)

Party	Candidate	Votes	Percentage of the vote	Change
Liberal Democrat	Jane Dodds	13,826	43.5	+14.3
Conservative	Chris Davies	12,401	39.0	−9.6
The Brexit Party	Des Parkinson	3331	10.5	+10.5
Labour	Tom Davies	1680	5.3	−12.5
The Official Monster Raving Loony Party	Lady Lily The Pink	334	1	+1
UKIP	Liz Phillips	242	0.8	−0.6

Turnout: 31,814 (59.6%); **Majority:** 1425

> ### Different viewpoint
>
> Why do you think people may vote differently in a by-election than at a General Election?
>
> Look at recent by-elections and compare the results with the previous and subsequent General Election results for the same seat to help you.

Parliamentary constituencies

The United Kingdom is divided into 650 single-member parliamentary constituencies such as those shown in Figure 13.1 relating to Birmingham.

The Boundary Commission reviews the size and boundaries of parliamentary constituencies and is carrying out a review that will be completed in 2023. The last possible date for the next General Election is December 2024 (for more information on this, see **https://boundarycommissionforengland. independent.gov.uk/home/2023-review**)

> ### Discussion point
>
> Some people argue that we need to change our voting system so that the number of MPs elected matches more closely the votes a party receives nationally. If Birmingham (see Figure 13.1) was turned into two constituencies each electing five MPs, what positive and negative issues do you think might arise?

Figure 13.1 Constituency map of Birmingham

Safe and marginal seats

Under the first-past-the-post system, some seats are called 'safe' seats because they are unlikely to change hands at the next election (see Table 13.3).

Other seats are marginal, meaning the winning candidate only has a small majority over the next candidate and therefore the seat may change hands at the next election. Some marginal seats are two-way marginal, meaning that either of two parties might win the seats (see Table 13.4); others are three-way marginal, where any one of three parties could win the seats (see Table 13.5). In Scotland, where the SNP is strong, it is possible to have four-way marginal seats.

Example of a safe seat: Liverpool Walton

Table 13.3 General Election results from Liverpool Walton, 2019 – a safe seat

Party	Vote	Percentage of the vote
Labour	34,538	84.7
Conservative	4018	9.9
Green	814	2.0
Liberal Democrat	756	1.9
Liberal	660	1.6

Table 13.4 General Election results from Bury North, 2019 – a two-way marginal seat

PARTY	VOTE	PERCENTAGE OF THE VOTE
Conservative	21,660	46.2
Labour	21,555	46.0
Liberal Democrat	1584	3.4
Brexit	1240	2.6
Green	802	1.7

Table 13.5 General Election results from Sheffield Hallam, 2019 – a three-way marginal seat

PARTY	VOTE	PERCENTAGE OF THE VOTE
Labour	19,709	34.6
Liberal Democrat	18,997	33.4
Conservative	14,696	25.8
Green	1630	2.9
Brexit	1562	2.7
UK Independence Party	168	0.3
Independent	123	0.2

VOTE FOR ONE CANDIDATE ONLY

1	BARLOW The Labour Party Candidate	Labour	
2	DAVEY Green Party	Green Party	
3	ELGOOD Liberal Democrats	LIBERAL DEMOCRATS	X
4	RALFE Independent		
5	WEATHERLEY The Conservative Party Candidate	Conservatives	

Figure 13.2 An example of a first-past-the-post ballot paper, where the voter places an X against the candidate of their choice

Other voting systems used in UK elections

Spec coverage
- Other voting systems used in UK elections, including proportional systems, and the advantages and disadvantages of each.

A variety of electoral systems is used for different elections and in different places in the United Kingdom. Each of the systems discussed below has its advantages and disadvantages, as shown in Table 13.6 (on page 124). Electoral systems broadly fall into two categories: **proportional** and non-proportional.

- **Proportional systems** – the number of votes given to a party at an election is reflected in the number of people elected. For example, if the House of Commons had 600 members and the Greens got 10 per cent of the vote they would expect to have 60 MPs.

- **Non-proportional systems**, like FPTP, rely on gaining the most votes in an individual constituency to win, so there is no link between the national vote for a party and the number of MPs elected.

In the 2015 General Election, UKIP gained 3.8 million votes, 12.6 per cent of the vote, but won only one seat under the FPTP system. The winning party, the Conservatives, achieved 11.3 million votes, 36.9 per cent, and won 331 constituencies. The Scottish National vote in 2015 was 1.4 million or 4.7 per cent of the UK vote and it won in 56 of the 59 Scottish constituencies.

In the 1951 and February 1974 General Elections, the party with the largest number of votes nationally didn't win the General Election as the party that got fewer votes won more seats. In 1951 Labour had more votes but the Conservatives had six more seats, and in February 1974 the Conservatives won more votes but Labour won five more seats.

Some countries have second ballots whereby if nobody gets 50 per cent plus one of the votes cast, there is a run-off ballot between the two candidates, similar to the **supplementary vote** system.

Table 13.6 Voting systems used in the UK

VOTING SYSTEM AND EXAMPLES	DESCRIPTION	ADVANTAGES	DISADVANTAGES
FIRST-PAST-THE-POST (FPTP) UK Parliament	The candidate with most votes wins. A non-proportional system. A referendum was held in May 2012 to change the way we elect Members of Parliament to the alternative vote system. The proposal was rejected.	The system is simple to use. The outcome is known quickly.	People can be elected on a minority of the vote. Governments are elected on a minority of the vote. Smaller parties are under-represented.
Local authority elections in England and Wales	Councils can choose to call an election every three years, or use a thirds system whereby one third of the members are elected each year. County councillors are elected every four years.		
SINGLE TRANSFERRABLE VOTE (STV) Northern Ireland Assembly Northern Ireland local councils Scottish local councils	Proportional system where the electors place candidates in number order. Each candidate must achieve a quota of votes to win. Votes above the quota are redistributed to the voters' lower choices.	Every vote does help elect someone. The result closely matches the votes cast for each party.	This system often leads to many parties electing candidates. Coalition governments are more likely. Results can take time to count.
SUPPLEMENTARY VOTE (SV) Directly elected mayors Police and Crime Commissioners	Voters have a first and second choice candidate. The winner must receive over 50 per cent of the votes. Lowest scoring candidates are removed and their second votes redistributed.	Ensures that the winner has over 50 per cent of the vote cast.	Often the winner relies on others' second choices.
ADDITIONAL MEMBER SYSTEM (AMS) Scottish Parliament Welsh Parliament Greater London Authority	Voters have two votes, one for a candidate and the second for a party list. The first votes operate as a FPTP system and the second act as a top-up vote to ensure that the overall vote is proportional when additional members are elected from the party list.	Ensures that the wishes of the voters are more closely aligned to the outcome.	Ends up with two types of elected member – one directly elected and another from a list.

The executive, the legislature and the judiciary

Spec coverage

- The difference between the executive, the legislature and the judiciary.

These are three key terms that relate to elements that make up our government system and the way it operates.

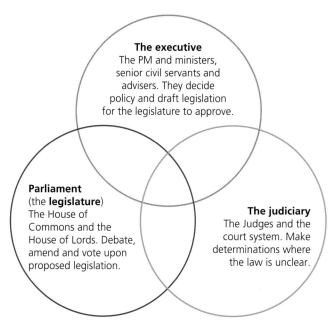

Figure 13.3 The separation of powers

The legislature

The **legislature** is the body that makes law. In the case of the UK it is Parliament sitting in Westminster, made up of the House of Commons and the House of Lords.

Figure 13.4 The Chamber of the House of Lords

The executive

The **executive** is the branch of government made up of the Prime Minister and other ministers, senior civil servants and policy advisers who draft and then, in the case of the civil service, implement the policy after it has been agreed by the legislature. Many decisions can be made by ministers and do not need to go before Parliament because the legislature has agreed that the minister has the power to act.

The expression the '**core executive**' is used to describe the very small number of those around the Prime Minister who are involved in major decision-making: that is, senior government ministers, who may vary according to the issue being determined, senior civil servants and advisers. Over the past 40 years, there has been increasing concern raised about the growth in numbers, role and importance of **special advisers**. Their role is to ensure that the political policy of the party is followed through in government.

Case study
Special Advisers

In November 2019, there were 108.4 full-time special advisers working across the whole of government. The total civil service had 413,910 full-time advisers at the same time.

The cost of special advisers is just under £10 million a year. They are paid between £40,000 and £145,000 a year. The Prime Minister has 44 special advisers, the Chancellor of the Exchequer has six, and the Foreign Secretary has four. Most other ministers have two special advisers. While they serve as civil servants, they are political appointments and change when there is a change of minister or government. In recent years the most well-known special adviser was Dominic Cummings, the leading special adviser to the Prime Minister.

Different viewpoint
Why do ministers need special politically appointed advisers when they have the civil service to support them doing their work?

The judiciary

The third element of the separation of powers is the judiciary, which comprises the judges and the legal process. The **Supreme Court** in the UK has limited powers to challenge laws made by Parliament. Decisions made by government ministers and by Parliament can be challenged in court and often legislation is not clearly worded, so judges have to make a determination regarding its meaning. While the judiciary is supposed to be separate and independent of the other two elements, it can become 'political' by the decisions it makes. If the government does not like the interpretation by the judges or the way the law has been interpreted, it can review the situation and draft new laws or regulations to achieve what was originally intended.

Figure 13.5 The Supreme Court of the United Kingdom

The separation of powers

This arrangement is the basis of a very important principle of government called 'the separation of powers'. Each of the three elements should be independent of the others and act as a system of checks and balances on the others to stop any one element having unbridled power. But there is overlap between these three elements in the UK because the executive is formed from the legislature, as all ministers are members of either the House of Commons or Lords, and the process whereby judicial appointments are made is established by Parliament. In the United States of America, this concept is seen more clearly whereby the President and executive are not a part of Congress, and the Supreme Court has the power to rule laws unconstitutional.

The nature of bicameral Westminster Parliament

Spec coverage
- The nature of bicameral Westminster Parliament; the respective roles, powers and relationships between the House of Commons and the House of Lords; the role of the monarch.

In the United Kingdom, Parliament is made up of two parts: the **House of Commons** and the **House of Lords**. This system of a two-chamber legislature/parliament is called bicameral (two chambers). It is a pattern followed in many other countries: for example, the Congress (Parliament) of the USA is made up of the House of Representatives and the Senate.

The House of Lords

Up until the early part of the twentieth century, it could be argued that the unelected House of Lords was more powerful than the elected House of Commons. Many Prime Ministers were members of the House of Lords. Today, the respective roles of the House of Commons and

the Lords are more clearly laid out, but there is still controversy about the membership of the House of Lords and its use of its powers. Table 13.7 indicates how the powers and membership of the House of Lords have been changed since 1911. At that time the House of Lords was composed of hereditary peers, peers elected as representatives by the Scottish and Irish peers, the **Lords Spiritual** (the 26 most senior Bishops of the Church of England), and four Lords of Appeal in Ordinary (senior judges), who had seats in the House for life. Politically at that time the House of Lords had a very large Conservative majority. The Labour Party had only just been formed. The other major party at that time was the Liberal Party, today's Liberal Democrat Party. The composition of the House of Lords in 2020 is shown in Table 13.8 on page 128.

Table 13.7 Changes in the powers of the House of Lords

DATE	EVENT
1911	The Liberal government was not able to get its budget though the House of Lords. An election was held and the Liberals were returned to power. The Liberals had the King's agreement to create new peers if the Lords refused again to pass the budget. The Parliament Act of 1911 stated that money bills can become law if not passed without amendment by the Lords within one month and that the Lords cannot veto most bills, but instead can only delay them for up to two years (or one month in the case of money bills). This curtailed the power of the Lords over taxation.
1949	The Labour government elected in 1945 decided to change the power of the Lords to delay laws from two years to one year.
1958	The Conservative government passed the Life Peerage Act whereby men and women could be a member of the House of Lords for their lifetime instead of being a hereditary peer whose title was passed on when the first person with the title died.
1963	The Peerage Act allowed members of the House of Lords to give up their titles and then be able to stand for election to the House of Commons. All Scottish peers also became members.
1968	The Labour government was unable to get through the House of Commons a bill reforming the House of Lords.
1999	The House of Lords Act removed all but 92 hereditary peers from the House of Lords, pending further reforms. These further reforms did not take place.
2005	The Constitutional Reform Act 2005 separated the House's judicial function from Parliament and ended the Lord Chancellor's combined role as head of the judiciary, a member of the executive and Speaker of the House of Lords.
2009	The judicial function of the House of Lords was transferred to the new Supreme Court.
2011	A draft bill was proposed to reform the House of Lords, proposing 80 per cent elected and 20 per cent appointed. The bill was dropped in 2012.
2014	The House of Lords Reform Act introduced the principle of resignation and allowed for expulsion under specified circumstances.

Table 13.8 The composition of the House of Lords in 2020

PARTY/GROUPS	LIFE PEERS	HEREDITARY PEERS	MALE	FEMALE	TOTAL
Conservative	209	46	188	67	255
Labour	174	3	118	59	177
Liberal Democrat	86	3	57	32	89
Crossbench	151	30	136	45	181
Non-affiliated	47	5	41	11	52
Bishops	–	–	21	5	26
Others	17	–	14	3	17
Total	**684**	**87**	**575**	**222**	**797**

Case studies

Stopping evictions during the Covid-19 pandemic

In September 2020, the government was defeated in the House of Lords on an amendment to the Civil Procedure. The Lords wished to amend new rules relating to the Covid-19 pandemic in order to extend the period of time when landlords could not evict tenants. This is an example of the formal language and style that has to be used in Parliament:

(Amendment No. 4) (Coronavirus) Rules 2020: To regret that the Rules will not continue to protect tenants from eviction, and to call on the government to amend the Housing Act 1998 to give courts temporary discretion on evictions. This was the 26th defeat for the government in the House of Lords during that parliamentary session.

Allowing 16-year-olds to vote in the EU Referendum

In November 2015, the House of Lords amended a bill about the EU Referendum to allow 16-year-olds to vote. The House of Commons had voted against this proposal prior to the bill going to the House of Lords. The government did not agree to the House of Lords' amendment and only those aged 18 and over were able to vote in the EU Referendum.

Different viewpoint

Many argue that the House of Lords should be abolished and that we should only have the House of Commons making decisions. Make a case for either abolishing or retaining the House of Lords.

Consider inviting in a member of the House of Lords who lives in your local area to talk about the work of the House.

These two case studies show the power of the House of Lords. The role of the House of Lords is to debate and revise legislation from the House of Commons. It can also propose legislation (normally about uncontroversial issues) and it carries out scrutiny functions similar to the House of Commons. At times, there are also joint committees of both Houses. A convention that assists the government in passing its legislation is called the **Salisbury convention** after the Marquess of Salisbury, who was the Conservative Leader in the House of Lords during the Labour government of 1945–51. It states that if proposed legislation was written into the manifesto of the party that won the election, the House of Lords should not oppose it.

Governments are often defeated on issues in the House of Lords as no single party in recent years has had a majority in the House.

The House of Commons

The House of Commons is the more important of the two chambers of Parliament.

It is an elected chamber currently made up of 650 members. The government is formed on the basis of the elections held to this chamber. The Prime Minister and most government ministers are members of this House. The last Prime Minister to come from the House of Lords was Lord Home in 1963, when he became Leader of the Conservative Party and Prime Minister. He used the 1963 Peerage Act to give up his title and stood in a by-election to become an MP.

From a government's perspective, the main function of the House of Commons is its ability to be able to vote the policy of the government into legislation. In the last resort, the House of Lords can only delay legislation for 12 months. The will of the House of Commons is always supreme.

Functions of Parliament

There are five key functions that Parliament performs, with the House of Commons being the more important of the two chambers:
1 Holding the government to account for its actions
2 Making and changing laws
3 Checking and challenging the work of government
4 Debating the important issues of the day
5 Checking and approving government spending.

Contemporary issues

- Recently there has been debate about reducing the number of MPs in the House of Commons to 600 and making the number of electors within each constituency more equal.

- There has also been prolonged debate about the role and size of the House of Lords, especially as no single party has a majority in the Lords.

- The House of Lords has the largest membership of any parliamentary chamber in a democracy in the world. The largest parliamentary chamber is the Chinese People's Congress with 2987 members.

- The number of members of the House of Lords has increased under each government in recent years.

- There have been scandals regarding expenses and payments in the Lords, as there have been regarding MPs. Members of the House of Lords receive no salary, unlike MPs, but are able to claim a daily allowance for attendance and living expenses.

The monarchy

The third element of our parliamentary system is the monarchy. The United Kingdom is a constitutional monarchy and citizens of the UK are subjects of the monarch. The role of the monarchy today is largely ceremonial. Monarchy is a traditional form of government whereby power is passed down through the family line, normally the male side of the family. In the UK, this was recently changed to follow the eldest child of the monarch, either male or female.

Over hundreds of years the power of the monarchy in the UK has been transferred to the elected government. Some countries still have a system of government based upon the monarch having absolute power. Examples include: Qatar, United Arab Emirates, Brunei and eSwatini (Swaziland).

In the UK, the monarch appoints a Prime Minister after each General Election. The monarch each year formally opens Parliament and reads the Queen's Speech. This is actually written by the government and sets out its legislative programme for the next 12 months. The monarch formally dissolves Parliament before a General Election. When a bill is passed by Parliament, the monarch formally agrees it – when it is given the Royal Assent. This changes a bill into an Act of Parliament, making it a law. The last time a monarch refused to give Royal Assent was in 1707.

The major political parties in the UK

Spec coverage

- The major political parties contesting UK General Elections; key philosophical differences between the political parties operating in UK General Elections.

The party-political system we have in the United Kingdom dates back to the mid-nineteenth century, when the political divide was between the Liberal Party (Whigs) and the Conservatives (Tories). 'Whig' and 'Tory' were earlier terms used to describe the two groups before formal parties were established to fight elections nationally. These were originally terms of insult. The term Tories (Tory) is still used as shorthand for the Conservative Party. Whigs were seventeenth-century Scottish rebels and the term 'Tory' originates from an Irish word for an outlaw or robber. Both of these parties developed during a period when large numbers of people were not allowed to vote.

At the turn of the twentieth century, a third party emerged supported by the trade union movement: the Labour Party. After the First World War, the Liberals went into decline and a **two-party system** emerged –

the Conservative Party and the Labour Party. In the 1951 General Election, these two parties between them gained over 96 per cent of the vote. It is called a two-party system because there are two major parties, each of which has a chance of winning a General Election.

Today, the UK has evolved into a **multi-party system** where there are still two major parties but also a number of other parties that achieve a sizeable vote at a General Election. In 2010, no one party won a majority of seats, so a coalition government was formed between the Conservatives and the Liberal Democrats who had won 57 seats at the 2010 General Election.

Philosophical differences

Traditionally politics has been described using terms like right and left, capitalist or socialist, mixed economy or free market. Today the divisions and philosophical differences between the parties are less discernable. Politicians have believed that to win elections they need not only to attract their own voters, be they a right-wing or left-wing party, but also to appeal to voters in the centre in order to get enough votes to win the election. This has led to voters often not being able to see much difference between the views and policies of the two major parties.

Tony Blair famously re-launched the Labour Party as New Labour and won three General Elections. In 1975, Margaret Thatcher became leader of the Conservative Party and moved the party to the right and won three General Elections. So clearly a number of factors influence whether a party is successful or not. Tony Blair would claim Labour won by moving to the centre and Mrs Thatcher would claim that her move to the right coincided with a change in the political climate in the United Kingdom, which matched her views. Traditionally, when discussing the views of political parties, the word 'ideology' is used (see below).

Three traditional political philosophy terms were used in the UK to describe our political parties. In the 1960s and 1970s, the parties could be linked clearly to a political philosophy.

- **Socialism** – seen as being on the left of the political spectrum. Parties on the left of politics range from Social Democrats to **Communists**.

- **Conservatism** – seen as being on the right of the political spectrum. Parties on the right range from Christian Democrats to **Fascists**.
- **Liberalism** – was associated with the Liberal Party, which was concerned about human rights and individual liberty, freedom and tolerance, and consent. Modern liberalism differs from classical liberalism, due to a greater emphasis on social and welfare issues.

Today's politics is not so clearly defined by ideological differences. In recent years 'populist' movements have from time to time dominated national politics. In the UK one such populist movement was UKIP. Later the Brexit Party took over the political space that had been occupied by UKIP. These parties focus on one issue that is dominant for a period of time, and the movements are often led by populist leaders who are experts at messaging. The AFD in Germany is another such political party that saw rapid growth due to its campaigns about immigration.

Discussion point

Where would you place the following parties on this example of a political spectrum?

- British National Party
- Brexit Party
- Conservative Party
- Green Party
- Labour Party
- Liberal Democrat Party
- Scottish National Party
- UK Independence Party

UK political parties today

When considering the state of UK politics today, it is helpful to review the political landscape in recent years.

A useful starting point is 1979. In that year the Conservatives won the General Election, defeating the Labour government. They were led by Margaret Thatcher, who became the first woman Prime

Minister in the history of the UK. She led the Conservatives to victories at the 1979, 1983 and 1987 General Elections. Her successor John Major won the 1992 General Election but lost power at the 1997 General Election.

The phrase '**New Right**' became associated with Thatcher's brand of conservatism, which she linked to elements of nineteenth-century liberalism. As well as winning power, Thatcher also saw part of her political mission as ending socialism as a political force. The New Right believed very strongly in a smaller state. They were suspicious of big government, strong on national defence and wanted fewer ties with the European Union. As a result, the New Right:

- provided fewer services and privatised many elements of the economy that at that time were owned by the government
- put an end to the 'nanny state', where they felt government intervened too much and stopped individual initiative
- curbed the influence of trade unions
- lowered tax rates and public spending
- balanced the government's budget and reduced borrowing
- emphasised individual liberty and choice.

During the Thatcher years, Labour moved to the left and this led to MPs defecting from the party and setting up the Social Democratic Party, which was modelled on many centre-left parties in Europe. In 1983, it fought the General Election as the Alliance in partnership with the Liberal Party. The two parties later merged to form what is now the Liberal Democrat Party.

In the 1990s under its new leader Tony Blair, the Labour Party re-branded itself New Labour and changed many of its policies to reflect the changes that had taken place under Mrs Thatcher, agreeing not to reverse most of the changes she introduced. New Labour remained in power from 1997 until 2010.

The Liberal Democrats entered into a coalition in 2010 with the Conservative Party, and lost most of its MPs in the 2015 General Election as its vote declined. Its vote and number of MPs has increased since 2015, but the party is yet to regain the influence it had in the last decade.

The Labour Party, after being defeated in 2010 and 2015, elected a new leader, Jeremy Corbyn, associated with the far left of the party. Following two election defeats, Jeremy Corbyn stood down as leader and was replaced by Sir Keir Starmer in 2020.

After the 2015 General Election the Conservative government pushed ahead with the proposal to hold a referendum about the UK's membership of the EU. In 1973, it was the party that took the UK into the then EEC, now the EU. In 2017 the Conservatives called a General Election and lost their majority but remained the largest single party. They remained in power with the help of the DUP. At the time of writing, the Conservative Party is on its third leader since the 2016 referendum, Boris Johnson, who has overseen the completion of the Brexit negotiations.

The 2019 General Election was dominated by the issue of Brexit (see Table 13.9). The Conservatives campaigned on the slogan of 'Get Brexit Done' and won a number of former Labour seats in the North of England. The Liberal Democrats, the most pro-European party, campaigned on the slogan: 'Stop Brexit – Build a Better Future'. The Labour Party tried to pursue issues relating to both Brexit and public services with its slogan: 'NHS Not for Sale', linking a possible threat to the NHS, post-Brexit, from a trade deal with the USA.

Table 13.9 indicates the policies of the three major UK parties at the 2019 General Election, which the Conservatives won with an overall majority of 81.

Table 13.9 Key policy pledges of political parties in 2019

POLICY	CONSERVATIVE PARTY	LABOUR PARTY	LIBERAL DEMOCRAT PARTY
Brexit	Get Brexit done without any delay.	Re-negotiate the terms of a deal with the EU.	Would hold a new referendum to remain in the EU.
NHS	50,000 new nurses, 40 new hospitals.	Increase spending by 4.3% a year.	1p extra on income tax to go to the NHS.
Taxation	No increases in income tax, NI or VAT.	Raise tax for those on £80k and more.	Replace business rates, increase corporation tax to 20%.
Economy	Make Free Trade agreements with other countries. Retake World Trade Organization seat. Support start-up and small businesses.	Nationalise the Royal Mail, buses, water and energy. Set up a National Investment Bank.	Invest £130bn in transport, energy, schools and homes.

Nationalist parties

From 1945 until 1974, the UK clearly had a two-party system. From 1974 until 2010, it had a two-and-a-half-party system, the half being the Liberal Democrats. Since 2010, we have a multi-party system, made up of two major (Conservatives and Labour) plus three minor (Liberal Democrats, UKIP and the Greens) plus a range of nationalist parties (SNP, Plaid Cymru and the Northern Irish parties).

The most recent change in the UK political landscape has been the rise of UKIP and the SNP. The United Kingdom Independence Party (UKIP) grew out of the Referendum Party, a group that wanted a referendum on the UK's membership of the European Union in the 1990s. It became increasingly successful in the proportional-representation-based European elections and now fights Westminster parliamentary elections. It got 12.6 per cent of the national vote, but won only one constituency, in the 2015 General Election. It is trying to broaden its base from simply being anti-EU, has adopted a number of right-of-centre policies and is perceived to be anti-immigration, especially with regard to the EU. In 2019, a new party emerged called the Brexit Party, led by Nigel Farage, the former leader of UKIP. It won the 2019 UK European Elections and fought in the 2019 General Election, but won no seats. The Brexit Party has now changed its name to Reform UK in order to contest local and parliamentary elections.

The Scottish National Party's main political platform is to achieve full independence for Scotland. Since 1997, Scotland has gained its own Parliament and controls a large number of public services. Until the 1960s, the Conservative Party, whose full title is the Conservative and Unionist Party – that is, in favour of the Union of England, Scotland, Wales and Northern Ireland – was the majority party in Scotland, sending most MPs to Westminster. From the 1960s until 2015, the Labour Party became the majority party in Scotland. In the 2015 General Election, the SNP won all but three seats in Scotland, even though the 2014 Referendum results were against Scottish independence by 55 per cent to 45 per cent. The SNP is the governing party in the Scottish Parliament. In policy terms, the SNP is seen as being to the left of centre in the political spectrum.

Plaid Cymru is the nationalist party of Wales, but it has not met with the same success as the SNP. Labour is the largest party in the Welsh Parliament. Plaid Cymru is seen as being to the left of the Labour Party.

> ## Discussion point
> In recent years there has been a growth in support for parties beyond the traditional three national parties. Why do you think parties like the SNP, Plaid Cymru and UKIP have gained support?

Government accountability

> ## Spec coverage
> - How Parliament works: scrutinising government and making it accountable; parliamentary questions, committees, debates.

Parliament has the function of both legislating and holding the government to account for its actions. In this section we will look at how Parliament holds government to account for its actions. How the legislative process operates is dealt with on page 136.

Members of Parliament – both in the Commons and the Lords – are able to ask ministers or the Prime Minister questions during their **question time** session in each chamber. These questions can be either oral or written. Oral questions require an oral statement in the chamber, while a written question means the Member wants a written reply.

Question time takes place for an hour from 2:35 p.m. on Mondays, 11:35 a.m. on Tuesdays and Wednesdays and 9:35 a.m. on Thursdays. Ministers from each government department attend the Commons on an agreed basis with the opposition to answer oral questions. Each major government department is allocated a particular day of the week. In the House of Lords, question time takes place at the start of business each day. If the minister is a Member of the Commons, a Member of the House of Lords who is a government minister in the same department answers questions.

Prime Minister's Questions (PMQs)

The Prime Minister answers questions from MPs every Wednesday from 12 p.m. until 12:30 p.m. when the House is sitting (**PMQs**). By convention, the first question asks the Prime Minister to list his engagements that day. The MP asking this question then asks their supplementary questions, which can be on any topic. The Leader of the Official Opposition, the second-largest party in Parliament, is then allowed to ask six questions, again on any topic of their choice. The leader of the next largest party in Parliament is then allowed to ask two questions. The rest of question time is then given over to backbench MPs (see page 136) to ask questions.

MPs have to place their names on the order paper (the agenda for PMQs) and it is up to the Speaker who is called to ask a question. The PM clearly has to be well briefed on a range of topical issues in order to answer the questions. Some questions from their own party's MPs will have been suggested by the Whips' Office (see page 136), so that they will have prepared responses. These questions are ones that either appear to praise the government or seek to embarrass the opposition. Most MPs are in the Chamber for this session, so it can become very noisy.

Figure 13.6 The House of Commons at Prime Minister's Questions

Select committees

Much of the work of Parliament is done in either House committees or joint committees of both Houses. There are committees established to consider draft legislation and these will be discussed in the section about legislation (see page 136). Regarding accountability, in 1979 the House agreed to set up **departmental select committees** that maintain oversight over the work of each government department. In the House of Lords, select committees cover areas including: science, economics, communications and the UK constitution. Each of the House of Commons select committees has a minimum of 11 members and the majority of the chairs of these committees are elected; the number of chairs is allocated by party size in Parliament. These committees have full powers to call witnesses and demand answers to their questions. The government must respond to the reports of the committees within 60 days.

Some select committees cross government departments, like the Public Accounts and the Environmental Audit Committees. These committees are staffed and can

appoint specialist advisers. There are also other select committees that assist with the working of Parliament and its business, like the Backbench Business Committee that can select motions for certain debates, both in the Chamber and in Westminster Hall. This committee considers **e-petitions** that have gained more than 100,000 signatories on the government website and decides whether they should be debated (see page 150).

Debates

Members of Parliament can also take part in parliamentary debates. Debates enable MPs and Lords to discuss government policy, propose new laws and discuss current issues. At the end of a debate there can be a division when a vote has to be taken. The opposition parties are allocated days when they can propose motions for debate.

The role of MPs

> ### Spec coverage
> - The role of MPs; representing their constituencies, debating policy, scrutinising legislation.

Members of Parliament are elected to represent their constituency and all the people who live in the constituency. MPs divide their time between working in Parliament and in their constituency and working for their political party. Some MPs hold ministerial posts or shadow ministerial posts (see page 136) with specific responsibilities, which take up a lot of their time. In recent years, there has been a lot of controversy about the pay and expenses of MPs and their outside interests.

As of April 2020, an MP's annual salary is £81,932 and they are able to claim expenses to maintain an office and staff, a home in either London or their constituency, and travelling costs to London and their constituency. All their expense claims are published and available on the Independent Parliamentary Standards Authority website. You can also find out what your MP is claiming on this part of the site: www.theipsa.org.uk/mp-costs/your-mp

The Prime Minister and other ministers receive additional pay beyond their MP's salary:

- Prime Minister: £75,440
- Senior ministers: £67,505
- Junior minister: Between £22,000 and £31,000.

Between June 2017 and the General Election in December 2019, MPs declared outside earnings of £8.4 million. Over half of this was declared by just 15 MPs. During this time, prior to becoming Prime Minister, Boris Johnson declared outside earnings of nearly £800,000.

Working in Parliament

When Parliament is in session, MPs spend a lot of their time working in the House of Commons. In 2017/18 Parliament sat for 103 days. This compares with a school year of 190 days. This work includes:

- dealing with constituency correspondence and issues
- raising issues affecting their constituents
- attending debates and voting on new laws
- attending functions both relating to their party politics and their political interests.

Most MPs are also members of select or standing committees, which look at issues of government policy or new laws.

Constituency work

Many MPs leave the House on Thursdays and return to their constituencies. They hold surgeries where they meet constituents and discuss their problems.

There will also be a round of functions to attend from schools to local businesses as well as party-political functions in the constituency.

The local MP is there to assist all constituents with their problems. It is no good writing to another MP who might support your ideas to resolve a local issue because parliamentary convention states that a constituent has to work with their own MP.

Many problems that MPs deal with are confidential and will not be made public. The MP may write to a government department or meet a minister on your behalf to resolve the issue. If it is an issue that can be made public, the MP can raise it in the House of Commons, where it becomes a part of the official record and can come to the attention of the media. You may give your MP the authority to raise the issue outside Parliament, to seek publicity for the issue.

MPs can also raise issues by:

- Questions – by asking ministers or the Prime Minister questions.
- Adjournment debates – held for 30 minutes at the end of each day. Members can raise any issue in this debate.

- Backbench debates – an MP can ask that the issue be raised in the time allocated for backbench debates. Thirty-five days a year are set aside for these debates.
- Private Member's Bill – an MP can put their name forward for the **Private Member's Bill** ballot that is held each year. If their name comes near the top of the list and the issue they want to raise is uncontroversial, they stand a reasonable chance of introducing a bill that will become law that parliamentary session.

The House of Commons is also a forum for national debate. If they 'catch the Speaker's eye' MPs are called to speak, often in important debates. The amount of time they can speak for is limited. MPs normally inform the Speaker in advance that they want to speak. The Speaker then decides who will speak and in what order.

When discussing Private Member's Bills, MPs can speak the bill out of time by talking and using all the time allocated for the bill and thereby allowing no time for a vote to take place. MPs also have an important role in scrutinising proposed legislation, both on the floor of the House and in committee. This work is more fully outlined in the section about legislation.

Ceremonial roles and key parliamentary roles

Spec coverage

- Ceremonial roles including Black Rod; key parliamentary roles including the Speaker, whips, frontbench and backbench MPs.

In order for Parliament to work successfully, it is supported by a large personnel. Some of these posts date back hundreds of years. Some are ceremonial, but today many also carry out important roles that enable Parliament to function.

The Speaker

The Speaker of the House of Commons is elected to the post by their fellow MPs. They chair debates in the Commons Chamber. The Speaker is the chief officer and has the highest authority in the Commons. They are expected to be politically impartial after they are elected to the chair. They are called Mr or Madam Speaker. They are not normally opposed at the General Election by the other major parties. The Speaker interprets the rules of the House. They can bar members, decide who speaks and can call ministers to the House to make statements. The Speaker represents the Commons to the monarch.

Commons Deputy Speakers

There are three Deputy Speakers who can also chair sittings of the House. They are elected by their fellow MPs. They are known as:

- the Chairman of Ways and Means
- the First Deputy Chairman of Ways and Means
- the Second Deputy Chairman of Ways and Means.

Once elected, these MPs withdraw from any active political role. Unlike the Speaker, they contest the next election under their party colours.

The Chairman of Ways and Means is chairperson of any committee of the whole House. The Chairman of Ways and Means has three distinct roles from the Speaker:

- Supervision of arrangements for sittings in Westminster Hall
- General oversight of matters connected with private bills
- Chair of the Panel of Chairs with general responsibility for the work of general committees.

The two other deputies may take the chair in the absence of the Chairman of Ways and Means, either in the Commons Chamber or in Westminster Hall, and exercise all the authority of the Speaker.

Lord Speaker

The **Lord Speaker** is elected by members of the House of Lords. Politically impartial, they are responsible for chairing the debates in the Lords chamber and offering advice on procedure.

The main responsibilities of the Lord Speaker include:

- Chairing daily business in the House of Lords debating chamber
- Chairing House of Lords committees
- Offering advice on procedure
- Formal responsibility for security in the Lords section of Parliament
- Speaking for the House on ceremonial occasions
- Acting as an ambassador for the work of the Lords, both at home and abroad.

Although the Lord Speaker chairs the Lords debating chamber, they have less authority than the Speaker of the House of Commons. Unlike the Speaker in the House of Commons, the Lord Speaker does not:

- call the House to order or rule on points of order
- call members to speak or select amendments.

Clerk of Parliaments

The Clerk of Parliaments is the most senior official in the House of Lords. The Crown appoints them as head of the permanent administration and the chief procedural adviser to the House.

The main functions of the Clerk of Parliaments are:

- accounting officer for the House of Lords
- employing staff in the Lords
- keeping the official records of the membership and business of the House
- offering expert advice on House procedure (the formal and informal rules of its everyday activities)
- ensuring the text of Acts is accurate.

Black Rod

Figure 13.7 Black Rod banging three times on the Commons door

Black Rod is responsible for the security of the House of Lords.

Black Rod is also responsible for and participates in the major ceremonial events at the Palace of Westminster. During the State Opening of Parliament, Black Rod is sent to the Commons Chamber to summon MPs to hear the Queen's Speech. The doors of the Commons are slammed in Black Rod's face to symbolise the independence of the Commons. Black Rod then bangs three times on the door with the rod. The door to the Commons Chamber is opened and the MPs follow Black Rod back to the Lords to hear the Queen's Speech.

Serjeant at Arms

The Serjeant at Arms is responsible for security and keeping order within the Commons section of Parliament.

The Serjeant at Arms' duties also involve carrying the House of Commons mace during the Speaker's procession before each day's sitting. The Serjeant, or a deputy Serjeant, sits in the Commons chamber and is responsible for security for the duration of the sitting. The Speaker can call upon them to escort people out.

Clerk of the House of Commons

The Clerk of the House is the principal constitutional adviser to the House of Commons. This post also involves management of contracts and leases regarding the property of the House of Commons.

Whips

Some of the other roles within Parliament are linked to the political parties.

Whips are MPs or Members of the House of Lords appointed by each party in Parliament to help organise parliamentary business and to ensure that their party's MPs turn out and vote according to the party's wishes. Every week, whips send out a notice (called 'The Whip') to their MPs and Lords detailing parliamentary business for the week and giving instructions on how to vote. Items are underlined as to their importance.

- A three-line whip is the most important: an MP is expected to vote according to the party's wishes.
- For a two-line vote it is important that an MP attends and votes.
- A one-line vote is the least important for an MP to attend.

Whips try to control their members. Often a pairing system is used, whereby an MP will agree with another MP not to vote on an issue as they need to be elsewhere at that time. As the two votes would cancel each other out, the whips will allow the MPs to be absent. In the House of Commons MPs have to be present and walk through the voting lobbies to exercise their votes. The term 'whips' relates back to hunting, where 'whippers-in' ensured that the pack of dogs kept together.

Frontbenchers and backbenchers

These terms refer to where people sit in the House of Commons and now relate to their seniority within a political party.

- **Frontbenchers** sit on the front green benches in the House of Commons. On the government side this is where ministers sit, and on the opposition benches it is where the shadow ministers representing the main opposition party sit.
- A **backbencher** is an ordinary MP who holds no government or opposition post so therefore sits behind the front bench on the backbenches.

The legislative process

All proposals for new laws (legislation) in the UK follow a similar pathway. There are different types of legislation that both Houses of Parliament consider.

Types of legislation

Bills (draft legislation) can be introduced by:

- the government
- individual MPs or Lords
- private individuals or organisations.

There are four different types of bill:

- **Public bills** – these change the law as it applies to the entire population and are the most common type of bill. They are proposed by government ministers.

- **Private bills** – these are usually promoted by organisations, like local authorities or private companies, to give them additional powers. They only change the law in regard to that one organisation or body.

- **Hybrid bills** – hybrid bills mix the characteristics of public and private bills. The changes to the law proposed by a hybrid bill would affect the general public, but would also have a significant impact on specific individuals or groups. An example of a hybrid bill is the construction of the HS2 rail line.

- **Private member's bills** – a form of public bill as they affect the entire population, but they cannot involve raising taxation. They are introduced by MPs and Lords who are not government ministers. They often are about social issues: for example, abortion, divorce or sexuality issues.

How laws are made by Parliament

Time is given over in the House of Commons for debates about both legislation and issues of the day. The Speaker, if requested, can call emergency debates to discuss urgent events. Ministers must be available to speak to the motion laid down to debate. Votes are often taken at the end of the debate and a record is maintained of how every MP has or has not voted in every division in the House. A formal record is also kept of every word spoken in the House and in its committees. *Hansard* is the official record of debates in the House of Commons and is published daily. The public is now also able to trigger debates in Parliament, using the e-petition system (see page 150).

The Green Paper
Often the government will publish a 'Green Paper', which is a discussion document about a possible new law, and MPs and others will be invited to comment upon its suggestions. It is called Green because the cover is green.

The First Reading (White Paper)
The government then publishes a 'White Paper', which is a proposal for a new law. This becomes a Bill (draft law) and is formerly announced (First Reading) in the House of Commons. No debate takes place at this time.

The Second Reading
This stage involves a debate upon the principle of the proposed legislation and a vote takes place at the end of the debate.

The Committee Stage
This stage comes next, where a group of MPs from all parties discuss the Bill in detail, line by line, and vote on amendments.

The Report Stage
The work of the committee is discussed and voted upon in the House of Commons.

The Third Reading (or Final Stage)
The amended legislation is voted upon and the legislation is then sent to the House of Lords, where all the same stages from First Reading to Third Reading are gone through. If the Lords make amendments, the Bill returns to the House of Commons where further votes take place until the Bill is accepted.

The Royal Assent
The legislation then receives Royal Assent – it is agreed and signed by the monarch – and then becomes law.

Figure 13.8 The Parliamentary process of law-making

Government formation

Spec coverage
- The formation of government by the leader of the political party with a majority in the House of Commons, or by a coalition of parties.

The Fixed-term Parliaments Act of 2011 meant Parliament was dissolved 25 working days before the General Election date. This Act was repealed in 2020 and the UK will return to the long-standing constitutional norm whereby the Sovereign may grant a General Election on advice from the Prime Minister. While MPs cease to be MPs, becoming only candidates if they are standing again, government ministers remain in post until the new government is formed. So the Prime Minister is still Prime Minister until they tell the monarch that they are unable to form a government.

After an election, the current Prime Minister goes to Buckingham Palace and informs the monarch of one of the following:

- That they have won a majority of 326 or more seats. The monarch then asks them to form a new government.
- That they have lost and that the monarch should ask the leader of the winning party to form a government.
- That no party has won a majority.

In the 2010 General Election, the Labour Party lost its parliamentary majority. The Conservatives won more seats but did not have an overall majority. Gordon Brown, the Labour Prime Minister, remained in office and tried to reach an agreement with the Liberal Democrats. If they had reached an agreement, the two parties would still not have had an overall majority. The Conservatives reached an agreement with the Liberal Democrats to form a **coalition government**. The two parties together had an overall parliamentary majority of 77 seats.

Once a new Prime Minister has been appointed by the monarch, they must then set about appointing their government. Senior government ministers are appointed first, then junior ministers. The whole process can take several days, as people do not always accept office or the office they are offered. The Prime Minister has to take a range of factors into account when appointing their ministers. Clearly some would have held the shadow post or the office prior to the General Election. The Prime Minister will wish to promote some and demote or sack others.

They may wish to include a variety of different opinions in their Cabinet or avoid splits in their government by either including or excluding certain people. Their own position may not be strong within their own party, especially if they have just won an election with a much-reduced majority.

In both 2017 and 2019, General Elections were called by the House of Commons, which voted by two-thirds to call the election – this was an option within the Fixed-term Parliaments Act. In 2017 the Prime Minister, Theresa May, lost her majority and governed after reaching an agreement with the DUP. In 2019, Boris Johnson called an election under the slogan 'Get Brexit Done' and the Conservatives won a large majority (see Table 13.10).

Discussion point

Should a General Election be held when the party in power chooses a new Prime Minister between elections?

Table 13.10 General Election results, 2019

PARTY	MPs ELECTED	PARTY VOTE (MILLIONS)	PERCENTAGE OF NATIONAL VOTE
Conservative Party	365	14.0	43.6
Labour Party	202	10.3	32.2
Liberal Democrat Party	11	3.7	11.5
Green Party	1	0.86	2.7
Brexit Party	–	0.64	2.0
Scottish National Party*	48	1.2	3.9
Democratic Unionist Party*	8	0.24	0.8
Sinn Féin*	7	0.18	0.6
Alliance*	1	0.13	0.4
Social and Democratic Labour Party*	2	0.11	0.1
Plaid Cymru*	4	0.15	0.5
Speaker	1	–	–

* Parties that only contest constituencies in a part of the UK: Scotland, Wales or Northern Ireland.

The role of the Prime Minister, Cabinet and ministers

Spec coverage

- The role of the Prime Minister, Cabinet and ministers.
- The power of the Prime Minister and Cabinet.

The phrase '*primus inter pares*', 'first among equals', has been used to describe the role of the Prime Minister. The phrase 'first among equals' implies that the Prime Minister is one of a team – that is, the Cabinet – and that the Cabinet is of equal importance to the Prime Minister. The phrase 'cabinet government' is often used to describe how the British system operates. Where members of the Cabinet agree important issues, they are then held by the concept of 'collective responsibility' to support the policy even if they personally do not agree with it. The role of a Prime Minister at a Cabinet meeting is to sum up the views of its members and state what he or she thinks the 'agreed' position is.

If ministers speak out in public against the Cabinet decision, they must resign. Recent Cabinet resignations have included Sajid Javid (the Chancellor of the Exchequer) and Amber Rudd (the Secretary of State for Work and Pensions).

Recently many Prime Ministers have been described as being 'presidential' in their way of working. This term relates to where the Prime Minister takes the lead on a number of policy issues, almost appearing not to involve the minister concerned, and in effect operates from Downing Street a duplicate government made up of special advisers. This style was associated with David Lloyd George during and after the First World War, Harold Wilson from 1964 to 1966, Margaret Thatcher from 1979 to 1991, and Tony Blair from 1997 to 2008. It was said that in the 'sofa-style' of government linked to Tony Blair, a very small group of people selected by him discussed policy issues and determined government policy.

The power of the Prime Minister and Cabinet

The power of a Prime Minister relates to their ability to choose their ministers and also sack their ministers.

They also have the power of patronage: the ability to fill a number of posts or recommend people for honours. They have the power to appoint junior ministers, senior civil servants, bishops and judges. In 2011, David Cameron gave up one of the most important powers of a Prime Minister: the ability to choose the date of the next election, when as a part of the coalition agreement, the Fixed-term Parliaments Act was passed, which set a date five years after the last General Election. This Act was repealed in 2020.

The Prime Minister's Office

Prime Ministers are supported by their own office support structure, which itself mirrors all the work of government. Although much of this work is coordinated through the Cabinet Office, the Prime Minister also has a private office staff who organise his or her schedule, but also provide a link to the party in Parliament and the country. A large media management team also supports the Prime Minister.

All Prime Ministers are constrained by the circumstances of their period of office. Margaret Thatcher was seen as a conviction politician who dominated her Cabinet and Parliament. This was partly because she commanded large majorities in the House of Commons, and the main opposition party did not pose an electoral threat to her position. Other Prime Ministers like James Callaghan (Labour) 1976–1979 had to act differently. He had a small, then no, parliamentary majority and faced major economic issues. John Major, 1990–1995, won the 1992 election with a small majority, then faced the exit of the pound from the Exchange Rate Mechanism and a party that became increasingly divided over the EU, as well as an opposition that was gaining support and had re-branded itself 'New Labour'.

The Cabinet

The Prime Minister appoints their own Cabinet. The current Cabinet consists of 21 other members, and there are then a further 97 junior ministers. The size of the Cabinet is not limited, but the number that can have a ministerial salary is. The senior posts within the Cabinet have traditionally been: the Chancellor of the Exchequer, the Foreign Secretary, the Home Secretary and the Defence Secretary.

While the Prime Minister chairs Cabinet meetings, there are also a number of Cabinet committees of groups of ministers that the Prime Minister agrees

to set up, and the Prime Minister appoints the chairs of these committees. The committees report to the Cabinet. Some of these committees are linked. There are also government taskforces that are set up to deal with specific issues. Each government department will have ministers attending some of these committee and taskforce meetings.

Figure 13.9 A meeting of the Cabinet

Examples of Cabinet committees and taskforces, 2020

- National Security Council
- Covid-19 Strategy
- EU Exit Strategy
- Domestic and Economic Strategy
- Climate Action Strategy
- Economic Operations Committee
- Union Policy Implementation
- National Space Agency
- Crime and Justice Taskforce
- Parliamentary Business and Legislation Committee

The Prime Minister does not have the constitutional authority a US President has. The Prime Minister is not directly elected by the voters. They are just a Member of Parliament. Their party can replace a Prime Minister without consulting the voters, as the Conservatives did in 1990, replacing Margaret Thatcher with John Major, and in 2016 and 2019, making Theresa May and Boris Johnson Prime Minister without a General Election. Labour did the same in 2007, when it replaced Tony Blair with Gordon Brown.

The organisation of government administration

Spec coverage

- The organisation of government administration into departments, ministries and agencies; role of the civil service.

Government in the United Kingdom is organised and delivered via government departments (ministries). In recent years, the size of many of these departments has decreased as many of the services they administer are now delivered via public bodies and agencies that spend public money but are run on business principles. Increasingly, the role of central government departments is the planning and commissioning of services for other bodies to run, which they then monitor to ensure they offer the public value for money. This is also increasingly the model used in local government.

Government ministers who are accountable to Parliament run the government departments listed in Table 13.11. They also work with many agencies and public bodies. The structure laid out in this table can vary from government to government. Departments can be re-named, merged or discontinued.

Table 13.11 The Prime Minister's Office at 10 Downing Street works with 23 ministerial departments

DEPARTMENT	NUMBER OF AGENCIES AND PUBLIC BODIES WORKED WITH
Attorney General	4
Cabinet Office	23
Department for Business, Energy and Industrial Strategy	41
Department for Housing, Communities and Local Government	12
Department for Digital, Culture, Media and Sport	45
Department for Education	18
Department for Environment, Food and Rural Affairs	33
Department for International Trade	
Department for Transport	24
Department for Work and Pensions	15
Department of Energy and Climate Change	9
Department of Health and Social Care	29
Foreign and Commonwealth and Development Office	12
HM Treasury	14
Home Office	30
Ministry of Defence	28
Ministry of Justice	33
Northern Ireland Office	3
Office of the Advocate General for Scotland	
Office of the Leader of the House of Commons	
Office of the Leader of the House of Lords	
Scotland Office	1 (public body)
UK Export Finance	1 (public body)
Wales Office	

Table 13.12 shows government-controlled bodies that are accountable to the departments shown in Table 13.11. For example, HM Revenue and Customs is linked to HM Treasury from Table 13.11.

Table 13.12 There are 20 non-ministerial departments

DEPARTMENT	NUMBER OF AGENCIES AND PUBLIC BODIES WORKED WITH
The Charity Commission	
Competition and Markets Authority	
Crown Prosecution Service	
Food Standards Agency	Works with 7 agencies and public bodies
Forestry Commission	Works with 2 agencies and public bodies
Government Actuary's Department	
Government Legal Department	
HM Revenue and Customs	Works with 2 agencies and public bodies
Land Registry	
NS&I (National Savings and Investments)	
The National Archives	
National Crime Agency	
Office of Rail and Road	
Ofgem	
Ofqual	
Ofsted	
Serious Fraud Office	
Supreme Court of the United Kingdom	
UK Statistics Authority	Works with 1 public body
The Water Services Regulation Authority	

Agencies

There are also 412 agencies and other public bodies and 98 high-profile groups, 12 public corporations, and the three devolved administrations that also work with the departments shown in Table 13.11.

Agencies are business units at arm's length from government that carry out specific functions or services on behalf of their client government department.

The term used to cover the range of differing agency arrangements is Non-Departmental Public Bodies (**NDPBs**). They are also known under the term **quango** (Quasi-Autonomous Non-Government Organisations). In recent years, the government policy has been to cut down on the number of government-linked quangos.

Examples of agencies:

- Air Accidents Investigation Branch
- Bank of England
- British Film Institute
- Criminal Cases Review Commission
- Imperial War Museum
- Sport England
- Welsh Language Commissioner

Public corporations

A public corporation is an organisation created by the state to carry out a public service. They operate as commercial organisations, for example:

- Historic Royal Palaces
- Civil Aviation Authority
- Channel 4
- BBC

High-profile groups

High-profile groups are specialist groups or posts within government that by regulation need to be consulted or which the government has decided to involve in consultation, delivering or monitoring services. Examples are:

- Government Chemist
- Civil Nuclear Constabulary
- Veterans UK

Role of the civil service

The civil service helps the government develop and implement its policy. The civil service also provides services directly to the public, including: running prisons; employment services; the benefits and pension system; and issuing driving licences. In recent years, the number of civil servants has declined as more government services are provided on an agency basis and their employees are then not directly employed civil servants.

Civil servants are *politically neutral*, are *impartial* and remain in post when governments change. They are also *anonymous* to the public, but increasingly those in NDPBs are becoming accountable and are often called before parliamentary committees. The civil service is made up of 25 professions, from engineers to procurement managers to lawyers. In 2019, there were 445,400 civil servants in post.

The Senior Civil Service (SCS) is made up of the top 5970 civil servants who devise policy and advise ministers. Civil servants in this group earn between £71,000 and £208,100.

Public Inquiries

When a government feels there are matters of public concern, it can establish a Public Inquiry, which collects evidence for a range of groups and individuals about a specific topic.

The Inquiry produces a report that may contain recommendations for government action. Several of the case studies mentioned in this book have led to Public Inquiries.

A judge or a senior ex-civil servant normally chairs the inquiries. The Reports are normally known by the surname of the Chair. Recently we have had the Leveson Report on Media Regulation, and the Francis Report on care at the Mid Staffordshire hospital. A Public Inquiry was also launched after the Grenfell fire in June 2017 (see page 91), but has not yet published its final Report.

These Inquiries can be expensive; the Saville Report on the events of Bloody Sunday cost £195 million. The Chilcott Report on the war in Iraq was established in 2009 and took seven years to complete.

Websites

UK government: www.gov.uk

BBC News: www.bbc.co.uk/news/election/2019/results

UK Parliament: www.parliament.uk

House of Lords: www.parliament.uk/lords

Electoral Reform Society: www.electoral-reform.org.uk

Courts and Tribunals Judiciary: www.judiciary.gov.uk

The Supreme Court: www.supremecourt.uk

The British monarchy: www.royal.uk

Prime Minister's Office: www.gov.uk/government/organisations/prime-ministers-office-10-downing-street

Parliamentary publications: www.publications.parliament.uk/pa/cm/cmregmem.htm

Activity

Consider as a class or a group writing to your local MP about an issue of concern. The issue can be local, national or international. Research your issue, ask the MP to respond to your questions and ask whether they will raise the matter with the appropriate minister. After any response, arrange for your MP to visit your school and discuss the issue with you. Keep a log of the process and ask the MP (when they visit or in a follow-up letter) about the process of citizens making their voice heard and how it might be improved.

Review questions

1. What description best fits the constituency where you live: a safe seat or marginal, and if marginal, what type?
2. What is a bicameral parliament?
3. Which political party has the third highest number of MPs in the House of Commons?
4. What is the job of Black Rod?
5. Who appoints the Prime Minister?
6. What is the Cabinet?
7. What is the function of a legislature?
8. What do the initials FPTP stand for?

Learning review points

- How do elections work in the UK?
- How do the different voting systems work?
- How does our two-chamber Parliament work?
- What political parties exist in the UK?
- How does the government work and pass laws?

EXAM PRACTICE

1. Explain what is meant by a 'coalition government'. (AO1) [2 marks]
2. Referring to the box above on Public Inquiries, discuss one advantage for a government and one advantage for the public, of holding a Public Inquiry. (AO2) [4 marks]
3. Justify why the House of Commons is more important than the House of Lords. (AO3) [8 marks]

Chapter 14: How do others govern themselves?

Key question

- How do others govern themselves?

Electoral systems and processes used in European parliamentary elections

Spec coverage

- Electoral systems and processes used in European parliamentary elections.
- The impact of these systems on the composition of political parties representing citizens.

In 2016, a referendum was held in the UK regarding its membership of the European Union. The result was in favour of the UK leaving the EU. The UK ceased to be a member of the EU in January 2020. The UK negotiated a transition period until January 2021, during which time negotiations would take place to agree a new treaty arrangement with the EU. Therefore, even though the UK was leaving the EU, it participated in the European Parliamentary elections that were held in June 2019 (see Table 14.1). Those who were elected as Members of the European Parliament (MEPs) in 2019 served in the European Parliament only until January 2020.

European Parliamentary elections

When elections were first held in the UK to the European Parliament, MEPs were elected using first-past-the-post (FPTP) in England, Scotland and Wales.

Table 14.1 The result of the 2019 European Parliament elections in Great Britain (Source: Press Association)

PARTY	SEATS WON	VOTE SHARE (%)
Brexit	29	31.6
Liberal Democrats	16	20.3
Labour	10	14.1
Green	7	12.1
Conservative	4	9.1
SNP	3	3.6
Plaid Cymru	1	1
Change UK	0	3.4
UKIP	0	3.3

In Northern Ireland, the single transferable vote (STV) system was used to ensure that by using a proportional system, the minority Nationalist community would gain one of the three seats. The European Parliamentary Elections Act of 1999 changed the voting system from FPTP to a **closed party list system**. The UK was split into 12 regions, with varying numbers of MEPs according to the population of each region. The closed list system allowed voters to use the single X system against the name of a party. Each party had a list of candidates it had placed in number order. The number of votes achieved by the party was then converted into the number of MEPs elected. If a party won two seats, candidates number 1 and 2 from its list were elected. Voters had no say in this system about whom they elected, only the party they supported. It was the party that decided which candidates were top or bottom of its list.

Every member of the EU must use a proportional system of voting but the actual system can vary from country to country.

Unlike General Elections, the turnout for European Parliamentary elections was always low (see Table 14.2 on page 144) – about the same level of turnout as for local elections in the UK.

The countries with the highest turnout in 2019 were Belgium with 88 per cent and Luxembourg with 84 per cent. The country with the lowest turnout was the Czech Republic, with 28.7 per cent. Unlike other elections in the UK, the voter was not electing anyone to be in power or to govern them by being a member of a government party.

Table 14.2 Voter turnout in the UK for European Parliamentary elections

ELECTION YEAR	PERCENTAGE TURNOUT (%)
1979	32.34
1984	32.57
1989	36.37
1994	36.43
1999	24.0
2004	38.52
2009	34.7
2014	35.6
2019	37.18

In the European Parliament, MEPs sit in **transnational groups**: that is, MEPs from at least seven member countries with at least 15 MEPs as members. The Parliament sits in a horseshoe design by party group.

Unlike other parliaments, the European Parliament meets in two places, Brussels in Belgium and Strasbourg in France. The European Parliament discusses and votes upon European legislation and directives, confirms the appointment of the European Commission and drafts the budget, but there is no government or opposition as in other parliaments.

The outcome of European Parliamentary elections was often very difficult to interpret in regard to domestic UK politics. It was often seen as a way of punishing the party in power in the UK. Also it was an opportunity to use your vote as a protest against the major parties. As no government was formed as a result of these elections, single-issue parties like the Brexit Party and the Greens did well. Also using a proportional system based upon a region list enabled parties that cannot win under the FPTP system to get candidates elected.

Discussion point

Why do you think so few people voted in elections to the European Parliament?

Political groups in the European Parliament

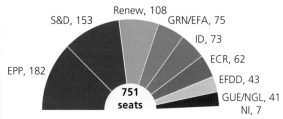

Figure 14.1 Political groups in the incoming European Parliament, 2019, including UK MEPs elected in May 2019

- **EPP** – Group of the European People's Party (Christian Democrats)
- **S&D** – Group of the Progressive Alliance of Socialists and Democrats in the European Parliament
- **Renew Europe** – Renew Europe Group
- **Greens/EFA** – Group of the Greens/European Free Alliance
- **ID** – Identity and Democracy
- **ECR** – European Conservatives and Reformists Group
- **EFDD** – Europe of Freedom and Direct Democracy
- **GUE/NGL** – Confederal Group of the European United Left – Nordic Green Left
- **NI** – Non-attached Members

In terms of UK political parties:
- Labour MEPs sat with the S&D group
- Conservative MEPs sat with the ECR group
- Liberal Democrat MEPs sat with the Renew Europe Group
- Brexit MEPs sat with the ID group

Democratic and non-democratic political systems

Spec coverage
- Key differences in how citizens can or cannot participate in politics in one democratic and one non-democratic political system that is outside the UK.

If asked whether we live in a democracy in the UK, most people would answer yes. If the follow-up question was 'How do you know?', what would be your answer? What are the vital ingredients that make up a democracy?

Some countries call themselves a democracy, but many would not think them democracies. What do you call a country that has some elements that we think are essential for a democracy, but not others? So when we try to categorise countries or systems of government, should we really talk about democratic, **non-democratic** and semi-democratic (somewhere in-between)?

Figure 14.2 identifies some of the key elements that are said to comprise a democratic system. Terms that may be associated with a non-democratic system are given in Figure 14.3 on the next page.

given in Figure 14.3 on the next page.

> ## Discussion point
> Do you think some elements listed in Figure 14.2 are more important than others in a democracy? Can a country or a political system call itself democratic if any of these elements is not allowed? Are political, legal and human rights all necessary components of a democratic system or can you have a democracy without all of these elements? So what do we mean by a non-democratic society or political system?

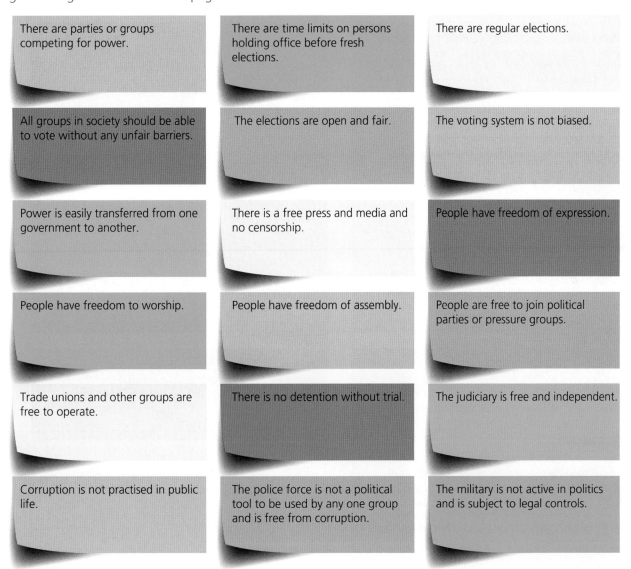

Figure 14.2 Democracy checklist

Absolute monarchy – a traditional form of government in which power is held by one family based upon a hereditary principle of power being transferred down a royal line. A small number of countries still have an absolute monarchy. Most monarchies now are called constitutional monarchies, where the monarch has passed all or most of their powers to an elected government and the monarch is a symbol of national unity. The UK is an example of a constitutional monarchy. Examples of absolute monarchies are Brunei, Oman, Qatar, Saudi Arabia, eSwatini (Swaziland).

Authoritarian rule – where power is in the hands of a leader or a small group that is not constitutionally accountable to the people. Authoritarian leaders rule outside the existing laws and legal framework. Citizens do not normally have a chance to free themselves of their rule by the electoral process. This form of rule is often seen when the military takes over a state. For example, the current government in Egypt was formed after a military takeover. Although after the takeover a President was elected, because he was the ex-military chief and because of the circumstances of the election and the situation in Egypt, there is a system of authoritarian rule in place.

Dictatorship – a system of government where there is rule by one person or group. In 2020 according to Freedom House there were 50 dictatorships in the world. There are 19 in Sub-Saharan Africa, 12 in the Middle East and North Africa, eight in Asia-Pacific, seven in Eurasia, three in the Americas and one in Europe. Examples include Belarus, Cuba, Myanmar and Laos. Many dictators also happen to be absolute monarchs or heads of single-party states.

Oligarchy – a system whereby the control of the state and economy is by a small group of well-placed, extremely wealthy insiders. These people could be formed from royalty or the wealthy, due to family ties, education or corporate power, or from the military. This system can sit alongside differing forms of democracy. It is often used to describe how the Russian system of government works alongside the elected government members.

Technocracy – a government system based upon people who are not elected but are technical experts in their field. A recent example would be in Ukraine in 2019, where newly elected former comedian President Volodymyr Zelensky called on the other parliamentary parties to contribute names of candidates for building a technocratic government.

Military – where the government is run by the military. The phrase 'military junta' is often used to describe the group of military officers running a country. Examples of military juntas are Myanmar and Sudan.

Aristocracy – government by the few, usually based upon inherited wealth and status in society. In the UK for many centuries this power of the nobility/aristocracy worked alongside the power of the monarch.

Theocracy – where the government of the state is held by religious figures whose beliefs dominate the governmental system. Examples are Iran and the Vatican.

One-party state – a system that allows only one political party to hold power. There may be elections, but the candidates will belong to the one party and there may be no choice of candidates on the ballot paper. Examples of one-party states are China, Cuba, Eritrea, Laos, Vietnam and the Western Sahara.

Figure 14.3 Terms that may be associated with a non-democratic system

Case study
Citizen participation in a democratic political system: The USA

The USA dates its democratic traditions back to 1787 and its founding Constitution, which is still used today as the reference for settling constitutional issues. From local to county to state to national government, elections are regularly held using the first-past-the-post electoral system. In some parts of the USA, judges are directly elected alongside the local sheriff (chief of police). The vote is secret and the counting of votes takes place under supervision. Citizens can stand for public office, many supported by one of the two major political parties: the Democrat or Republican Party.

The media is free to express opinions about candidates and policies. The public are allowed to protest and join campaign groups to lobby about issues. There are many private interest groups representing business groups, unions and others who lobby government. Political action committees allow the public to donate funds and to support political causes or election campaigns.

The public are also able to challenge government decisions through the courts. Citizens are free to express their opinions and are not subject to arbitrary arrest or detention for expressing political views. Citizens have the freedom to participate or not in the political process.

Increasingly, the power of participation for citizens is via the internet, which allows them to bypass traditional media formats. President Trump used his Twitter account to directly communicate with his supporters, rather than have the media report what he wanted to say. This also allowed for his supporters to spread on his views and also to communicate with him. In 2020, he had over 87 million followers on Twitter. In 2021 Donald Trump was barred from many social media platforms, including Twitter and Facebook.

In November 2020, Donald Trump failed to get re-elected when he lost the presidential election to his Democrat opponent, former Vice President Joe Biden.

(Source: adapted from **www.uscis.gov/sites/ default/files/document/lesson-plans/Intermediate_ RightsandResponsibilities_handouts.pdf**)

Different viewpoint

- How does the democratic process in the USA differ from that in the UK? Are there any elements of the US system that the UK should adopt? Consider contacting the US Embassy in the UK to answer any questions you may have.

- Campaigning in the USA is very expensive, so to get elected candidates need the support of very wealthy people or groups who will fund their campaign.

- The electoral system favours a two-party system so it is difficult for other parties or independents to get elected.

- The media is increasingly important in setting the political agenda and promoting its own views, as it is not bound by the concept of political balance. In the UK TV channels are regulated and have to be politically balanced in their reporting; this is not the case in the USA.

Case study
Citizen participation in a non-democratic state: North Korea

North Korea is a nuclear-armed state, and according to Human Rights Watch is the world's most repressive state. Interestingly, the formal title for the state is the 'Democratic People's Republic of Korea' (DPRK).

Its leader – Kim Jong-un – is a part of a family dynasty who have ruled North Korea since 1948. He is head of the Workers' Party of Korea, the only political party allowed. The Party exercises total control over all aspects of life in the country.

The government restricts all civil and political liberties, including freedom of expression, assembly, association and religion.

It prohibits any political opposition, independent media, civil society and trade unions. The media is controlled, as is access to the internet.

There is arbitrary arrest and punishment, including executions.

The state requires unpaid labour from its citizens. Movement within the country and to other countries is restricted. The Korean government has signed several international human rights treaties, but refuses to implement them.

North Korea does hold elections and everyone aged over 17 must vote. There is no choice of candidate and turnout is always close to 100 per cent. Approval for the government is unanimous.

(Source: adapted from **www.hrw.org/world-report/2019/country-chapters/north-korea** and **www.libertyinnorthkorea.org/learn-nk-challenges**)

Different viewpoints

- The word 'democratic' appears in the formal name of the country. In what ways, if any, can North Korea claim to be a democratic state?
- In what ways do the workings of North Korea differ from those of the USA?
- Can a one-party state claim to be democratic?

Websites

Freedom House: www.freedomhouse.org

Global Witness: www.globalwitness.org/en

Amnesty International UK: www.amnesty.org.uk

European Parliament: www.europarl.europa.eu/portal/en

Activity

Using Figure 14.2 on page 145, select four countries in the world and research how you would grade them against the democratic checklist.

Learning review points

- How does the European Parliament election system differ from the UK Parliament election system?
- What is the difference between a democratic and non-democratic system?

Review questions

1 What type of electoral system is used to elect members of the European Parliament?
2 What is meant by the term a 'transnational political group'?
3 Name an example of an absolute monarchy.
4 Which group is most powerful in a theocracy?

EXAM PRACTICE

1 Name the party that won the most seats in the UK European elections of 2019. (AO1) [1 mark]
2 Referring to the definition of a 'technocracy' on page 146, consider one advantage and one disadvantage of such a form of government. (AO2) [4 marks]
3 Analyse the benefits of living in a democracy. (AO3) [8 marks]

Chapter 15: Bringing about political change

Key question

- How can citizens try to bring about political change?

How citizens can contribute to parliamentary democracy

Spec coverage

- How citizens can contribute to parliamentary democracy and hold those in power to account.

In a liberal democracy, the citizen is seen as being at the heart of political power. The citizen through their vote provides legitimacy to those who win an election. As we live in a representative democracy, the citizen can often appear to be at arm's length from their elected representatives. It is seen as a duty of a citizen in a democracy to take part in the political process to ensure that their voice is heard. By registering to vote and voting at local and national elections, a citizen is conferring their legitimacy on our democracy.

Citizens can become more active than just voting at election times. They can join a political party or a pressure group to campaign to bring about change. Through that support and membership they can take part in forms of action that seek to influence decision-makers. Citizens can lobby their representatives to ensure that they are aware of their views. Increasingly, lobbying is undertaken using technology rather than by a formal meeting in the lobby of the House of Commons.

The ultimate power the citizen has in regard to holding those in power to account is how they use their vote at an election. If a citizen feels strongly enough about an issue, they can stand for election themselves.

Martin Bell, a former BBC correspondent, stood in the 1997 General Election in the Tatton constituency against the sitting Conservative member, Neil Hamilton, who had been accused of accepting money from the then owner of Harrods. Martin Bell stood as an independent candidate on a clean up politics platform, and promised to take no party whip if elected and only to serve for one Parliament. Both the Labour and Liberal Democrat candidates stood down at the election. Martin Bell won the seat with 29,334 votes to Neil Hamilton's 18,277 votes. Martin Bell stood down at the 2001 General Election, and the Conservatives have held the seat at each subsequent General Election.

Figure 15.1 Martin Bell in the white suit confronting his Conservative opponent Neil Hamilton

Dr Richard Taylor, a retired medical consultant, was so concerned about the changes taking place at his former hospital, he decided to stand in the General Election in the Wyre Forest constituency on a pro Health Service platform as an independent candidate.

He won the seat in 2001, held it in 2005, but narrowly lost in 2010 (see Table 15.1).

Table 15.1 Wyre Forest General Election results 2001, 2005 and 2010

	2001	2005	2010
Conservative	9,350	13,489	18,793
Labour	10,857	10,716	7,298
UKIP	368	1,074	1,498
Dr Taylor	28,487	21,708	17,270
Liberal Democrat	—	—	6,040

In 2010, Lady Sylvia Hermon, the MP for North Down in Northern Ireland since 2001, left the Ulster Unionist Party and remained as an independent MP until she retired in 2019, winning as an independent in the 2010, 2015 and 2017 General Elections.

Methods of improving voter engagement

Spec coverage

- How digital technology, social media and other methods are being developed as a means to improve voter engagement and the political participation of citizens.

In response to low voter turnout at elections and increasing levels of political apathy, strategies are being used to try to increase citizen action and campaigning.

Traditionally, letter-writing was the method people used to contact political figures about particular issues. One international charity, Amnesty International, developed letter-writing into a powerful campaigning tool. People were encouraged to write letters to governments when political prisoners were unjustly imprisoned, calling for improvements in their conditions in prison or for their release. The charity has been incredibly successful in freeing many people based on this public pressure.

Today, people are turning to technology to campaign about political issues. It is now possible to have a subject debated in Parliament if you are able to get 100,000 people to sign an e-petition. The government website https://petition.parliament.uk explains how to go about creating an e-petition:

How petitions work

- *You create a petition. Only British citizens and UK residents can create or sign a petition.*
- *You get five people to support your petition. We'll tell you how to do this when you've created your petition.*
- *We check your petition, then publish it. We only reject petitions that don't meet the standards for petitions.*
- *The Petitions Committee reviews all petitions we publish. It selects petitions of interest to find out more about the issues raised. It has the power to press for action from government or Parliament.*
- *At 10,000 signatures you get a response from the government.*
- *At 100,000 signatures your petition will be considered for a debate in Parliament.*

Debates

- *Petitions that reach 100,000 signatures are almost always debated. But we may decide not to put a petition forward for debate if the issue has already been debated recently or there's a debate scheduled for the near future. If that's the case, we'll tell you how you can find out more about parliamentary debates on the issue raised by your petition.*
- *MPs might consider your petition for a debate before it reaches 100,000 signatures.*
- *We may contact you about the issue covered by your petition. For example, we sometimes invite people who create petitions to take part in a discussion with MPs or government ministers, or to give evidence to a select committee. We may also write to other people or organisations to ask them about the issue raised by your petition.*

The Petitions Committee

The Petitions Committee can:

- *write to you for more information*
- *invite you to talk to the Committee in person about your petition – this could be in Parliament or somewhere else in the UK*
- *ask for evidence from the Government or other relevant people or organisations*
- *press the Government for action*
- *ask another parliamentary committee to look into the topic raised by a petition*
- *put forward a petition for debate.*

The Petitions Committee is set up by the House of Commons. It comprises up to 11 backbench Members of

Parliament from Government and Opposition parties. The number of committee members from each political party is representative of the membership of the House of Commons as a whole.

Standards for petitions

We'll only reject your petition if it is:

- *not clear what you're asking for*
- *about something that the UK Government or Parliament is not responsible for*
- *about something that's the responsibility of a devolved body (e.g. the Scottish Parliament)*
- *about a purely personal issue*
- *confidential, libellous, false or defamatory*
- *contains language that may cause offence, or is provocative or extreme in its views, deceptive or misleading*
- *advertising or spam*
- *nonsensical or a joke*
- *party political*
- *about honours or appointments – there's a different way to nominate someone for an honour*
- *breaks the law or violates intellectual property rights*
- *covered by a court order or injunction or is about a case that's active in the UK courts*
- *potentially confidential, commercially sensitive or might cause someone distress or financial loss*
- *names people working in public bodies (except for senior management)*
- *names family members of elected officials or people working in public bodies*
- *names someone who has been accused of a crime, or contains information that may identify them*
- *a Freedom of Information (FOI) request – there's a different way to make an FOI request.*

If we reject your petition, we'll tell you why. If we can, we'll suggest other ways you could raise your issue. We publish the text of petitions that we reject, as long as they're not illegal, offensive or confidential.

Between June and October 2020, 19 e-petitions were debated in Parliament. Thirteen of these concerned issues relating to Covid-19. The one with the highest number of signatures, 238,573, wanted to extend paid maternity leave by three months in light of the pandemic.

The highest number of people signing an e-petition to date was in 2019. It was about revoking Article 50 and remaining in the European Union. The petition was signed by 6,103,056 people. In its response the government stated that, 'This Government will not revoke Article 50. We will honour the result of the 2016 referendum and work with Parliament to deliver a deal that ensures we leave the European Union.'

Many pressure groups also use digital technology, both as a means of informing members and to gain support but also as a campaigning tool. For example, Compassion in World Farming recently presented to the European Commission in Brussels a Cow On Tour petition, signed by 176,062 European citizens. Its campaign aimed to stop the export of live animals for slaughter. To highlight the plight of live animals that are moved from country to country in poor conditions before being slaughtered, Compassion in World Farming sent a statue of a tethered cow around European cities.

Another campaigning group, www.change.org, claims to be the world's largest petition platform, which to date has empowered 400 million people, over 19 million in the UK alone, to campaign and win victories on issues they care about.

A UK-based campaigning platform is 38 degrees (see page 36), which has sponsored over 15,000 online campaigns. Currently there are 274 active campaigns on its website: https://home.38degrees.org.uk/news

Case study

The power and influence of social media

Many citizens now use social media platforms to make their views known about issues, and many celebrities have large followings on social media. In 2019, David Beckham was the most followed UK celebrity influencer on Instagram, with 59.7 million followers.

Facebook, for example, has approximately 2.6 billion users out of a world population of 7.8 billion.

Many now raise concerns about the openness of these platforms and the ability of groups and countries to try to influence opinions and events like the 2016 UK referendum, or the 2016 and 2020 US presidential elections.

Different viewpoint

Who should be accountable for what appears online – the person writing the material or the owners of the social media platforms?

Consider looking at the Facebook vs the Australian government controversy that occurred in February 2021 when drafting your response.

Action to bring about political change

Spec coverage

- The different forms of action citizens can take to hold those in power to account for their actions; how the citizen can contribute to public life by joining an interest group or political party: standing for election; campaigning; advocacy; lobbying; petitions; joining a demonstration; volunteering.

You have seen in earlier sections how citizens can hold those in power to account by joining a political party, standing for election and writing petitions. Campaigning, demonstrating and volunteering are other methods that citizens can use to contribute to public life. Each of these has benefits but also drawbacks in regard to achieving its aims. Volunteering during the pandemic to help others in the community indicated the strength of community spirit in many local areas.

Campaigning

When citizens are trying to influence the actions of government, either at a local, national or international level, action can take many forms. What can start as a local initiative by an individual can turn into a community group action, and if it benefits from publicity can turn into an international campaign. Such an example started in the small town of Modbury in South Devon.

Case study
Plastic bags

In 2007, Rebecca Hoskings, a wildlife photographer, was concerned about the effects she saw of plastic waste on sea life around Hawaii when she was filming for the BBC. She convinced the BBC to commission a programme about the issue. In her home town of Modbury she persuaded all 43 shops to stop handing out plastic carrier bags, initially for a trial six months. The ban has now become permanent. The local butcher said it saved him issuing 100,000 bags a year. As the publicity grew about the issue, other towns in the UK and worldwide joined the campaign. There are now numerous national and international websites and campaigns about plastic waste and the damage it causes, especially to wildlife.

In 2015, in the UK a new law came into effect forcing large shops to charge at least 5p for every plastic bag they issued to customers. In its first three months of operation, the large supermarkets saw an 80 per cent decline in the number of plastic bags they used.

According to the government, the average person in England now buys just four single-use bags a year from the main supermarkets, compared to 140 in 2014. The government hopes that the extension of the bag charge to all retailers will further discourage the use of single-use bags and prevent plastic waste, and instead encourage the use of long-lasting reusable bags. Since 2015, UK consumers have used 9 billion fewer single-issue bags.

Different viewpoint

Why do you think this campaign was so successful?

Demonstrating

Case study
Extinction Rebellion

Unlike other campaigns that want to change government policy, the Extinction Rebellion movement is different. It has no formal structures and has been a worldwide movement. It is politically non-partisan, and uses non-violent direct action and civil disobedience to persuade governments to act on climate change and the ecological emergency.

It has three demands:

1   It wants governments to tell the truth about the climate and ecological emergency.

2   It wants governments to act now to halt biodiversity loss and reduce greenhouse emissions to net zero by 2025.

3   It wants governments to be led by the decisions of a Citizens' Assembly on issues of climate and ecological justice.

On 31 October 2018, a group of activists assembled on Parliament Square in London and announced a Declaration of Rebellion against the UK government. Within a few weeks 6000 supporters had gathered in London and blocked five major bridges in protest. Supporters superglued themselves to the gates of Buckingham Palace as they read letters to the Queen. Within a short period of time, due to the publicity and the influence of social media, the campaign became global.

The movement is now international – it is estimated that some 250,000 people in more than 1000 groups across 75 nations are a part of Extinction Rebellion today.

Different viewpoint

Why do you think the Extinction Rebellion movement grew so quickly and spread across the world?

Volunteering

Some citizens try to make a difference by volunteering.

- VolunteerMatch will link you to a volunteering opportunity that suits your interests: www.volunteermatch.org
- The UK government has its own web pages that promote the idea of volunteering:
  - If you are aged 16 to 17, the government has sponsored the National Citizen Service programme, which is locally based and involves an element of volunteering.
  - If you prefer to work overseas, the UK government has an International Citizen Service programme for those aged 18 to 25.
- Volunteering England provides a web-based platform for a number of voluntary organisations in the UK that seek helpers. Here are some examples from its website:

Every 45 seconds someone in the UK finds a volunteering opportunity thanks to Do-it. Do-it is the national database of volunteering opportunities. Search more than one million volunteering opportunities by interest, activity or location and apply online.

ivo is a social network for the community-minded, connecting people and organisations that want to make their world a better place. It allows you to search through 25,000+ volunteering opportunities and jobs available in the not-for-profit sector.

CharityJob is the UK's busiest site for charity jobs and volunteering opportunities. It regularly has more than a thousand voluntary, internship and trustee positions available across 27 job categories. If you are looking to volunteer in the UK or for opportunities abroad, then CharityJob might just have the perfect role for you.

How-tos are written by people with real-world experience on subjects that matter to you. These guides are wiki-based so you can update them and even add your own.

Roles played by groups in providing a voice for society

Spec coverage

- The roles played by public institutions, public services, interest and pressure groups, trade unions, charities and voluntary groups in providing a voice and support for different groups in society.

A range of bodies and organisations exist to assist in ensuring the citizen's voice is heard and their rights are protected.

The following case studies are examples of how different bodies and groups provide a voice for the citizen.

Discussion point

What forms of discrimination and unfairness still exist in the UK?

How do you think they should be tackled?

Case study
The Equality and Human Rights Commission

The Equality and Human Rights Commission is a government-funded quango, which was established by law. Parliament gave the Commission the job of challenging discrimination and protecting human rights in the UK. The Commission's work covers the whole of the UK and it has a network of regional offices throughout the country.

The Commission's aims are as follows (taken from its website www.equalityhumanrights.com):

- Ensure people's ability to achieve their potential is not limited by prejudice or discrimination.
- There is respect for and protection of each individual's human rights, and for the dignity and worth of all.
- Each individual has an equal opportunity to participate in society.
- There is mutual understanding between groups based on understanding and valuing of diversity and on shared respect for equality and human rights.

We have different duties in the three areas of our mandate.

Equality and diversity

- We must promote understanding, encourage good practice, and promote equality of opportunity; promote awareness and understanding of rights through publishing independent reports; provide independent assistance to victims of discrimination; and work towards the elimination of unlawful discrimination and harassment.

Human rights

- We must promote understanding of the importance of human rights through teaching, research and public awareness and educational programmes; promoting awareness, understanding and protection of human rights and efforts to combat discrimination.
- Ensuring compliance among public bodies with their existing statutory human rights obligations and the equality duties, by monitoring and enforcing compliance with the current legislative framework including the Human Rights Act.

Good relations

- We must promote understanding of the importance of good relations; encourage good practice; work towards the elimination of prejudice, hatred and hostility; and work towards enabling participation.

Across all three areas of our mandate we must:

- Monitor the law: monitor the effectiveness of existing statutes.
- Monitor progress: identify relevant changes in society; define the outcomes we seek and indicators of progress; consult and involve the public and take account of representations; monitor progress and publish a report on progress to Parliament.
- Plan ahead: prepare and publish a plan of activities, priorities and principles; revise the plan as necessary.

We can:

- provide assistance to those taking legal proceedings in relation to equality
- take legal cases on behalf of individuals or intervene in litigation to test and extend the right to equality and human rights
- apply to the court for injunctions and interdicts [a court order forbidding an act] where we consider it likely that an unlawful act will be committed
- set up inquiries to investigate the behaviour of institutions
- enforce the public sector equality duty, issuing Compliance Notices where we believe the law has been breached
- award grants to organisations
- provide education and training
- produce guidance and statutory codes of practice to support individuals and organisations to comply with the law and promote good practice, and
- use our influence and authority to lead new debates, building our arguments from the evidence we collect and publish.

The Commission is a very powerful body as it is a statutory body, established by an Act of Parliament. It has powers to work on behalf of individual citizens and groups of citizens and, through its legal powers and the use of the court, to both bring about change and ensure enforcement of existing rights.

Different viewpoint

Are laws and government bodies the best way to change people's attitudes about equality issues?

Case study
Greenpeace

Greenpeace is an international pressure group that ensures it has no links with any governmental body, so it is free to campaign on environmental issues. It investigates, exposes and confronts environmental abuse, and champions environmentally responsible solutions. Greenpeace encourages its supporters to assist it in its work. It suggests:

- joining your local Greenpeace group/network
- inviting a Greenpeace speaker to talk to a community group
- getting active as an individual
- working for Greenpeace
- joining its political lobbying network
- volunteering in the office
- applying for direct action training
- helping raise funds for Greenpeace
- taking up a Greenpeace internship
- working overseas and at sea for Greenpeace.

On its website Greenpeace outlines how it takes action to make change happen.

Greenpeace intervenes at the point where our action is most likely to provoke positive change – whether this is intervening at the point of an environmental crime, targeting those who have the power to make a difference, engaging people and communities who can leverage change, or working for the adoption of environmentally responsible and socially just solutions.

Investigations

Investigations are a fundamental part of Greenpeace's campaigns. Through investigations we can expose those responsible for environmental destruction and shed light on the areas of operation that they would rather stay in the dark.

Our investigations provide research, evidence and intelligence about environmental crimes and their perpetrators to inform and enable our campaigns. Using a variety of techniques from field work, satellite imagery, business and financial analysis, and working with whistleblowers, our investigations provide the facts and evidence Greenpeace needs in order to bring about change. Our investigations have led to Royal Dutch Shell being driven from the Arctic, UK plastic waste being banned from Malaysia, and a huge area of the Arctic Ocean being declared off-limits to industrial fishing.

Campaigning at Greenpeace is based upon the following elements:

Informed research

All of Greenpeace's work is guided by and informed by science and research. We use facts and peer-reviewed research conducted by scientists all over the world to inform our campaigns and policies.

The Greenpeace Research Laboratories form part of the Science Unit of Greenpeace International. Based at the University of Exeter in the UK, the laboratories provide scientific advice and analytical support to Greenpeace campaigns

worldwide, over a range of disciplines. The laboratories are equipped with hardware for the analysis of heavy metal and organic contaminants in a range of environmental samples. An extensive database of scientific literature has been built up since 1986.

Lobbying

Our political unit in the UK works with people across the political and policy arena in Westminster and across Britain. We meet with politicians to build political support for our campaigns, produce and disseminate reports and briefings, organise events for MPs in Westminster and at Party Conferences, and make submissions to consultations and committee inquiries.

We work hard behind the scenes at climate conferences, and engage policy-makers and diplomats at international forums like The Convention on the Conservation of Antarctic Marine Living Resources to encourage countries across the world to work together.

Peaceful direct action

Taking peaceful, non-violent direct action has always been at the heart of Greenpeace's work. Greenpeace was founded in 1971 by a small group of people who set sail in an old fishing boat to try and stop a US nuclear weapons test on an island off the coast of Alaska.

Direct action is about physically acting to stop an immediate wrong at the scene of the crime. Ordinary people around the world can act to confront those in positions of power with their responsibility for stopping global environmental destruction. We act to raise the level and quality of public debate. Above all, we act to provoke action from those with the power and responsibility to make change happen.

Guiding all of our actions, always, is a commitment to nonviolence and personal responsibility.

Our fleet of ships allows us to take action and bear witness at the scenes of environmental crimes around the world, often in remote and difficult-to-reach places.

(Source: **www.greenpeace.org.uk/about-greenpeace/how-we-create-change**)

This case study indicates the methods you may wish to apply when carrying out your own Citizenship Investigation.

Different viewpoint

Greenpeace is seen as a very successful pressure group. Why do you think it is so successful?

Case study
Black Lives Matter

In recent times across the globe a campaign has developed and grown based upon the slogan 'Black Lives Matter'. Originating in the USA in 2013, after the death of Trayvon Martin, its mission is encapsulated within its slogan. The campaign aims to combat racial discrimination and counter acts of violence against people on the basis of their race.

Following the death of George Floyd in May 2020, aged 46, the campaign became global. After being arrested by police outside a shop in Minneapolis, Minnesota, USA, social media footage showed a white police officer kneeling on Floyd's neck while he was pinned to the floor. Mr Floyd said more than 20 times that he could not breathe as he was restrained by the officers. The officer held his knee on Floyd's neck for seven minutes and 46 seconds.

This event sparked marches and rallies around the world. In the UK, players took the knee (knelt down on one knee) before football matches to combat racism. One aspect of the BLM movement in the UK has centred upon the nature of historic public statutes. In Bristol, protesters pulled down a statute of Edward Colston, a benefactor to the city in the eighteenth century whose wealth was linked to the slave trade.

Different viewpoint

We have laws in the UK that protect individuals and their rights. Why is it that there is still a need for a campaign like Black Lives Matter?

Case study
Citizens Advice

Citizens Advice is a charity whose work involves a large number of volunteers. It receives funding from the government, among other bodies. In most towns and cities of the UK there are Citizens Advice offices. Many people turn to them to seek help and advice on everyday issues, such as housing, benefits entitlements, poverty, legal advice and consumer issues. It works with some of the most disadvantaged in society. Research shows that its clients are five times more likely to live in poverty than the average member of the UK population. Citizens Advice also provides educational services to the general public, and campaigns on social issues.

Formerly known as the Citizens Advice Bureau, Citizens Advice was established in 1938 in order to assist with the needs of the civilian population if there were to be a war. It has always been staffed by volunteers.

In the 1950s, the government decided to stop funding the service, but it was able to carry on thanks to support from charities and other groups such as the Nuffield Foundation, Carnegie Trust and the Joseph Rowntree Foundation.

In 1960, the government restored funding to Citizens Advice. In 2019–20, Citizens Advice helped millions of people. The charity's work included:

- 34,500,000 visits to its website
- 1,344,000 people helped face-to-face
- 1,010,000 people using its phone service
- 483,000 people contacting its consumer helpline
- 436,000 people getting help by email or webchat
- 97,000 witnesses helped through the Witness Service.

In total, Citizens Advice helped 2.8 million people in person, or by phone, email or web chat. The charity provided support in 2540 locations across England and Wales, with 21,400 volunteers and 8150 staff. Its income in 2018/19 was £110 million. The bulk of its income still comes from the government, but much of this funding is now linked to specific services that the organisation offers, such as money and pension advice.

Different viewpoint

Why is it important for the government to fund a body like Citizens Advice?

Case study

Age UK

Age UK is a UK-based group of charities that are concerned about the rights of the elderly. As well as providing help and assistance, it is a campaigning body. Age UK is the largest charity in the UK devoted to helping people make the most of later life. Like Citizens Advice, it has 130 local Age UK groups providing help and advice in communities. Although Age UK is probably best known for its network of 450 shops, staffed by volunteers, it also carries out a lot of other services. The charity offers internships and office roles, trains those who work with the elderly, endorses commercial products for the elderly and carries out research about seniors.

Different viewpoint

Why are volunteers important to a charity like Age UK?

Consider inviting in to your school or making contact with a local representative to ask them to discuss the work of their organisation.

Case study

The Women's Institute (WI)

The Women's Institute was formed in 1915 to help revitalise rural communities and to help women become more involved in food production during the First World War.

Today the WI has more than 230,000 members and over 6300 branches. As well as being concerned with food, it is also a campaigning organisation. It is non-political, but its voice is heard by government because it represents such a broad band of public opinion.

Recent campaigns supported by the WI include:

Food Matters

This campaign is about reducing food waste and tackling food poverty. The WI is encouraging its members and supermarkets to cut food waste and work more widely to address the issue of increasing food poverty.

SOS for Honeybees

Since 2009, the WI has been campaigning to raise awareness of the plight of bees and how we can take action to increase the UK honeybee population.

No More Violence against Women

This campaign encourages WI members to raise awareness and take action to end the scourge of violence against women.

Can men join the WI?

The WI was established to provide a strong female community offering women educational opportunities and a chance to make a difference in their local community. The WI is an educational charity and UK charitable law allows organisations to state that their membership is single-sex. The WI welcomes men to attend many of its courses and events but they cannot become members.

Different viewpoint

Do you think there is still a role for an organisation like the WI in the twenty-first century?

Consider inviting in to your school or making contact with a local representative to ask them to discuss the work of their organisation.

Websites

Surfers Against Sewage: www.sas.org.uk

VolunteerMatch: www.volunteermatch.org

NCVO: www.volunteering.org.uk

UK government: www.gov.uk/volunteering

Equality and Human Rights Commission: www.equalityhumanrights.com

Citizens Advice: www.citizensadvice.org.uk/about-us

Greenpeace UK: www.greenpeace.org.uk

Age UK: www.ageuk.org.uk

The Women's Institute: www.thewi.org.uk

Review questions

1 How does Greenpeace differ from the Equality and Human Rights Commission?
2 What are the thresholds regarding e-petitions being acted upon by Parliament?
3 Identify one method the government has introduced to encourage voter engagement with the democratic process.
4 What services does Citizens Advice offer?

Learning review points

- How can citizens take part in the democratic process?
- How do pressure groups and other bodies hold those in power to account?

Activity

Investigate one of the organisations described in this chapter. Draw up a list of criteria you think are important in deciding whether an organisation is successful. Present to your class an account of its campaigning success.

EXAM PRACTICE

1 Identify one reason why the internet is important for pressure and campaign groups. (AO1) [1 mark]
2 Referring to page 150 and the text about e-petitions, discuss your own idea for an e-petition. (AO2) [4 marks]
3 Examine the advantages and disadvantages of demonstrations as a means of protest. (AO3) [8 marks]

This chapter outlines the requirements of the Active citizenship section of Question Paper 1, which accounts for 25 per cent of the total marks awarded for the GCSE.

Active citizenship

The assessment for this GCSE specification is divided into two question papers and each paper is divided into two parts. Each part is worth 40 marks and 25 per cent of the total GCSE assessment. Active citizenship is the title given to Section A of Paper 1. You have to answer two sets of questions. The first relates to campaigning and active citizenship, which is about your understanding of the skills and processes related to active citizenship, and includes source material about a real or imagined case study of active citizenship. The second part of Section A questions you about the Investigation you have undertaken.

Citizenship case studies

On the next two pages you will find out about three active citizenship case studies. Once you have read through each case study, you will carry out an activity and answer questions about it.

In this section, we are going to identify the key questions that need to be asked and investigated when looking at a case study of people trying to make a difference.

All three case studies outlined here involve citizens trying to make a difference, locally, nationally or globally. The outlines are about the methods, processes and skills that had to be applied to achieve their aims.

Case study
HS2 protests

HS2 is a transport project to improve the rail infrastructure between London, the Midlands and the North of England. The first phase from London to Birmingham is due to be opened in 2026. Once the other sections further north are opened, it is claimed that it will help regenerate the economy in the North of England.

Those opposed to HS2 formed the Stop the HS2 campaign. Since the project began, they have cast doubt on the economic benefits. They argue that the true cost will far exceed the estimate, and so far they have been proven correct. The expected final cost is estimated to have risen from £40bn to £110bn. The campaigners also claim that the disruption and loss of homes along the route are not worth any possible gain. Over 600 homes will have to be demolished. If there is this amount of money available, the protesters state that it would be better spent on other line improvements across the whole country and that this would achieve a better economic return.

The Stop the HS2 campaign saw local and national protesters, as well as affected MPs, join together to try to prevent the legislation required for the development. However, in February 2020, Parliament passed the legislation for the HS2 project to go ahead as planned.

Case study

Greta Thunberg: How one person is trying to make a difference

In May 2018, a 15-year-old Swedish schoolgirl, Greta Thunberg, won a newspaper competition after writing an essay about climate change. In August of that year each week she left school and started protesting outside the Swedish Parliament in Stockholm holding a poster that said 'School Strike for Climate'. She said she would go each week until the Swedish government met its carbon emissions targets agreed at the Paris Climate Change Conference in 2015.

Her protest went viral via the internet, and other children around the world began to copy her protest. By December 2018, over 20,000 students globally had joined her campaign. She met fellow students across Europe who were protesting, travelling by train to join them so that she limited her impact on the environment.

Greta took the whole of 2019 off school to continue campaigning, attending key climate change conferences and joining student protests around the world. She campaigns for governments and businesses to cut their carbon emissions more quickly and for banks, companies and governments to stop investing in fossil fuels. She asks that instead they invest in sustainable technologies and research, and in restoring nature.

In September 2019, she travelled to New York to speak at a UN climate change conference. Again, she refused to fly and instead travelled across the Atlantic Ocean in a racing yacht. As she arrived it was a signal for millions across the world to take part in a climate strike.

Speaking at the UN conference, she criticised politicians, saying, 'How dare you? I shouldn't be up here. I should be back in school on the other side of the ocean, yet you all come to us as young people for hope. How dare you?' The then US President Donald Trump criticised her comment saying she 'must work on her anger management problem'.

In response Greta messaged, 'When haters go after your looks and differences, it means they have nowhere left to go. And then you know you're winning. I have Asperger's and that means that I'm sometimes a bit different from the norm. And – given the right circumstances – being different is a superpower.'

In 2019, Greta was named the *Time* Person of the Year.

Case study
National Farmers' Union

Sign the food standards petition now!

I want the food I eat to be produced to world-leading standards.

Our Government should ensure that all food eaten in the UK – whether in our homes, schools, hospitals, restaurants or from shops – is produced in a way that matches the high standards of production expected of

UK farmers. Covid-19 has highlighted the importance of food security and traceability.

I believe the UK Government should seize the opportunities of 'Global Britain' to promote sustainable models of production and consumption across the world.

Farming throughout the UK has high standards of safety and welfare with an ambition to be net zero in greenhouse gas emissions by 2040. There are very strict controls on farming methods allowed in the UK and I expect the same of all food that is imported here so that the food I eat is safe, traceable and produced to high welfare and environmental standards.

Before the UK begins to negotiate trade deals with countries around the world, I call on the UK Government to put into law rules that prevent food being imported to the UK that is produced in ways that would be illegal here.

(Source: **www.nfuonline.com/news/latest-news/
food-standards-petition**)

This petition gained over 1 million signatures within 48 hours. It is sponsored by the National Farmers' Union (NFU), which is seen as an insider pressure group that acts as one of the representatives for the agricultural industry and is consulted by government on farming matters.

This is an example of an issue that has arisen due to Brexit. The UK now has to negotiate trade agreements with other countries, instead of having the EU negotiate them on the UK's behalf. The UK has, in the past, been at the forefront of demanding high animal welfare standards, to our country in the agricultural industry and bans the use of certain chemicals and additives in our food. The NFU is concerned that other countries, particularly the USA, want to be allowed to export their food products, which don't meet our current food welfare standards, to our country. Normally, as an insider group, it would speak to the government and its views would carry a lot of weight. However, this petition is a sign that it believes it has to campaign in the same way as a campaigning pressure group in order to get the government to listen to its point of view. The issue for the government is that food imports are a small element of what could be an important trade agreement with a major importer of British goods and services.

Activity

In your exam, you will be asked questions about a case study of citizen action. If you consider the following questions, you will be prepared to answer any questions on the case study that you may be set.

Case study questions to consider

1 **Issue** – Is it clear what the campaigners/protesters are concerned about?

2 **Aim** – What is the group trying to achieve?

3 **Target groups** – Has the group identified target group(s) it needs to influence, in order to achieve its aim(s)?

4 **Opposition** – What groups oppose the views of those who are campaigning?

5 **Methods** – What methods of campaigning do the protesters use?

6 **Role of the media** – Do the campaigners try to achieve media coverage and is this coverage helpful?

7 **Organisation** – Do the campaigners belong to formal groups and is there a structure they are all working within?

8 **Membership** – Is there a formal membership structure to the campaign, and what is the size and composition of the membership?

9 **Finance** – How do the campaigners fund their actions?

10 **Public impact** – What is the public perception of the campaign and the methods it is using?

11 **Achievement** – Did the campaign achieve its aims?

12 **Citizenship processes** – What citizenship processes were involved in this campaign?

13 **Citizenship skills** – What citizenship skills were successfully applied?

Copy out the following table. Complete the table by carrying out more research on each of the three case studies on pages 161–63, to answer each of the 13 questions on page 164. Use the web links below the table to help you.

	Greta Thunberg	HS2	National Farmers' Union
1 Issue			
2 Aim			
3 Target groups			
4 Opposition			
5 Methods			
6 Role of the media			
7 Organisation			
8 Membership			
9 Finance			
10 Public impact			
11 Achievement			
12 Citizenship processes			
13 Citizenship skills			

Useful web links

Greta Thunberg:
- **https://fridaysforfuture.org**
- **https://time.com/person-of-the-year-2019-greta-thunberg**
- **www.bbc.co.uk/news/newsbeat-53902468**
- **www.npr.org/2019/09/23/763452863/transcript-greta-thunbergs-speech-at-the-u-n-climate-action-summit?t=1602667497774**

HS2:
- **www.gov.uk/government/organisations/high-speed-two-limited**
- **http://stophs2.org**
- **www.bbc.co.uk/news/magazine-24159571**

NFU:
- **www.nfuonline.com/news/latest-news/food-standards-petition**
- **www.countrysideonline.co.uk/back-british-farming/food-standards-petition**
- **www.thelondoneconomic.com/news/full-list-of-mps-who-voted-to-lower-our-food-standards-during-the-covid-pandemic/26/05**
- **www.itv.com/news/2020-10-12/commons-defeat-for-brexit-food-standards-amendment-despite-warnings-over-chlorinated-chicken**

Your Investigation

The second part of the first section of Question Paper 1 asks questions about your Investigation. You must undertake an Investigation of a citizenship issue either on your own or with others to gain this GCSE qualification.

1 Understand the range of methods and approaches that can be used by governments, organisations, groups and individuals to address citizenship issues in society, including practical citizenship actions

This element also relates to how groups and formal bodies operate. While you will develop understanding of this element through the core content relating to each theme, you are most likely to develop your understanding through the fifth section, which is assessed in Part A of Paper 1.

Table 16.2 indicates some of the methods and approaches with which you need to be familiar. Some of the methods and processes are common to more than one category, but the methods may be used in a different way.

2 Formulate citizenship enquiries, identifying and sequencing research questions to analyse citizenship ideas, issues and debates

This element relates to your citizenship Investigation – the approach you should take, whatever type of Investigation you undertake. (see Table 16.1)

3 Present your own and other viewpoints and represent the views of others, in relation to citizenship issues, causes, situations and concepts

This element can be demonstrated in the written examination papers and your own active citizenship Investigation.

4 Plan practical citizenship actions aimed at delivering a benefit or change for a particular community or wider society

This relates to the ability to plan practical citizenship actions.

Examples may include: collecting a petition to raise awareness of an issue, volunteering with others to carry out a community project or attending a meeting to speak on behalf of others.

5 Critically evaluate the effectiveness of citizenship actions to assess progress towards the intended aims and impact for the individuals, groups and communities affected

While this element relates to your own active citizenship Investigation, it could also relate to case study or source-based questions within the written papers. The intention of this skill is to measure your ability to understand how well any citizenship actions you are taking are progressing towards your goal, and how these actions impact upon the people and groups involved in your action.

Your Investigation is divided into three stages, each comprised of two parts: 1) Investigate, 2) Take action, 3) Reflect.

AQA provides an online booklet for you to record the evidence that you gather about your Investigation.

Your Investigation must relate to an element or elements of the AQA specification.

The exemplar Investigation on page 168 is based upon a local case study.

Table 16.1 Approaches to the Investigation

ACTIVITY	COMMENTARY
Formulate citizenship enquiries	What is the issue you are concerned about?
	Does it subdivide into several elements or issues?
	Have you thought through the possible directions an Investigation might take you?
Identify and sequence research questions	Following on, what evidence or materials do you need to help you investigate the issue?
	Have you thought through a route map of questions you need answered to enable you to formulate a judgement and conclusion?
Analyse citizenship ideas, issues and debates	Have you identified the citizenship element within the Investigation?
	Have you considered a range of ideas and views about the issue, even ones that you may disagree with?

Table 16.2 Examples of methods and approaches

EXAMPLES OF METHODS AND APPROACHES		COMMENTS
Government	Consultation	Government often consults widely about proposals or changes before preparing legislation. Formal consultation can take place via the publication of a 'Green Paper' – ideas for legislation.
	Legislation	Government, if it wishes to bring about change, introduces a bill before Parliament, which goes through several stages and votes before receiving the Royal Assent and becoming an Act of Parliament (legislation).
	Publicity and education	Government will also use public funds to campaign for or promote issues, like road safety or health.
	Financial support	Government makes funding available to many organisations to support their work.
	Taxation	Governments can seek to change public attitudes through the use of taxation policies, for example changing the duty on tobacco, alcohol, fuel or the use of sugar can impact on people's behaviour in relation to those products.
Organisations	Publicity	For many organisations that wish to influence public opinion, publicity regarding their work in the media is an important campaigning tool.
	Sponsorship	Sponsorship or endorsement by others or celebrities can enhance an organisation's reputation and credibility.
	Education	Many organisations wish to educate the public about their work and encourage participation. Often they will employ staff purely to promote their educational programmes, for example the RSPCA.
	Membership	By encouraging corporate or individual membership, a group can gain in status. Bodies like the National Trust, with a membership of 4.2 million, gain status through the size of their membership.
	Protest actions	Organisations often take action to promote their aims, from petitioning to lobbying. This is usually done in a lower-key way than that undertaken by groups. Many organisations have insider status in that they work with or are supported by government.
	Legal redress	Organisations will often use the legal system to safeguard or promote the issue that concerns them.
Groups	Publicity	Both national and local groups wishing to pursue a cause or make a change need to promote themselves. They can either create their own publicity or seek media coverage and also try to promote themselves via social media.
	Membership	All groups need to attract supporters/members to enable them to function and promote their cause. Many groups may not have a formal membership structure but work with supporters.
	Sponsorship	Depending upon the nature of the cause a local group may seek sponsorship, but often sponsors will be reluctant to support the work of some pressure groups.
Individuals	Working with others	An individual may often have to work with others to try to bring about change.
	Establishing a formal group	If they gather sufficient support, individuals may decide to formalise their campaign by establishing a named group.
	Media attention	Unless they have sufficient finance to promote themselves, individuals will need media attention to help promote their cause. Many individual campaigners use social media for both promotion and crowd funding.
	Lobbying	Individuals often use lobbying especially in regard to a local issue; they may try to meet with their local council or councillors, their MP or MEP to seek support and assistance.
	Forms of protest	Often an individual is able to promote and gain media attention by the means of protest they use. For example, a well-supported petition or a publicity stunt can gain media coverage or form a basis for a social media item.

Exemplar Investigation

Background

- The Labour-controlled council in Exeter has decided to go ahead and redevelop what is the current Exeter Bus and Coach Station, which is adjacent to a recently re-developed shopping centre that includes a John Lewis store.

- The council is planning to build a new indoor swimming pool and other leisure facilities.

- Business leaders have welcomed plans for this long-awaited redevelopment.

- The site will also contain a new bus station and a mix of new shops and restaurants. It is planned that the pool will be opened within two years.

- Many people are opposed to this development for a variety of reasons.

- Both the Conservative and Liberal Democrat groups on the council oppose this development.

- Many are concerned about the cost of the project. In 2016, the pool and bus station complex were budgeted to cost £26m. This was to be paid for using funds from the New Homes Bonus and the Community Infrastructure Levy, so there would be no direct cost to the council-tax payer. The cost is now estimated to be over £52m and the council expects to have to borrow up to £18m to meet the extra cost.

- Many residents are concerned about the new traffic management system that will be introduced as a result of the development.

- Others feel that the town needs a new pool, but that this is the wrong site and the pool should be built alongside the current athletics facilities further out of town. Some swimmers are concerned that the pool may not be large enough to hold national and international competitions.

If this was the scenario in your local town, you as a young person may have views or concerns about this type of development.

Figure 16.1 Exeter Bus and Coach Station

Prior to starting your Investigation

You have to decide whether you want to undertake this work alone or with others. Both have benefits and drawbacks and may depend upon the issue you wish to investigate.

Some points to bear in mind when thinking about working alone or with a group:

On your own or with others?
You can complete your Investigation on your own, but by working with others you may achieve more and create a greater impact.

How many people should you work with?
Too few and the workload is higher and there are problems if someone drops out or doesn't complete their work. Too many and the group can be difficult to co-ordinate. Also, who takes charge?

What skills are you looking for from the team?
Some may be good at research, others may have IT skills, others may be good at working with people, others at coming up with ideas.

Stage 1: Investigate

Decide on the question or issue

Look at a copy of the current GCSE specification and consider any issues that interest you. The issues may be local, national or global, or any combination of the three.

A question is where you are seeking an answer, some information or to raise a doubt about an issue or a problem that needs to be resolved.

A hypothesis is where you wish to examine and test a theory, proposition or idea. It is used as a starting point for further investigation.

You have decided to investigate issues relating to a swimming pool development.

This is a local issue and relates to the workings of local government, which is a part of the Politics and Participation section of work.

Questions one could pose are:

- Does the pool offer value for money?
- Is the pool in the right place?
- Does the town need a new pool?

Remember to keep your questions quite small as this work is only 15 per cent of the total assessment and you need to be able to complete the work in the time your school allows you.

Stage 1: Investigate

Carry out the research

Gather your secondary research materials

Consider the sources that are available to you. Consider issues such as validity, reliability, accuracy, currency and bias.

What primary source information do you need?

After reviewing your secondary evidence you may require primary source material and evidence.

Range of evidence and sources

Have you ensured that you have used a range of sources that are up to date? Evidence that may refute your initial ideas about your question/issue should not be disregarded.

The results

What were the results from your secondary and primary research? Are they clear or unclear? Is there a logical progression? Can the results be bunched around key elements of your question or issue?

The conclusions

Looking at the results, what conclusions can be drawn? How do these conclusions relate to your question/issue? Do your original thoughts about the issue still stand or does the evidence take you in another direction?

You need to think about information you need to gather that relates to the initial question that you have posed. Possible sources: the local council, the developers, the local media, opposition councillors, sporting groups in the town, bus companies, the local Chamber of Trade. Some of these materials, like interviews with people, are primary sources. Others, like newspaper cuttings, are secondary. **Primary sources** are original information or data or the results of interviewing people. **Secondary sources** are materials that others have already collected: newspaper articles, internet stories or radio or TV interviews.

After reviewing all your evidence, you might decide to change the focus of your Investigation and decide to find out what young people at your school feel about the proposed development and feed this information back to the council.

Stage 2: Take action

Plan the action

> ### What do we mean by 'taking action'?
> Presenting a case to others, organising an event, representing the views of others, carrying out a consultation, writing a policy proposal or a review of a policy, setting up an action group. Which is most suited to your question or issue?

> ### Create an action plan
> Break down the action you wish to take into a sequence of bite-sized pieces and resolve who is doing what and when they have to complete their task – an action plan.

> ### Get approval
> Ensure that your teacher has approved your course of action. Ensure you have identified everyone you need to speak to so that any permissions can be sorted out in advance of your action.

> ### Review your planning
> Ensure everybody understands what they have to do. If issues arise, have you considered other options? Have you ensured that the action relates to your question/issue and that it can achieve its aims?

You have now decided to gather information in the form of a survey and give it to the council, showing the views of young people about the swimming pool development.

- What needs to be done?
- The school needs to agree you can do this.
- You need to agree a time scale to complete the task.
- Do you want to have speakers coming into school or just have a static display about the pool?
- Do you write a background leaflet to help inform students?
- How many students are going to be asked their views? You need enough to make the results reliable.
- What form will your questionnaire take: written survey, a number of questions or an online response format, or in-depth interviews with a small number of fellow students?

Stage 2: Take action

Carry out the action

> ### Reviewing the action plan
> Is the action plan up to date? Is there a clear line of communication between group members? Is someone in charge and able to make changes if need be?

> Have you set yourself targets in regard to your action so that you know you have succeeded? Have you ensured that all those outside your group who are involved in the action are aware of their role and have been contacted?

> Have you considered how others view your action? Have you built into your action plan gathering data, opinions or views from others about your action? This information will be helpful when you think about evaluating your action.

> Now carry out your planned action.

- Have you ensured that you or the group know what to do and that you have clearly planned for most eventualities?
- Have you ensured that the questions you are asking are not biased and will give useful data?

Stage 3: Reflect

The impact of the action

Gathering the evidence

Did you remember to seek others' views about your action? Is this information in a data format that will give you evidence you can use? Has each member of the group written or spoken about their contribution and views?

Successful?

To what extent was your action successful? Did it achieve the aims you set yourselves? Is there evidence to support your view about its degree of success?

Achievement

To what extent did your action make a difference? To what extent did the action relate back to the points raised by your research and your question/issue?

- You now need to collate all your results and ensure that all the elements fit together. You need to consider whether you achieved what you set out to do.
- Did you present your evidence to the council? Did you consider making a press release to the local paper about what you were doing and what the results were of your survey? Where did you send it?

Stage 3: Reflect

Evaluate the whole process

Reflect

What were the successful elements of the Investigation? What things could have been improved? What is the evidence to support your statements?

In relation to the question/issue, what conclusions did you reach after you had taken the action? Do you feel you made a difference? If so, how?

This Investigation enabled you to develop your citizenship knowledge and apply your understanding of citizenship skills, processes and methods to a real-life issue of your choice. What have you learnt and/or gained by doing this work?

Reflecting upon your Investigation, how do you think it could have been improved?

- Topic choice
- Question/issue(s)
- Research element
- Reviewing the evidence to draw conclusions
- Deciding on a form of action, taking action, working with others and the impact of my actions
- What conclusions can be drawn from this work?

Remember to keep a clear focus on what you want to achieve and limit the task to what is achievable within the time and resources you have available. Keep some record of what you have undertaken. Make use of the AQA Investigation Portfolio to record your progress. The main thing is to enjoy what you are doing and try to make a difference!

Glossary

Advocacy – speaking out to promote a cause or an issue.

Agencies – organisations and bodies that are a part of a major institution, for example the UN or EU.

Aggravating circumstance – something that makes a crime more serious.

Anarchy – a system where no form of government operates; when there is a total breakdown in society; for example, after a civil war a state of anarchy is said to exist.

Apathy – a lack of interest by citizens in the electoral and political process.

Apartheid – a system of government in South Africa based upon the separation of racial groups within different communities and a governmental system based on power being held by the minority white population.

Backbencher – a member of the House of Commons who is not a government minister or opposition spokesperson. They sit behind the front row of seats in the Chamber, hence the name backbencher.

Barrister – graduates who become specialists in a narrow aspect of the law and are employed by solicitors on behalf of their clients to represent them.

Battery – occurs when a person intentionally or recklessly inflicts unlawful force. You can be charged with assault and battery, or just assault or just battery.

Bicameral – the name given to a parliament made up of two chambers, like the UK system with the House of Commons and the House of Lords.

Boycott – refusing to buy goods or use a service in order to achieve a desired political outcome. The original term related to Captain Boycott, an Irish landowner whose tenants refused to pay their rent.

Brexit – a slogan used by the Leave campaign in the 2016 EU Referendum to signify its aims. The 'Br' stood for Britain or the UK, and 'exit' for leaving the European Union.

British values – the values that are associated with living in modern-day Britain.

Budget – an annual statement made by the Chancellor of the Exchequer to the House of Commons about the taxation policy for the forthcoming year.

By-election – an election held in a seat after the retirement or death of the sitting member.

Central government – term used to describe the government of the United Kingdom.

Chief constable – the chief police officer within each regional police force.

Citizens Advice office – locally based offices of Citizens Advice, a registered charity that provides advice, support and help related to a range of issues including legal, financial and consumer, and issues relating to local authorities and central government services.

Citizenship – a legal status conferred by a state upon members of the state, indicating their membership of the state.

Civil law – the type of law that deals with disputes between individuals when damages are awarded.

Civil service – employees of the state who administer public policy.

Closed party list system – the electoral system used in England, Scotland and Wales to elect MEPs.

Coalition government – a government formed by more than one party. The parties agree on a policy platform and each holds posts within the government. These arrangements can be for a fixed term or for a full Parliament, as in 2010.

Codification – in a legal context it is the bringing together or organising of separate elements into a single document or system.

Command economy – a national economy where all elements of the economic system are controlled by the government.

Common law – law based upon judges' rulings in court.

Commonwealth Charter – a document that lays down the principles associated with Commonwealth membership.

Communism – a classless system where there is no private property, the means of production are collectively owned, and the only political party is the Communist Party, e.g. Russia (until 1991) and China.

Competence – relates to areas of policy delegated by countries to the EU.

Conservatism – an eighteenth-century political ideology based upon a traditional belief in the family, the Church and nationalism. It has a paternalistic approach to community affairs. This ideology has evolved to encompass parties from the New Right to the Christian Democrats.

Constituency – a named geographical area consisting on average of between 56,000 voters in Wales and 72,200 in England, who elect a single MP to the UK Parliament. All parliamentary boundaries are currently being reviewed and will be finalised in July 2023, with the aim that all constituencies (with the exception of those composed of islands) will consist of around 73,000 electors.

Core executive – the most important policy-makers within the executive around the Prime Minister.

Council of Europe – was founded in 1949 and is an intergovernmental organisation that aims to promote human rights, democracy and the rule of law within its 47 member states. This body established the European Convention on Human Rights.

Council of the European Union – meetings of ministers from member states of the EU.

Councillor – a citizen who is elected to serve on local councils.

Criminal law – the type of law where individuals are charged by the state with an offence and if found guilty are punished by the state.

Crossbench – a group of members in the House of Lords who do not belong to any political grouping but operate as a formal group. For example, ex senior civil servants belong to this group.

Crown Prosecution Service (CPS) – an independent government body that determines whether charges should be brought. It prosecutes cases in the courts on behalf of the state.

Custodial – a sentence that involves imprisonment.

Declaration of the Rights of Man and of the Citizen 1789 – following the French Revolution, the new National Assembly declared that: 'the ignorance, neglect, or contempt of the rights of man are the sole cause of public calamities and of the corruption of governments, have determined to set forth in a solemn declaration the natural, unalienable, and sacred rights of man.'

Democracy – a political system based upon the concept of people having the power to decide through an open and fair electoral system, where electors can choose from competing political parties or groups. The word comes from the ancient Greek for people and power.

Departmental select committee – a committee of the House of Commons made up of MPs who monitor the work of a government department and publish reports on the work of the department.

Deterrence – a principle associated with sentencing policy. It aims to reduce levels of crime as a result of those considering a criminal act not carrying out that act due to the nature of the sentence they will receive.

Devolution – the transfer of power from a greater body to a lesser body, e.g. the UK Parliament granting powers to Scotland.

Devolved and reserved powers – devolved powers are those transferred by the UK government to the devolved governments. Reserved powers are those that are still held by the UK government.

Devolved government – name given to the bodies created under the policy of devolution, e.g. the Scottish Parliament.

Direct democracy – a system of government where all citizens take part in decision-making. A modern form of direct democracy is the use of referendums.

Directly elected mayors – posts within local councils in England and Wales that are directly elected by the voters. They are responsible for the running and direction of their local council. It is one of several ways in which local councils can be organised. One of the first to be created was the Mayor of London.

Director of Public Prosecutions (DPP) – head of the Crown Prosecution Service (CPS) in England and Wales. The DPP is appointed by and responsible to the Attorney General but is independent of government.

Discrimination – treating a person or group of people unfairly on the basis of their sex, gender, race, etc.

Either-way criminal offence – can be dealt with either by magistrates or before a judge and jury at the Crown Court. Such offences include theft and handling stolen goods. A defendant can insist on their right to trial in the Crown Court. Magistrates can also decide a case is so serious that it should be dealt with in the Crown Court – which can impose tougher sentences if the defendant is found guilty.

The Electoral Commission – a government-established body that monitors and oversees all UK elections and referendums.

E-media – all forms of media related to the internet; e stands for electronic.

Emigration – when people leave their own country to live permanently elsewhere.

Employers' association – industry- or regionally based bodies that seek to represent the interests of groups of employers.

E-petition – a way citizens can request Parliament to debate an issue. If a petition attracts 100,000 signatures, a committee of MPs decides whether it is suitable for debate in Parliament.

Equality – the concept that everyone should have an equal opportunity to make the most of their life and talents.

Equality Act 2010 – brought together 116 pieces of legislation to provide Britain with a new discrimination law to protect individuals from unfair treatment. Promotes a fair and more equal society.

Equality and Human Rights Commission – established in 2007, it took over the work of three previous equality organisations: the Commission for Racial Equality (CRE), the Disability Rights Commission (DRC) and the Equal Opportunities Commission (EOC), as well as taking on responsibility for protecting and promoting equality and human rights for everyone. It is a statutory non-departmental government body.

Euro – the common currency used by the Eurozone (19 members of the EU).

European Arrest Warrant – a system within the European Union that allows a police force in one country to request a police force in another to arrest someone and extradite them.

European Commission – appointed officials from member countries of the EU who draft policy initiatives and direct the workings of the EU.

European Convention on Human Rights – a convention that lays down basic human rights. It is based upon the UNDHR, and is overseen by the Council of Europe.

European Council – meetings of the heads of government of EU member states.

European Court of Human Rights – Court of the Council of Europe that sits in Strasbourg and rules on the European Convention on Human Rights. It must not be confused with the European Court of Justice, which is the court of the European Union.

European Parliament – the directly elected Parliament of the European Union.

Executive – an element of government made up of government ministers, advisers and senior civil servants who determine the policy of government.

Fairness – treating people equally and according to the circumstances.

Fascism – a state that is headed by a dictator and in which the state has control over everything, often forcibly, e.g. the interwar period in Italy, Germany and Spain.

Federalist – a person or view that supports greater EU integration, leading to a United States of Europe.

'First instance' case – where trials are first held.

First-past-the-post – an election system based upon the person with the highest number of votes cast being elected.

Freedom – the ability to act, speak or think as one likes.

Frontbencher – a government minister or shadow minister who sits on the front row of seats in the House of Commons chamber facing each other across the table in the chamber.

G7 – a forum for the leaders of the seven richest countries in the world to meet and discuss economic and political issues. Its members are Canada, France, Germany, Italy, Japan, the United Kingdom and the United States. The EU President of the Commission also attends.

General Election – an election when the entire UK Parliament is elected. Under the Fixed Term Parliaments Act 2011, elections were held after a fixed five-year period from the previous election, but this Act was repealed in 2020.

Geneva Conventions – the most important conventions relating to how civilians and others should be treated during a time of war.

Global identity – the concept that some aspects of identity are now global in nature.

Gross Domestic Product (GDP) – the value of all the goods and services created in a country, normally measured on an annual basis.

Gross National Income (GNI) – GDP minus income earned by non-residents plus income received from non-residents.

Group identity – the identity associated with belonging to a group.

Hague Convention – deals with the rules governing the conduct of war.

Hard power – the ability to use military or economic power to achieve one's aims.

House of Commons – the first chamber of Parliament, made up of 650 elected members. The government is formed based on the composition of this chamber. It is a legislative chamber that also holds the government to account.

House of Lords – the second chamber of Parliament. Since 1911, it is far less important than the House of Commons. Its main purpose is as a revising chamber. Made up of non-elected members.

Human right – a fundamental right that every person is entitled to have, to be or to do.

The Human Rights Act (HRA) – passed in 1998 and came into force in 2000. This Act brought together numerous pieces of human rights legislation and gave UK citizens easier access to the European Court of Human Rights.

Humanitarian aid – non-military aid given to countries and people in need, for example food, shelter, medical help.

Identity – the characteristics that determine whom or what a person is.

Immigration – the movement of people who come to live permanently in a foreign country. For example people from Hong Kong moving to live permanently in the UK.

IMPRESS – the official press regulator.

The Independent Press Standards Organisation (IPSO) – set up to handle complaints and conduct investigations into standards and compliance.

Indictable – a serious criminal offence that must be heard in a Crown Court.

Individual liberty – the concept that in a modern democracy people have the freedom to make their own choices and decisions.

Inflation – a rise in the average level of prices over a set period of time, which also corresponds to a fall in the purchasing power of your income.

International Criminal Court – set up in 1998 to try persons indicted for crimes against humanity or war crimes. By 2020, 120 nations had agreed to work with the Court.

International Humanitarian Law (IHL) – a body of law associated with international disputes and the conduct of war and people affected by war.

Judiciary – the part of the UK system of governance that is responsible for its legal system and that consists of all the judges in its courts of law.

Jury service – citizens are required to serve on juries as a civic duty. Twelve people serve. They are selected at random from the register of voters.

Justice – behaviour or treatment that is morally right and fair.

Lay member – a person who serves on a body/organisation but is not a qualified professional within the specialism of that body. They are there to represent the wider general public.

Legal executive – legally qualified specialists employed largely by solicitors.

Legislation – or statute law; laws passed by Parliament.

Legislature – a body, normally elected, that decides upon the laws that apply to a state. In the UK, Parliament is the legislature; in the USA, Congress is the legislature.

Liberal democracy – a system of government based upon representative democracy and linked to freedoms and rights for citizens.

Liberalism – a political philosophy dating from the eighteenth century, based on individual liberty, freedom of worship and free trade. It evolved into social liberalism, with a concern for welfare rights. It encompasses Liberal, Free Democratic and Radical parties.

Local election – elections held for councillors to local councils, held on a fixed date in May after the fixed term of office has expired.

Lord Speaker – the Speaker of the House of Lords.

Lords Spiritual – the 26 bishops of the Church of England who are members of the House of Lords.

Magistrate – part-time community volunteers who determine verdicts and sentences in local Magistrates' Courts.

Magna Carta – known as the Great Charter, signed by King John in 1215. It established the rights and powers of the King and the people of England.

Manifesto – a document produced by a political party at the time of an election, outlining the policies it would like to introduce.

Market economy – a national economy where most of the economy is run by the private sector and the state owns and runs limited elements.

Mass media – the means of communicating to a large number of people at the same time, e.g. television, newspapers, the internet.

Mediation – a process of involving outsiders in a dialogue to try to resolve a dispute between two parties.

Member of Parliament (MP) – a citizen elected to Parliament who serves as a Member of Parliament, normally as a member of a political party.

Migration – the movement of people out of one country and into another.

Mitigating circumstance – something that makes the charge or the offender's culpability less serious.

Mixed economy – a national economy that has some elements run and owned by the state and others run by the private sector.

Multicultural society – a society that comprises people from a range of cultural, ethnic and religious backgrounds.

Multiculturalism – a concept regarding the co-existence of diverse cultures in a society. A multicultural society is one in which these different groups live side by side and there is a mutual respect for each group's culture and traditions.

Multi-party system – a political system where several parties are vying for power.

Multiple identity – the concept that a person can assume different identities at different times and in different situations.

NACRO – a body that seeks to represent the views of offenders.

National identity – an identity associated with being a citizen of a specific country.

Nationalised – where the state owns and runs a part of the economy.

Nature v. nurture – a debate about whether a person's personality and identity are most affected by their biological background or by the way in which they are brought up.

NDPB – a Non-Departmental Public Body, formerly a quango. *See Quango.*

Neighbourhood Watch – a voluntary scheme in which people in a given area work with the police to help reduce crime.

Net migration – the difference in the number of people coming to live in a country and the number who leave a country to live in another country.

New media – all non-traditional forms of media.

New Right – a view of conservatism linked to Margaret Thatcher and the Conservative Party in the UK and Ronald Reagan and the Republican Party in the USA. The New Right ideology argued for less state provision, less state interference in business and lower taxation, in order to increase national wealth and allow for greater personal empowerment and social mobility.

Non-custodial – a criminal sentence that does not involve imprisonment.

Non-democratic – a system of government that lacks some or all of the elements that make up a democratic political system.

Non-governmental organisation (NGO) – can be national or international. Many of them are charities that provide services to those in need, similar to those provided by government. Many work with government agencies and can receive funds from government.

Ofcom – the Office of Communications: a government regulator for elements of the media industry.

Office for National Statistics (ONS) – a government body that collects and provides background data.

Petition of Right 1628 – a petition to King Charles I by Parliament demanding in return for taxation a number of basic human rights.

PMQs – 30 minutes each Wednesday when the Prime Minister faces questions from MPs in the chamber of the House of Commons. Six questions are allocated to the Leader of the Opposition.

Police and Crime Commissioner – a directly elected official who is responsible for the running of a regional police force outside London.

Police community support officer – officers who are police-trained and uniformed, but do not have police powers. Employed by each regional police force.

Pressure group – an organised body of citizens who share a common interest in an issue and promote their cause through a variety of actions.

The Prime Minister – the head of government in the UK; the monarch is Head of State. In the USA, the President holds both posts. The Prime Minister is normally the leader of the largest party in the House of Commons and is an MP. They are appointed by the monarch after a General Election and have the title First Lord of the Treasury.

Principle – a basic truth or idea that underpins a system of beliefs associated with a given society.

Private Member's Bill – a bill, a draft for a law, that is proposed by a Member of Parliament. A lottery is held each year and if an MP comes out towards the top, they stand a chance of their bill becoming law.

Proportional representation – a system of voting whereby the number of people elected relates to the number (percentage) of votes cast.

Proxy – in regard to voting, allowing another to vote on your behalf. You have to officially apply and nominate a named person to be your proxy.

Quango – a Quasi-Autonomous Non-Government Organisation. These are bodies that work with government, sometimes carrying out services on behalf of government and funded by government, but partially independent from government. Government now uses the term 'NDPBs' to describe them, as the word 'quango' has become associated with negative media coverage of these bodies.

Queen's Counsel – barristers may apply to become QCs, or KCs if there is a king on the throne. This is recognition that they have become experts in their specialist field.

Question time – the time allocated each week in Parliament where ministers face questions from Members of Parliament and are held to account for their actions.

Real government spending – the change in the amount a government spends after taking account of inflation.

Recorded crime – crimes that are reported to and recorded by the police.

Referendum – a vote on a single issue, where governments or other bodies wish to seek the views of electors on an issue, for example the 2016 referendum on the UK's membership of the European Union.

Rehabilitation – an aim of sentencing, seeking to change the behaviour of the offender.

Reparation – where an offender has to pay towards the damage they have caused.

Representative democracy – a system of government where citizens are elected to represent others in an assembly. A UK example of such a citizen would be an MP or councillor.

Responsibility – the state or fact of having to do something.

Right – a moral or legal entitlement to have or do something.

Rule of law – a basic principle of a democratic society that the law applies equally to all people.

Salisbury convention – a post-war convention whereby the House of Lords does not vote down a proposal from the Commons if it was in the election manifesto of the government.

Sanctions – measures taken by a state against others to achieve a change in policy or action.

Secondary action – when a worker not directly involved in a trade dispute takes action to support other workers.

Security Council – the major decision-making body of the United Nations. Made up of five permanent members and ten elected member countries. The UK is one of the permanent members.

Social media – the ways in which people interact with each other on the internet, for example Twitter and Facebook.

Socialism – a political ideology dating mainly from the nineteenth century, based upon the common ownership of the economy, equality and opportunity. It encompasses parties ranging from Communists to Social Democrats.

Soft power – the ability to influence others through the influence of your culture, political and foreign policy values.

Solicitor – mainly law graduates who cover a range of legal work, both civil and criminal, and have to be formally qualified.

Sovereignty – the power and authority that a country has to make decisions about itself and its relations with others.

The Speaker – a Member of Parliament elected by other members to chair the proceedings of the House of Commons and manage the business of the House.

Special adviser – specialist and political advisers to ministers and opposition spokespersons; they can have temporary civil service status, paid for by the taxpayer.

Special constable – volunteers who help the police on a part-time basis in their local community. They do not have police powers.

Strike – the withdrawal of one's labour; refusing to work.

Supplementary vote – a voting system used in the UK where voters have a second vote that is used in the election process if no candidate gets 50 per cent of the first-choice votes (see page 124).

Supreme Court – the final court of appeal in the UK for civil cases, and for criminal cases from England, Wales and Northern Ireland. It hears cases of great public or constitutional importance that affect the whole population.

Tiers – another term for levels of government.

Tolerance – a concept based upon the idea that in a modern society people show understanding of others with differing views and opinions.

Trade union – an organisation that employees join to provide collective representation with employers regarding, for example, pay, conditions of employment, and health and safety issues. An example would be the RMT (the National Union of Rail, Maritime and Transport Workers), which represents those working on the London Underground.

Trades Union Congress (TUC) – a national body representing most trade unions in the UK.

Traditional media – newsprint, radio, television, cinema.

Transnational group – a political grouping in the European Parliament made up of MEPs from several countries.

Two-party system – a political system that is dominated by two political parties, each of which may at some time form a government.

Ultra vires – acting beyond your legal power or authority.

United Nations Charter – a document that lays down the aims of the United Nations.

Universal Declaration of Human Rights – an international law setting out a set of universal human rights under the auspices of the United Nations.

US Declaration of Independence 1789 – a declaration related to the founding of the United States of America following the War of Independence from Britain. The Declaration protects freedom of speech, freedom of religion, the right to keep and bear arms, the freedom of assembly and the freedom to petition.

Values – standards of behaviour that are accepted by a society.

Veto – the ability to be able to vote down any decision.

Volunteering – giving your time without pay to help others.

Voter turnout – the number of voters who actually vote, against the total number who could vote, normally expressed as a percentage.

Whips – Members of Parliament appointed by their party leader to organise their MPs, ensuring their attendance and their vote.

Index

absolute monarchy 146

Abu Qatada 80

accountability 106, 113, 132–3

active citizenship 161–71
  case studies 161–4
  investigation 166–71

additional member system (AMS) 124

adjournment debates 134

adult social care 117

Advertising Standards Authority (ASA) 22

advocacy 172

Afghanistan 32

Age UK 159

agencies 172

aggravating circumstance 172

Alternate Dispute Resolution (ADR) 56, 57

Amnesty International 150

anarchy 94, 172

ancillary orders 73

apathy 172

apartheid 32, 172

arbitration 56, 57

aristocracy 146

authoritarian rule 146

backbench debates 134

backbenchers 134, 136, 172

Banksy 44–5

barristers 55, 172

battery 172

BBC 17, 18, 37

Bell, Martin 149

bicameral 172

Black Lives Matter 158

Black Rod 135

Blair, Tony 89, 96–7, 130, 131, 138, 139

Boundary Commission 122

Bourne, Katy 86

boycotts 32, 40, 172

Brexit 28–9, 131, 143, 151, 172
  referendum 19, 28, 110, 128

Brexit Party 130, 132

British Bill of Rights 79–80

British Board of Film Classification 22

British Constitution 96–100

British values 1–2

Broadcast Advertising Clearance Centre 22

Brown, Gordon 137, 139

budgets 105, 115, 172

burglary 69

business rates 115

by-elections 121, 122, 172

Cabinet 96, 139

Callaghan, James 139

Cameron, David 11, 28, 96, 139

Campaign to Protect Rural England (CPRE) 42

campaigning 88, 151, 152–3

celebrity influencers 40, 152

censorship 21, 22

central government 102, 172

Chairman of Ways and Means 135

Chancellor of the Exchequer 96, 115, 139

CharityJob 154

chief constables 172

Chilcott Report 142

child benefit 119

child protection 82

children's rights 3, 95

Churchill, Winston 26, 94

citizen journalism 16, 22

Citizens Advice 55, 158, 172

Civil Aspects of International Child Abduction 82

civil law 55, 59, 172

civil partnerships 89

civil service 98, 100, 141–2, 172

Clegg, Nick 96

Clerk of the House of Commons 136

Clerk of Parliaments 135

closed party list system 143, 172

coalition governments 137, 172

codification 173

collective responsibility 138

combined authorities 104

command economy 116, 173

common law 64, 173

Commons Deputy Speakers 135

Commonwealth 26–7
  Charter 173

communism 173

communities
  community cohesion 11, 12
  participation in 2, 43

community sentences 75

Compassion in World Farming 151

competence 173

conciliation 56, 57

Confederation of British Industry (CBI) 66

Conlon, Gerry 89

conservatism 130, 173

Conservative Party 79–80, 129–30, 131

constituency 173

constitutional monarchies 146

Constitutional Reform Act (2005) 100, 127

Corbyn, Jeremy 29, 131

core executive 173

corporation tax 115

Council of Europe 26, 49, 54, 77, 79, 173

Council of the European Union 26, 173

council tax 115

councillors 36, 173

Countryside Alliance 42

county councils 103

Covid-19 pandemic 116, 117–18, 128, 151

crime 67–71
    age of offenders 71
    punishments 49, 72–4, 75, 80
    sentencing 71, 72, 73–4, 75
    types of 67–8
Crime and Disorder Act (1998) 76

crime statistics 70–1

Crime Survey for England and Wales (CSEW) 67, 68, 69

Criminal Justice Act (2003) 72

criminal law 55, 59, 173

crossbench 173

Crown Prosecution Service (CPS) 53–4, 173

cultural identity 7–8

custodial sentencing 173

death penalty 49, 72

debates 133, 134, 137

Declaration of Independence, USA 99

Declaration of the Rights of Man and of the Citizen 1789 173

Defence Secretary 96, 139

defence spending 117

democracy 1, 11, 173
    concept of 93–5
    criteria 145
    participation in 36–45
demonstrations 40, 153

Department for International Development 33

departmental select committee 173

deportation 50

Detention and Training Orders 75

deterrence 173

devolution 7, 102, 107, 173

devolved government 106–9, 173

devolved and reserved powers 173

dictatorship 94, 146

direct action 157

direct democracy 93, 174

directly elected mayors 174

Director of Public Prosecutions (DPP) 53, 174

disability rights 95

Disasters Emergency Committee (DEC) 33

discrimination 174

discrimination legislation 49–50

dispute resolution 56, 57

district councils 103

diversity 155

divorce 59

Do-it 154

duties 2

economic rights 63

education 6, 70, 80, 105, 117, 120, 155

either-way criminal offence 174

elections 38–9
    by-elections 121, 122
    European Parliamentary elections 143–4
    general elections 97, 110–11, 112, 121, 123, 124, 138
    local elections 110, 112
    safe/marginal seats 123
    turnout 38–9, 112–13
Electoral Commission 113, 174

electoral systems 121–3, 124, 143–8

e-media 16, 40, 174

emergency debates 137

emigration from UK 9, 174

employers' associations 66–7, 174

English votes for English laws (EVEL) 110

e-petitions 133, 137, 150, 151, 174

Equal Partnership campaign 89

Equal Pay Act (1970) 3, 48, 66, 95

equality 2, 3, 47, 95, 155–6, 174

Equality Act (2010) 2, 48–9, 95, 174

Equality and Human Rights Commission 49, 155–6, 174

euro 174

European Arrest Warrants (EAWs) 50, 174

European Commission 26, 174

European Convention on Human Rights (ECHR) 26, 49, 64, 77, 79–80, 81, 174

European Council 26, 174

European Court of Human Rights 26, 54, 77, 79, 174

European migrant crisis 44–5

European Parliament 26, 143–4, 174

European Union (EU) 9, 25–6, 32, 79
    UK and 19, 27–8, 30, 128
Exeter Bus and Coach Station investigation 168

Extinction Rebellion 153

fairness 47, 174

fascism 174

federalist 175

first-instance case 175

first-past-the-post (FPTP) system 121–3, 124, 143, 175

Fixed-Term Parliaments Act (2011) 121, 137, 139

Food Matters campaign 159

food standards petition 163

Foreign, Commonwealth and Development Office (FCDO) 33

Foreign Secretary 96, 139

Francis Report 142

freedom 175

Freedom of Information Act (2000) 18

freedom of the press 18

freedom of speech 2, 95

frontbenchers 136, 175

G7 175

GDP (Gross Domestic Product) 24, 113–15, 175

General Agreement on Tariffs and Trade (GATT) 27

general elections 97, 112, 121, 123, 124, 138, 175
  selection of candidates 110–11
Geneva Conventions (1949) 81–2, 175
global identity 3, 14, 175
GNI (Gross National Income) 113, 175
Good Friday Agreement 31, 106
government 100, 102–20
  accountability of 132–3
  administration, organisation of 140–2
  devolved government 106–9
  executive 100, 125, 174
  formation of 137
  income 115, 116
  judiciary 98, 100, 125, 126, 175
  legislative process 136–7
  legislature 97, 100, 125, 176
  local government 102–6
  multi-party system 130
  organisation of powers 109–10
  party-political system 129–32
  power of 96
  selection of candidates 110–11
  service provision 115–16
  spending 113–14, 116, 117–19
  two-party system 129–30
Greater London Authority (GLA) 104–5
Greenpeace 156–7
Grenfell Tower fire 37, 91
Grenfell United 91
group identity 3, 13, 175
Guildford Four 89
gun ownership 49, 99
Hague Convention (1899 and 1907) 81, 82, 175
Hansard 137
hard power 24, 175
hate crimes 67
Her Majesty's Official Opposition 97, 132–3
Hidden Housing Scandal campaign 92
high-profile groups 141
Hillsborough disaster 90
Holyrood, *see* Scottish Parliament

Home Secretary 96, 139
House of Commons 97, 109, 110, 127, 128–9, 132, 133, 134–6, 175
House of Lords 97, 111, 127–8, 129, 132, 133, 135, 175
housing benefit 119
HS2 scheme 118, 161
human rights 37, 49, 155–6, 175; *see also* European Convention on Human Rights
Human Rights Act (HRA, 1998) 37, 62–4, 79, 80–1, 175
humanitarian aid 175
hybrid bills 136
identity 3, 6–14, 37, 175
immigration 7, 9, 10–11, 175
IMPRESS (press regulator) 21–2, 175
imprisonment 72–3
income tax 115
Independent Parliamentary Standards Authority (IPSA) 20
Independent Press Standards Organisation (IPSO) 21–2, 175
indictable 175
individual identity 3
individual liberty 1, 175
industrial action 65, 66
inflation 175
INQUEST 88
insider groups 41–2
Institute of Directors (IoD) 66
interest groups 41
International Committee of the Red Cross 82
International Criminal Court (ICC) 50, 82, 175
International Humanitarian Law (IHL) 81, 175
international organisations 24–35
  disputes and conflicts 30–2
  NGO response to humanitarian crises 33–5
  role of UK 24–7
  UK and EU 27–30
International Red Cross/Red Crescent movement 34, 82

International Security Assistance Force (ISAF) 25
Interpol 50
Iraq War 30–1
ivo 154
Jamieson, David 87
Johnson, Boris 28, 29, 33, 96, 106, 131, 138, 139
jury service 47, 84–5, 175
justice 47, 176
justice system 52–60
  rights and entitlements at differing ages 58–9
justices of the peace (JPs)/magistrates 47, 85–6, 176
Khan, Sadiq 106
Kony, Joseph 82
Labour Party 65, 129–30, 131
Law Lords 100
lay members 176
Leader of the Official Opposition 132–3
leafleting 40
legal executives 55, 176
legal representatives 55
legal rights 49–50, 58–9, 63
legal system 36, 46–50, 54, 55, 84–92
  court structure 56
  democratic and citizenship actions 91–2
  fundamental principles of law 46–8
  police 52–4
  rights in local to global situations 49–50
  role of citizen in 84–7
  role of groups in 88–90
  rules and laws 48–9
  in UK 59–60
legislation 176
Leveson Inquiry 21, 142
LGBTQ rights 63–4
liberal democracy 93, 149, 176
Liberal Democrat Party 131
Liberalism 130, 176
Lloyd George, David 138
lobbying 40, 149, 157

local elections 110, 112, 176
local government 102–6
London boroughs 103
London riots (August 2011) 70
Lord Speaker 135, 176
Lords of Appeal in Ordinary 127
Lords Spiritual 111, 127, 176
magistrates/Justices of the Peace (JPs) 47, 85–6, 176
Magna Carta 62, 99, 176
Make UK 66
Major, John 131, 139
manifestos 97, 115, 128, 176
market economy 116, 176
mass media 16–18, 176
    newspapers 16–17, 18, 19, 20, 21, 22
    television 16, 17, 18
May, Theresa 9, 29, 96, 138, 139
mayors 103, 106, 107, 124
Médecins Sans Frontières (MSF) 35
media 16–22, 40, 106
    censorship of 21, 22
    e-media 16, 40
    and EU membership 19, 28
    and political agenda 44–5
    regulation of 20–1
    role of 18–20
mediation 31, 56, 57, 176
Members of the European Parliament (MEPs) 143
Members of Parliament (MPs) 36, 132, 176
    accountability 113
    constituency work 134
    expenses 18, 20, 122, 129, 133
    outside earnings 134
    and PMQs 132–3
    role of 133–4
    work in Parliament 134
metropolitan districts 103
migration 176
military juntas 146
Minister of Defence 96, 139
ministerial departments 140
Miscarriages of Justice Organisation (Mojo) 89

mitigating circumstance 176
mixed economy 115, 176
modern-day democracies 93–4
monarchy 94, 98, 129, 146
morals/moral values 2
multi-cause groups 41
multicultural society 176
multiculturalism 2, 11, 13, 176
multi-party system 130, 176
multiple identity 176
NACRO (prison reform group) 74, 176
National Assembly, Wales 106–7, 108, 109
National Citizenship Service programme 42
National Crime Agency 98
national debt 115
National Farmers' Union (NFU) 163
National Health Service (NHS) 119, 131
national identity 3, 7, 8, 11, 13, 14, 176
National Infrastructure Commission 118
National Insurance 115
nationalised 176
nature v. nurture debate 13, 176
negotiation 56, 57
Neighbourhood Watch 87, 176
net migration 9, 176
New Labour 130, 131
new media 16, 177
New Right 131, 177
newspapers 16–17, 18
    censorship of 21, 22
    and EU membership referendum 19, 128
    Leveson Inquiry 21, 142
    MPs' expenses 18, 20
    phone hacking 20
No More Violence against Women campaign 159
non-custodial sentences 73, 75, 177
non-democratic political system 145, 148, 177

Non-Departmental Public Bodies (NDPBs) 141, 176
non-governmental organisations (NGOs) 33–5, 177
non-ministerial departments 141
non-proportional voting systems 124
North Atlantic Treaty Organization (NATO) 25, 32
Northern Ireland 8, 60, 143
    Good Friday Agreement 31, 106
    local government 103, 104
Northern Ireland Assembly 106–7, 108, 109
North Korea 148
Ofcom 22, 177
Office for National Statistics (ONS) 7, 177
Official Opposition 97, 132–3
oligarchy 146
ombudsmen 56, 57
one-party state 94, 146
opposition parties 97
outsider groups 41–2
Oxfam 34
Parliament, Westminster 96, 100, 102
    bicameral nature 126–9
    ceremonial roles 135–6
    functions of 129
    key parliamentary roles 134–5, 136
    law-making 137
    sovereignty of 97
parliamentary constituencies 121, 122
participation in democracy 36–45
    citizens' contribution to 149–50
    opportunities and barriers 36–41
    role of organisations 41–2
party-political system 129–32
patronage 139
PAYE system (Pay As You Earn) 115
peace-keeping missions 25
Pearle 66
personal rights 63
personal social services 117
Petition of Right 1628 177

petitions 40, 163
    e-petitions 133, 137, 150, 151
    standards for 151
Petitions Committee 150–1
phone hacking scandal 20
Plaid Cymru 132
police 52–4, 98
police community support offi-
    cer 177
Police and Crime Commissioners 41,
    52–3, 86–7, 177
political parties 41, 42, 97, 129–32
    Brexit Party 130, 132
    Conservative Party 79–80, 129–30,
        131
    differences between 130
    Labour Party 65
    Liberal Democrat Party 131
    New Labour 130, 131
    Plaid Cymru 132
    Referendum Party 132
    Reform UK 132
    Scottish National Party (SNP) 132
    Social Democratic Party 131
    UKIP 28, 42, 124, 130, 132
political rights 63
population
    age distribution 6–7
    changes in 8–10
    by ethnicity 10–11
    immigration 7, 10–11
pressure groups 40, 41, 42, 151,
    156–7, 177
presumption of innocence 47
Prime Minister 96, 138–9, 177
Prime Minister's Office 139
Prime Minister's Questions
    (PMQs) 132–3, 177
principle 177
prison, function of 71
Prison Reform Trust (PRT) 74
prisoners, votes for 80
private bills 136
private member's bills 134, 136, 177
proportional voting systems 123,
    143, 177
proxy 177
public bills 136

public corporations 141
public inquiries 142
quangos (quasi-autonomous
    non-government organisa-
    tions) 141, 155, 177
Queen's Counsel (QCs) 55, 177
question time 132, 177
race audit (2017) 3
racial equality 3, 95
Rashford, Marcus 44
real government spending 177
Recall of MPs Act (2015) 113, 122
recorded crime 68, 177
Referendum Party 132
referendums 22, 31, 94, 124, 177
    on devolution 106, 107, 109
    on EU membership 19, 28, 110,
        128
    local referendums 106
    on Scottish independence 113,
        132
Reform UK 132
regional identity 8
rehabilitation 177
religious rights 63
reparation 177
representative democracy 93, 121,
    149, 178
reserved powers 107
responsibilities 2, 95, 178
returning officers 111
rights 2, 62–7, 178
    children's rights 3, 95
    disability rights 95
    legal rights 49–50, 58–9, 63
    LGBTQ rights 63–4
    right to die 49
    right to representation 64–7
    rights of women 3, 95
    see also human rights
rule of law 1, 95, 178
St Lucia 26
Salisbury convention 128, 178
sanctions 32, 178
Save our Forests campaign 36
Save our Human Rights Act cam-
    paign 37

Save Staffordshire Countryside and
    AONB campaign 37
Save the BBC campaign 37
Saville Report 142
Scotland 8, 60
    independence referendums 113,
        132
    local government 103, 104
    National Parliament 106–7, 108,
        109
Scottish National Party (SNP) 132
Scottish Parliament 106–7, 108, 109
second ballots 124
secondary action 178
secret ballot 121
Security Council 178
select committees 133
Senior Civil Service (SCS) 142
separation of powers 100, 125, 126
sexual rights 3, 95
Sierra Leone 32
single-issue groups 36, 41, 42
single-tier authorities 103, 178
single transferable vote (STV) sys-
    tem 124, 143
Single Union Agreement 66
Social Democratic Party 131
social media 14, 16, 44, 147, 158, 178
    campaigns 19, 43, 82, 153, 167
    celebrity influencers 152
    censorship of 22
social protection spending 117
social services 117
socialism 130, 178
soft power 24, 178
solicitors 55, 178
SOS for Honeybees campaign 159
sovereignty 178
Speaker of the House of Com-
    mons 134–5, 178
special advisers 125, 126, 178
special constables 85, 178
Starmer, Keir 131
state pension age 119
statute law 64
Stoke-on-Trent Pathfinder 12

Stonewall 63

Stop the HS2 campaign 161

strike action 65, 66, 178

supplementary vote system (SV) 124, 178

Supreme Court 97, 100, 126, 178

Surfers Against Sewage (SAS) 43

Syria 34

taxation 115–17, 131

Taylor, Richard 149

technocracy 146

terrorism 13, 22

Terrorism Act (2006) 22

Thatcher, Margaret 130–1, 138, 139

theocracy 94, 146

38 Degrees 36–7

Thunberg, Greta 162

tolerance 2, 178

Tories, *see* Conservatives

trade unions 40, 63, 64–6, 178

Trades Dispute Act (1906) 65

Trades Union Congress (TUC) 65, 178

traditional media 16, 178

transnational group 178

tribunals 56, 57, 85

Trident nuclear programme 118

two-party system 129–30, 178

two-tier systems 103–4, 178

UK Official Development Assistance (ODA, 2019) 33

Ukraine 35

ultra vires 178

UN Security Council 24

unitary authorities 103, 109

United for Grenfell 37

United Kingdom Independence Party (UKIP) 28, 42, 124, 130, 132

United Nations (UN) 24–5, 32, 77

United Nations Charter 24, 178

United Nations Convention on the Rights of the Child 80

United Nations Day 24

United States of America (USA) 24, 25, 31, 82, 147, 158, 163

Declaration of Independence 99, 179

gun ownership 49, 99

Universal Declaration of Human Rights (UDHR) 24, 49, 77, 78, 178

universal human rights 77–82

international law in conflict situations 81–2

international treaties 77–81

university tuition fees 120

value-added tax (VAT) 115

values, British 172, 179

veto 179

victims of crime 87

volunteering 42, 154, 179

voting 112–13, 121

improving voter engagement 150–2, 179

voting age debate 112

voting systems 121–3, 124, 143

Wales 8

local government 104

Parliament 106–7, 108, 109

Plaid Cymru 132

war crimes 82

wealth, distribution of 7

welfare policies 118–19

welfare rights 63

Welsh Parliament 106–7, 108, 109

Westmill wind farm 43

Whigs (Liberal Party) 129

whips 136, 179

whistleblowers 49

Wilson, Harold 138

Windrush generation 9

witnesses 87

Women's Institute (WI) 159

Women's rights 3, 95

working tax credits 119

World Trade Organization (WTO) 27, 50

Youth Court 74–5

youth justice system 74–6

youth offending teams (YOTs) 76

The Publishers would like to thank the following for permission to reproduce copyright material.

Photo credits: page 1 © Cate Gillon / Getty Images News / Getty Images; page 7 © False Economy; page 13 © luckybusiness / 123RF.com; page 17 Ofcom, News consumption in the UK 2020; page 19 © Andrew Milligan / PA Images / Alamy Stock Photo; page 20 (bottom) © Leon Neal / AFP / Getty Images; page 20 (top) © Mark Makela / ZUMA Press, Inc. / Alamy Stock Photo; page 24 © Melvyn Longhurst / Alamy Stock Photo; page 34 © Danuta Hyniewska / SuperStock; page 37 (bottom left) © Ron Evans / Alamy Stock Photo; page 37 (bottom right) © Amer Ghazzal / Shutterstock; page 37 (top left) © Liberty; page 37 (top right) © Mark Thomas / Shutterstock; page 41 © Ollie Millington / Getty Images News / Getty Images; page 42 © Ashley Cooper / Alamy Stock Photo; page 43 (bottom) © Anthony Upton / PA Images / Alamy Stock Photo; page 43 (top) © Derek Gale / Alamy Stock Photo; page 44 (top) © Sander Chamid / Nippon News / SCS / AFLO / Alamy Live News / Alamy Stock Photo; page 45 © THOMAS LOHNES / AFP / Getty Images; page 50 Coláiste Éamman Rís, Cork City www.cercork.ie; page 62 © Chronicle / Alamy Stock Photo; page 65 (bottom) © The Unite, © RMT; page 65 (middle) © Mark Kerrison / Alamy Live News / Alamy Stock Photo; page 65 (top) © David Cheskin / PA Images / Alamy Stock Photo; page 70 © Lewis Whyld / PA Images / Alamy Stock Photo; page 78 © TERMCAT (CC BY 4.0); page 79 (left) © JAM WORLD IMAGES / Alamy Stock Photo; page 79 (right) © FREDERICK FLORIN / AFP / Getty Images; page 84 © IE235 / Image Source Plus / Alamy Stock Photo; page 85 Jeffrey Isaac Greenberg 18+ / Alamy Stock Photo; page 86 © Albanpix / Shutterstock; page 87 © David Mansell / Alamy Stock Photo; page 88 Zethu Maseko / INQUEST; page 89 (bottom) © Chrysoulla. Photography; page 89 (top) © John Minihan / Evening Standard / Hulton Archive / Getty Images; page 90 © Shutterstock / REX; page 91 © Tommy London / Alamy Stock Photo; page 92 © CHRISTOPHER FURLONG / Getty Images News / Getty Images; page 94 (bottom left) © EPA / Epa European Pressphoto Agency b.v. / Alamy Stock Photo; page 94 (bottom right) © Pool / Supreme Leader's Press Office / Anadolu Agency / Getty Images; page 94 (top left) © Olivier Douliery / Pool / CNP / dpa picture alliance / Alamy Stock Photo; page 94 (top right) © Keystone Pictures USA / Alamy Stock Photo; page 96 (left) © EPA / Epa European Pressphoto Agency b.v. / Alamy Stock Photo; page 96 (middle) © Michael Tubi / Shutterstock.com; page 96 (right) © PA Images / Alamy Stock Photo; page 98 © Alastair Grant / WPA Pool / Getty Images News / Getty Images; page 99 © IanDagnall Computing / Alamy Stock Photo; page 106 © Mark Thomas / Alamy Stock Photo; page 108 (bottom left) © Robertharding / Alamy Stock Photo; page 108 (bottom right) © Chbaum / stock.adobe.com; page 108 (top left) © M Ramírez / Alamy Stock Photo; page 108 (top right) © Roger Gaisford / Alamy Stock Photo; page 118 (top) © Xinhua / Alamy Live News / Alamy Stock Photo; page 125 © John Stillwell / PA Images / Alamy Stock Photo; page 126 © Alex Segre / Alamy Stock Photo; page 133 © UK Parliament / Jessica Taylor / Handout / Xinhua / Alamy Stock Photo; page 135 © STEFAN ROUSSEAU / AFP / POOL / Getty Images; page 139 © ssJonathan Buckmaster / Pool / REUTERS / Alamy Stock Photo; page 148 © Ron Harvey / Everett Collection Inc. / Alamy Stock Photo; page 149 © David Kendall / PA Images / Alamy Stock Photo; page 150 © amer ghazzal / Alamy Stock Photo; page 151 © Compassion in World Farming; page 153 (bottom) © Malcolm Park / Alamy Live News / Alamy Stock Photo; page 153 (top) © John Cancalosi / Alamy Stock Photo; page 156 © Greenpeace UK; page 157 (left) © Mark Kerrison / Alamy Live News / Alamy Stock Photo; page 157 (right) Will Rose / Greenpeace; page 158 © UK Sports Pics Ltd / Alamy Live News / Alamy Stock Photo; page 159 (bottom right) National Federation of Women's Institutes (NFWI); page 159 (left) National Federation of Women's Institutes (NFWI); page 159 (top right) © Alekss / stock.adobe.com; page 161 © Julie Edwards / JEP News / Alamy Stock Photo; page 162 (bottom) © Jemal Countess / UPI / Alamy Stock Photo; page 162 (top) © Jasper Chamber / Alamy Stock Photo; page 163 Toby Lea / National Farmers Union; page 168 © Washington Imaging / Alamy Stock Photo.

Acknowledgements: The Publishers would like to thank the following for permission to reproduce material in this book. Page 9 (top) Windrush Scandal, Windrush generation: Who are they and why are they facing problems?, Published 31 July 2020, © BBC; page 9 (bottom) Impact of Immigration on UK Economy by Tejvan Pettinger, August 1, 2019, © http://economicshelp.org, and Migration Statistics Quarterly Report: Dec 2016, Office of National Statistics; page 18 UK national newspaper circulation figures for January 2020; page 32 War in Afghanistan, The National Army Museum; page 33 Statistics on International Development, Provisional UK Aid spend 2019, © Crown Copyright. Contains public sector information licensed under the Open Government Licence v3.0; page 37 SAVE STAFFORDSHIRE COUNTRYSIDE & AONB by Paul Woodhead; page 43 Coronavirus: Pandemic 'causing new wave' of plastic pollution, August 31, 2020, © BBC; page 44 Alix Culbertson, Migrants from Banksy-funded boat stranded as Italy and Malta refuse safe port, charity says, August 30, 2020, © Sky UK;

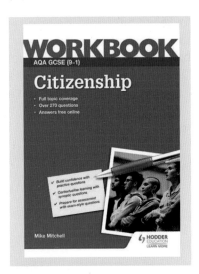